Heart Journey

Heart Journey

a spiritual journey into the heart of abundance
and the manifestation process
through desire, surrender, and greater love
for oneself,
for one another,
and for God

Mary Juno
M.A. Counseling Psychology

Twin Stars Unlimited
Clinton, CT

Published by Twin Stars, Unlimited
P.O. Box 301
Clinton, CT 06413
maryjuno@maryjuno.com
htttp://www.maryjuno.com

All rights reserved. No part of this book may be reproduced or used in any form or by any means – graphic, electronic or mechanical, including photocopying, mimeographing, recording, taping or information storage and retrieval systems – without written permission from the author. A reviewer may quote brief passages.

ISBN 978-1-930310-13-1

Printed in the United States of America

Copyright 2011
by Mary Shea
All rights reserved.

For all those
who ever reached past
the pain of vulnerability
to love well,
and in the midst
of that courageous act
discovered the great joy that comes
from opening the heart.

Dedicated
to my three sons

Stephen

Joseph

James

I am sincerely grateful for the
support and expertise of my editor,
Margaret Rose Fortier.

Her excellent questions and comments
helped me to clarify and expand on
the concepts presented in Heart Journey.
She had the uncanny ability to understand
what I wanted to write and the skill to
get me to write it.

Contents

Heart Journey: Introduction
Everyday Experiencing of God xxiii
Co-creative Partnership xxiv
Manifesting Abundance xxiv
The Heart Journey Contract xxv
Heart Journey as the Beginning of a Sacred Partnership xxv
Heart Journey as a Spiritual Path xxvi
Developing Two-Way Communication xxvi
The Importance of Surrender xxvii
The Twelve Co-creative Thought Transformations xxvii
Eight Stages of Heart Openness xxviii
The Results xxviii
Growing into Surrender xxix
Shared Abundance xxix
Love is Essential xxx
Personal Experience xxx

Part One
The Initiation

Chapter One: Learning to Ask
Asking as an Initiation into a Spiritual Path 3
From the Piscean Age to the Age of Aquarius 4
Co-creating Shared Abundance 4
A New Noncompetitive Paradigm 5
   An Example of Abundance through Attraction 6
The Image of God as Loving 7
Asking for Material Possessions and Money 8
   An Example of Asking for Money 9
Asking for Assistance 10
   An Example of Asking for Information 10
How Asking can Create Intimacy with God 11
The Need for Cleansing 11

Chapter Two: Surrendering the Results
How Heart Journey is Different 13
The Importance of Surrender 14
   An Example of Surrender to Divine Creativity 15
How the Process of Surrender Begins 15

Chapter Three: Heart's Desire
- Desire as the Basis for Asking 17
- Heart's Desire 17
- False Desire 18
- The Ineffectiveness of What You Don't Want 18
- Victimization Versus Co-creation 18
  - *Example of Victimization Versus Co-creation* 19
- Styles of Discernment 20
  - Strong Desire 20
  - Confusion and Uncertainty 20
  - Strong Surrender to God's Desire 21
- Methods for Determining Heart's Desire or Surrender 22
  - Listening within and the Inner Voice 22
  - Recognizing Passion 23
  - Personal Symbolism 23
    - *Example of Personal Symbolism* 23
- Moving Ahead Regardless 24
- Final Steps and Confirmation 24

Chapter Four: Negating the "Gimme God" Image
- Surrender 26
- No Guarantees 27
  - *An Example of Acceptance and Reorientation* 27
- Simple is Best 29
  - *An Example of a Simple Contract* 29
- A True Partnership 30
- The Untrue Partnership 31
- Manifestation Takes Time 31
- Heart Openness 31
- Spiritual Development 32
- Sharing 32
- Conclusion 33

Chapter Five: Pre-contract Considerations
- The Purpose of the Heart Journey Contract 34
- Spiritual Diet 34
- Heart Journey Participation 35
- Be Positive 36
- Translating Desire into Thought 36
- Be Concrete and Specific 37
- Concrete and Specific Examples 37
- But Don't be Too Specific 38

TABLE OF CONTENTS

Divine Upgrades 38
    Example of an Upgrade 39
A Focused, Sustained Thought 39
The Role of Emotion 40
Necessary Components for Manifestation 40
Surrender Contracts 41
Make This Journey Your Own 41
Love as a Remedy 42
Retaining What you Already Have 42
"Be Careful of What you Ask for" and Other Fears 43

Chapter Six: Composing Your Contract
Contract Media 44
Contract Formats 44
Types of Contracts 45
    Individual Contracts 45
    Relationship and Group Contracts 46
    Business or Professional Contracts 46
    Health and Healing Contracts 46
Prioritizing, Evaluating and Organizing Your Intentions 47
    Prioritize 47
    Evaluate Desire 47
    Organize 47
Multifaceted Requests 48
Before Writing or Composing Your Contract 52
Pay Attention while Writing 52
Technical Writing Tips 52
    Make "I" Statements 53
    Use Present Tense 53
    Do Not Use Negatives 53
    Use Positive Language 54
    Intentions, Not Vows 54
    Be Flexible 54
    Leave Plenty of Room For Upgrades 55
    Qualify Your Contract 55
    Gratitude 55
    Offering 55
    Reflection and finalization 55
Examples 56
    The Written Contract: 56
    The Symbolic Visual Contract 57

  A Garden Contract 57
 Empowering the Heart Journey Contract 58

Chapter Seven: Creating a Ritual
 Instructions 60
 Considerations when Planning Your Ritual 61
  Location, Location, Location 61
  Timing 61
  Participation 62
  Preparation 62
 Sensory Elements in Your Ritual 63
  Sight 63
  Sound 63
  Smell 63
  Touch 63
  Taste 63
 During the Ceremony 63
 Following the Ceremony 64

Part Two
The Co-creative Partnership and Manifestation Process

Chapter Eight: Communicating with God
 Introduction 67
 The Importance of Communication 68
 Sharpen Your Ability to Listen 69
  Listening 69
  Talking to God 70
   Example of Listening 70
 Develop a Common, Meaningful Language 71
  Symbols 71
   Example of Symbolism 72
  Signs 73
   Example of a Sign 73
  Coincidence 74
  Ease 74
   Example of Difficulties and the Lack of Success 75
  God Whispers 76
   Example of God Whispers 76
  Lucid Dreaming 76
   Example of Lucid Dream Communication 77

Visions	77
Example of a Vision without Significance	78
Stranger than Fiction Communication	78
The Ballad of Mildred	78

Chapter Nine: The Nature of Communications

Introduction	82
Distinguishing Characteristics	82
What Divine Communications Are Not Like	83
Never Meant to Control	83
Not About Others	83
Never Critical	83
Will not Flatter Your Ego	83
No Fear-based Messages	84
Rarely Predictive	84
Won't Condone Your Anger	85
What Divine Communications are Like	86
Loving	86
Uplifting and Challenging	86
Encouraging and Supportive	87
Insightful and Wise	87
Example of Insight and Wisdom	88
Protective	88
Example of Protection	88
Humorous Example	89
Energetic Example	89
Rational Versus Irrational	90

Chapter Ten: Communication Guidelines

Establishing Guidelines for Communication	91
Choose a Specific Symbol with a Specific Meaning	91
Examples of Symbolism	92
The Rule of Three	92
Milestones of Success	94
Asking for Wisdom	96

Chapter Eleven: The Process of Manifestation

Introduction	97
The Four Elements Needed for Manifestation	98
Desire Tempered by Surrender	99
A Focused and Sustained Potent Thought	101

    Flow 102
        Example of Manifestation within the Flow 103
    Avenue for Manifestation 104
        Example of Following Blindly 106
    Gratitude 108

Chapter Twelve: Troubleshooting Communication
    Introduction to Troubleshooting 110
    Start Troubleshooting by Communicating with God 111
        Assess the Strength of the Connection 111
        Evaluate the Nature of the Communications 112
        Falling into Prediction 115
        Faith in Your Co-creative Partner 116

Chapter Thirteen: Troubleshooting Desire & Surrender
    Troubleshooting the Four Elements Needed for Manifestation 118
    Problems Related to Desire 119
        Too Strong Desire and Clinging to Expectations 119
        Weak Desire 121
        A Comment About Passion 122
        Conflicting Desires and Overly Complex Contracts 122
        Sabotaging Fears and Other Negative Emotions 123
    Problems Related to Surrender 125
        Inability to Surrender Control 125
        Weak Surrender to God's Desire 127
    The Swing of the Pendulum between Desire and Surrender 129

Chapter Fourteen: Troubleshooting Thoughts
    Introduction to Problems Related to a Focused, Sustained Thought 130
    Problems Related to Focusing Your Thought 130
        Rigid and Narrow Focused Thoughts 131
        Example of Overcoming Resistance 132
        Inability to Focus and a Lack of Specificity 132
    Problems Related to Sustaining a Focused Thought 135
    Problems Related to Thinking 136
        Excessive Thinking 136
        Rationalism and the Need for Logical Explanations 137
        Example of Surrender to a Divine Upgrade that is Irrational 138

Chapter Fifteen: Troubleshooting Flow
    Introduction to Problems with the Flow 140

    Moving Against the Flow...141
    Unresponsive Flow 142
    Slow Moving and Stagnant Flow 144
    Delays, Interference, and Incorrect Timing...146
        Example of Delay, Interference, and Incorrect Timing................................148
    Quick Flow and the Need to be Prepared 148
        Example of Quick Moving Flow 149

Chapter Sixteen: Troubleshooting the Avenue for Manifestation
    Introduction to Problems with the Avenue for Manifestation 150
    Problems with Instant Gratification...151
        1. The inability to cope with delayed gratification....................................151
        2. A tendency to choose only simple, effortless desires 151
        3. Limited communication with the co-creative Partner..........................151
        4. Lack of spiritual growth and maturity..152
        5. Ego inflation...152
    Problems with Delayed Gratification 153
        1. Procrastination and an Inability to Follow Through.............................154
        2. Counterproductive Character Traits and Self-Sabotage 155
        3. Lack of Sincere Effort 156
        4. Impatience and Overcompensation 156
        5. Lack of Essential Skills...157
        6. Preconditions..158
        7. Chaos, Disorganization and Other Distractions....................................159
        8. Complexity...161
        9. Renegotiation 161
            Example of Renegotiation..162
        10. Never Getting Started..163
            1. Your Startup Plan 164
            2. God's Plan 164
            3. Feedback Regarding Actions and the Need for Consistency.........................165
            4. Temporary Stoppage 165
            5. Testing the Waters 165
        11. Lack of Financial Support...166
        12. Lack of Moral or Ethical Integrity..167
    The Delicate Art of Skillful Navigation..167

Chapter Seventeen: Health, Healing, & Death
    Disclaimer..169
    Bringing God into the Healing Process 169
    Illness and Causality 170

Physical Contributions to Disease 170
Emotional Contributions to Disease 171
   Example of Physical Healing 171
Health Warnings 173
A Different Kind of Healing 174
   Example of Finding a Healer 174
Healers and Healing 175
Routines for Weight loss, Addictions, and Good Health 175
On Death and Dying 176
   1. Physical assistance with the illness 177
   2. Letting go 177
   3. Your journey to the other side 177
      Example of the Power of Love in the Afterlife 177
      Example - Uncle Frank's Journey Out of Dementia and into Glory 178
      Example - The Nature of Choice at the Moment of Death 178
      Example - My Father's Passage into the Hands of the Angels 179

Part Three
Spiritual Development and Heart Openings

Chapter Eighteen: Twelve Co-creative Thoughts
Introduction 183
Twelve Alchemical Thought Transformations 184
1st Co-Creative Thought Transformation 185
   Old thought: The Do-It-Yourself Fantasy 185
   Alchemical Transformation: Learning to Attract, Opening to Receive 185
      Example of Attracting and Receiving 186
   The Process of Attraction 186
2nd Co-Creative Thought Transformation 187
   Old thought: Even Steven Reward System 187
   Alchemical Transformation: Receive More than Your Fair Share 187
3rd Co-Creative Thought Transformation 189
   Old thought: The Mental Ghetto 189
   Alchemical Transformation: Silence and Reflection 189
      Example of Inspiration in the Silence 191
4th Co-Creative Thought Transformation 192
   Old thought: Disabling Need or Dependency 192
   Alchemical Transformation: Self-sufficiency Moving to Wholeness 192
5th Co-Creative Thought Transformation 193
   Old thought: Reality Deception 193
   Alchemical Transformation: Multidimensional Perception 193

    Example of Shifting Realities 195
    Example that Spans Distance and Space 196
  6th Co-Creative Thought Transformation 197
    Old thought: Mental Constructs 197
    Alchemical Transformation: Open Mindedness 197
      Example of Preconceptions Resulting in Resistance 198
      Example of a Mystical Hawaiian Journey 199
  7th Co-Creative Thought Transformation 200
    Old thought: Judgment 200
    Alchemical Transformation: Compassion 200
      Example of Judgment 202
  8th Co-Creative Thought Transformation 203
    Old thought: Possessiveness and Control 203
    Alchemical Transformation: Honoring 203
      Example of Control 206
  9th Co-Creative Thought Transformation 208
    Old thought: Ego Armada 208
    Alchemical Transformation: Egoless 208
      Example of My Own Egotistic Folly 210
  10th Co-Creative Thought Transformation 211
    Old thought: Guilt 211
    Alchemical Transformation: Forgiveness 211
      Step one 211
      Step two 212
      Step three 212
      Step four 212
      Step five 213
  11th Co-Creative Thought Transformation 215
    Old thought: Distrust 215
    Alchemical Transformation: Trust and Faith 215
      Example of Trust in God 217
  12th Co-Creative Thought Transformation 218
    Old thought: Self 218
    Alchemical Transformation: No-Self 218
      Example of Shape-Shifting 219
Final Words 220

Chapter Nineteen: Eight Stages of Heart Openness
Introduction 221
Signs of an Opening Heart 222

Stage One: Cognizance of Heart Closure 222
Stage Two: Heart Vulnerability 224
   Example of vulnerability 226
Stage Three: Spiritual Input, Thoughts, Emotions, and the Physical 227
   Spiritual Input and the Spiritual Level 228
   Thoughts and the Mental Level 229
   Emotions and the Emotional Level 230
   Body and the Physical plane 231
Stage Four: Harmonizing the Four Levels of Experience 232
   Spiritual Input and the Spiritual Level 232
   Thoughts and the Mental Level 232
   Emotions and the Emotional Level 233
   Body and the Physical Plane 233
Signs of an Open Heart 234
   Stage Five: Receiving Abundance 235
   Stage Six: Channeling Abundance 237
      Example of Receiving 239
   Stage Seven: Spiritual Stress Test and Surrender 239
      Inability to manifest 240
      Situational test 241
      Test of service to others 242
      Example of Service to Others 242
      Health issue test 243
      Relationship issue 244
   Stage Eight: Acceptance and Generation 244
Beyond Stage Eight 245

Chapter Sixteen: Spiritual Evolution
Desire versus Desireless 247
Definition of Surrender 248
Definition of Abundance 248
The Process of Attraction 249
Duality and Consciousness 249
Love and Non-duality 249

Index
Index 251

Heart Journey

Heart Journey: Introduction

Heart Journey is first and foremost a love affair, a love affair with the Divine, Spirit, or God if you will, the greatest lover of all, no matter what name you use or what religion you practice. But Heart Journey is not about religion and it is not about God's name. It is about experiencing God in a new way, experiencing God as an abundant, generous lover, and co-creative partner.

God is many things to many people, a protector, a guide, a healer, comforter, father, mother, savior, redeemer. To others, God is a not so kind, a judge who extracts payment for sins and transgressions. But to mystics, God is, has been, and always will be the Beloved. The ancients, saints, vowed and professed, or simply the highly spiritual have seen this side of God. No one can read the poems of Rumi or the works of Julian of Norwich and not hear the romancing of God "the Lover."

Everyday Experiencing of God

Heart Journey is about that side of God, God the Beloved, and the everyday experiencing of God by the ordinary person living an ordinary life. One does not need to enter a monastery or shun all worldly possessions to enter into a love affair with God. It is time for the lay person, the householder, the parent, the common person to have a direct and mystical relationship with God. Divine intimacy is what Heart Journey is about. Opening to feeling God's love and guidance while carrying out daily activities is the accessibility Heart Journey seeks to bring about. God can be experienced at any moment as tangible, real, enticing, and beneficent.

Most of those who come to Heart Journey don't come seeking a love affair with God. They do not even perceive the possibility initially and generally not for a while. It is a part of the journey that sneaks up on you and surprises you with its warmth and caring. God is not distant or uninvolved. God is responsive, attentive, and generous. God is listening, hears your prayers, understands what you need, and responds. This will take you by surprise one day, that anyone, human or in spirit would care that you have what you need for the next step on your journey, or that you don't have what you need when you are set to head off in the wrong direction. Everything unfolds as it should, in the correct manner, and with the right person or people at an appropriate time for your highest good and the highest good of all involved. You will be astounded when you experience the smallest detail falling into place by chance. Though you may pass it off as a coincidence, when it continues to happen regularly you will know that it is nothing less than the caring touch of a guiding force.

Co-creative Partnership

Heart Journey is a hands-on Divine experience that helps you foster direct communication with God through a co-creative partnership. You grow into it and with it by opening your heart. The love affair grows with your ability to love and be loved. With time, the connection and interaction intensifies as your awareness of subtleties and acceptance of mystery matures. Mysticism, by definition, is about mystery and what can be experienced, but not explained. Mystical experiences are beyond words and can only be partially conveyed through poetry, music, or art. Additionally, mystical experiences are not causal. There is no one-on-one direct relationship between cause and effect in mysticism. Occurrences are coincidental. You set the stage and when the conditions are right mystical experiences may or may not arise, but your ability to perceive them increases as your level of awareness deepens. Heart Journey is a format for setting the stage and deepening your level of awareness. It is a process for the development of a sacred, mystical relationship with God more than any co-creative goal or material desire you might conceive. This is not obvious to the beginner setting out on the Heart Journey path, but it is the truest, most powerful, and enduring aspect.

Manifesting Abundance

What many come for and are drawn to in Heart Journey is the desire for abundance and the ability to manifest one's heart's desire, whatever that might be, through attraction and the co-creative process. In addition to being a love affair with God, Heart Journey is about opening to receiving, receiving what you ask for, and receiving beyond your wildest dreams. It truly is. The truth is a good lover receives as well as gives. A good lover is loved as well as loving. There is no greater lover than God. When your heart is open, all things flow, and you receive as easily as you give, give as readily as you receive, and eventually there is no distinction. All movements are one breath within the co-creative process of manifestation. Abundance is born in the heart and increases through sharing. When you share your abundance and the ability to manifest, Divinity has a human face and good fortune magnifies, touching all involved. Love grows.

The Heart Journey Contract

How does this all come about? Where do you begin? The process is actually quite simple at the start and as ancient as the Bible. It is written in the scriptures,

> *Ask and it shall be given you; seek and ye shall find; knock and it shall be opened unto you.* (Matthew 7:7, King James Version of The Holy Bible)

All you need to do to begin your Heart Journey and initiate a co-creative partnership with God is to formally "ask." It's that simple.

Asking takes the form of a Heart Journey contract in Chapter Six: Composing Your Contract. You enter into a co-creative partnership with God by writing or composing a request, (some would call it a wish list), that expresses in words or symbols what you want to manifest in your life. Your request or Heart Journey contract is a reflection of your heart's desire. Stated or implied in your contract is an invitation to God to walk with you hand-in-hand as your partner in this manifestation process. By means of this simple act you initiate and access a broad interaction with this side of God as lover and co-creative partner. Together you birth a new reality, one filled with limitless potential and miracles. It is love which drives this relationship and opens you to receiving; it is love which enhances this birthing and manifestation process; and it is love that awakens you to the possibility that something better can and does exist, something beyond your own ability to create by yourself or even dream of. Through the simple act of asking, you begin to awaken to the experience of being guided, protected, gifted, and cherished, hence the beginning of your love affair with God.

Heart Journey as the Beginning of a Sacred Partnership

What you need to realize at the outset and before you begin to write your heart's desire contract is that Heart Journey is a rich and enlightening co-creative dance between two partners. You are not just on the receiving end. God is not simply a supplier. God is your partner in this venture and the co-creative partnership is like a marriage. As in any marriage or collaborative effort, pulling together is a learning process. There will be times when you will need to take the lead. At other times, yielding will be crucial. You must stay conscious of the flow of power and bring all your skills, knowledge, and love to bear on the development of a sacred relationship. At the same time, learning to trust will be essential to your progress.

On the wedding day and for the duration of the honeymoon period, each marriage is consumed with expectations and fantasies about how perfect everything will be. Even in the best of marriages, the reality is never a mirror of the fantasy. There will always be things to work out. It is the same with Heart Journey. Your intention, your desire, your wish list is like the initial expectations and fantasies fostered on any wedding day. Once the honeymoon is over, you must do the work of building a strong and lasting partnership. You will need to put in the effort and take action when the ball is in your court, or master patience and the art of surrender when the next move is up to God.

All great marriages and partnerships are works of art in progress. When a marriage is good and truly loving, it becomes much better than either spouse could have imagined. The two individuals grow in their ability to love, accept, honor, share power, and combine forces. When it all comes together, the union becomes sacred and fosters contagious abundance, joy, and love. The same is true of your co-creative partnership with God when you learn the same lessons, only the rewards are greater.

Once you have composed and activated your intention, it is your responsibility to grow in your ability to love, accept, honor, and share power with your co-creative partner. God already loves you, accepts you, honors you, and shares power. You do have free will. God has been putting forth the effort for a long time. It will be your job to learn to open widely, receive fully, trust deeply, listen with great clarity, and then heed.

Heart Journey as a Spiritual Path

Heart Journey is a spiritual teaching in how to ask for your heart's desire. The material in this book will guide you step-by-step in the formulation of your contract and its subsequent activation. There are guidelines and examples of actual requests others have made. Once you have formulated your contract you will want to ritualize its initiation. Since you are confirming your spiritual connection to God, this should be a time of celebration and sacredness. You can have your own private ceremony or join with others. Tips for creating your own ritual are given.

But the most important part of Heart Journey is yet to come, i.e., the development of your co-creative partnership with God while you learn and practice the art of manifesting your heart's desire. What is needed for manifestation to occur is clearly defined in the text. Four necessary elements are required. These are discussed in Chapter 11: The Process of Manifestation. The practice will be demonstrated and clarified through true life stories.

Developing Two-Way Communication

Central to Heart Journey and spiritual growth is the co-creative partnership. For this to evolve, communication is essential. Most of us know how to pray and talk to God, formally or informally. But for manifestation to occur and the co-creative partnership to develop, communication needs to be a two-way street. One must learn to listen and hear God's whispers.

Chapter 8: Communicating with God will focus on this direct exchange with God, how to become aware of communication as it occurs, and the forms it might take. Conversation can be subtle, but its hallmark is the emphasis on wisdom, guidance, and lovingness. In Chapter 9: The Nature of Communications, discussion will focus on what exchanges with God are like and what they are never about. Clear distinctions are made. Fostering good two-way communication enables the co-creative partnership with

God to deepen. It also promotes spiritual learning. Direct experience is the essence of mysticism and central to the insights and enlightenment fostered in all spiritual pilgrims throughout time.

The Importance of Surrender

Heart Journey is not just about desire and manifestation. Desire is always balanced by surrender as discussed in Chapter 2: Surrendering the Results. "Not my will, but Thy Will," is innate to Heart Journey and essential to the manifestation process. The two, desire and surrender, go hand-in-hand. The pendulum constantly swings back and forth between these two points. Mastering surrender might seem like a daunting task, but it is presented differently in Heart Journey. God has a better idea! Surrender opens you to "Divine upgrades." You only need to be upgraded once to see the wisdom of handing over the helm to God and letting your ego take a back seat.

Surrendering the ego occurs gradually as you learn to accept and yield. This happens even though it is the ego which gets you into Heart Journey in the first place. You want. You need. You desire. So you write a wish list and ask for help. You invite God in and the journey begins. What starts out looking like a ticket to the better life you envisioned, can end up being a ticket to a better life you could not have imagined in your wildest dreams. The intention is the hook for many, the opening. It gets you in at ground level. But some time, some day, in some way, when you let go, love well, and least expect it, God surprises you with a tangible sweetness that clearly lets you know that you are cared for and even treasured. A miracle occurs. You get much more than you asked for. Once that happens, you get very clear, really fast about who you want running the show. From that time on, the ego does not stand a chance. You are willing to let go and let God. Guidelines for surrender and examples will be given to make the process of surrender easier, more understandable, and even advantageous.

The Twelve Co-creative Thought Transformations

There are twelve co-creative thought transformations associated with Heart Journey that you must cultivate and adopt. These are presented in Part Three: Spiritual Development and Heart Openings. They will assist you in the process of manifestation of abundance, spiritual development, heart openness, and communication with God. Each one is an insightful "Ah-hah!" or enlightened transformation of a lower, more commonly held, negative and counterproductive thought pattern. The corresponding twelve lower and limiting thought patterns need to be released. They will derail your Heart Journey, impede the process of manifestation, and sabotage the co-creative partnership. As you progress, you will come to see that you do not need or want these lower thoughts, and each one can be replaced by a better idea!

For example, the first lower thought pattern to be released is the "Do-it-Yourself Fantasy." You must abandon your checklist of "things I must do to make this happen."

Though you will be doing your part and share of the work in Heart Journey, you will not be working alone. God is your co-creative partner and results do not depend solely on your efforts. Letting go of a "go-get'em" approach to manifestation will naturally lead you to the enlightened co-creative thought pattern of "Learning to Attract, Opening to Receive." Heart openness increases abundance. The power to attract is a product of an open heart. It is central to the process of manifestation and is a little-used inner muscle you will be strengthening. The guidelines in Heart Journey will help you to do this.

Another lower, limiting thought pattern you will be releasing and replacing is the "Mental Ghetto." How can you hear your co-creative partner when your mind is cluttered with gossip and negativity? Each of the higher thoughts is a key step along the Heart Journey path that you will be glad to take.

Eight Stages of Heart Openness

And finally, Heart Journey discusses and defines the process of opening your heart while you develop spiritually. There are "Eight Stages of Heart Openness", the highest being the "Acceptance and Generation." Progress through the stages is not necessarily linear. You might experience several of the levels in one day, moving forward and then falling back, but with time, you will remain at higher levels of heart openness for longer periods of time. It is then that your ability to manifest improves to the point of benefiting others.

The Results

I have been asked if Heart Journey comes with a guarantee, like you write an intention and as soon as you sign it, God is duty bound to fulfill your request. Heart Journey doesn't work that way, and in my experience, God doesn't either. For that I am grateful. God is a much better creator than any of us will ever be. As creators, we have small and limited abilities next to what God can do. We need only gaze at a sunset or witness a child being born to know that. There are breezes, colors, mountains, flowers, and the delicate balance of nature. None of us has that kind of know-how or power. We might be creative with words, a paintbrush, or a tune, but we're not and never will be that creative or imaginative. We could not have created one percent of what exists. This gives one pause. The smart person on a Heart Journey yields the lead consistently to a far greater and better Creator.

Have I seen individuals get what they asked for item by item? Yes, I have. I have seen some people manifest a list in four days. Have I seen people who did not get what they asked for at all? Yes, I have. I personally have been disappointed, but in most instances grew to understand the wisdom of the results and/or was glad for the way things turned out. We all know people who have prayed with all their hearts only to be denied. It does happen that some come up with nothing even after the simplest request. Results can be incredible. Sometimes a request lays fallow because it was not is the best interest or highest good of all involved. Sometimes the process takes much longer than expected, even years. There will be troubleshooting chapters for those who are becalmed, but there are no guarantees.

In certain instances individuals have gotten much more than they asked for, different from what they expected, but also much better. The most loving people, those who wrote their intentions and gently placed them in God's care, those who trusted totally, waited patiently, acted responsibly, did their part, and loved well, did the best. In some cases, they did not get what they asked for; they got something instead or better, a richer, more loving experience than they could have imagined. Heart Journey opens you to receiving and being loved at higher and stronger levels, sometimes beyond your ability to conceive.

Growing into Surrender

It is possible and it has happened that the love grew to be so strong and the receiving so overwhelmingly abundant that individuals left all intentions behind and simply said "Yes" to whatever God had in mind or heart. There was no risk in doing so because this Being, this Force, this loving, creative Potential we call God loved them better than they could love themselves. God had a better idea, a better plan. Love opened them to seeing this movement, prepared them for receiving the gifts, and enabled them to cast their egotistical perspective aside, and seize the sacred opportunity to surrender and simply accept whatever was offered. Desire fell away completely into surrender. All spiritual journeys eventually lead to this point of total surrender. Heart Journey is no different.

Shared Abundance

The love God bestows on you cannot be contained. Heart Journey is not just about the abundance and love you receive, it is also about the abundance and love that can pour through you, overflowing and filling the lives of those around you. You cannot receive this much and not pass it on. Abundance becomes a river. There is no way you can own it. There is no way it can be limited. It pours in and out of your heart as lovingness and kindness. In fact, the more you pass on, the more you will receive. And the more you say yes to receiving, the more abundance and love will flow, filling you and spilling over to those you care about and even some that you don't. The entire system moves on the wings of love. This has nothing to do with religion and nothing to do with evangelizing. There is nothing for you to teach or even share. It is all a wordless transfer, a peaceful, open, and loving presence that is soothing to all you contact. Your calmness and state of mind, your trust in the future, and lack of fear, your grace and kindness enhance exchanges with others who see you as nonthreatening and beneficent. You become a better person as the grace of God works through you allowing Divinity to touch those around you.

This process of receiving and sharing abundance becomes as natural and easy as breathing in and out. Through your dedication to the co-creative process and the task of loving well, higher love enters the world. Everything around you can begin to soften, receive, and benefit. The bottom line in a global sense is that love grows, peace arises, and God's grace becomes stronger on the planet. The world becomes a better place. Divinity infuses humanity. And it can all start with you and your wish list!

Love is Essential

However you look at it, love is essential to the process, and not just love for God, but also love for your fellow wo/man and love for yourself. Love creates conductivity, enabling the movement of abundance in and out of your heart and through every fiber of your being and life. Love for others allows abundance to reach others enhancing the flow. The more that is shared, the more that is created. Your loving abilities can impact family and friends in a positive way. Only an open heart can take this much in and give this much out, hence the name Heart Journey.

Not everyone will have such a powerful experience, but it is attainable by ordinary people who strive to love well and beyond their originally perceived capacity. There are many options and stages to the Heart Journey. There are many ways for the journey to progress once it is started, but all roads lead to God on the wings of love, whether you get what you ask for or not. Surrender and acceptance are as valid and fruitful a path as desire and abundance.

Personal Experience

At one point in my life, I worked with a desire coach and a spiritual director. It was very difficult for me to desire anything at that time, I was so conflicted. I could not think in terms of requesting anything from anyone, even God. It was not a healthy or spiritual place to be since I was not balanced. I had no options, no way to gauge my co-creative interaction with God.

One day my desire coach said to me, "You can desire a diamond tiara and have it be a spiritual experience." I had a hard time accepting this. I immediately backed away from her as if what she had said was the most nonspiritual and unenlightened thought I had ever heard. I curled into a fetal position. But, she was right. Spirit-based desire, tempered with the right amount of surrender, and in keeping with a co-creative partnership with God is always a spiritual experience, no matter what you desire, and regardless of whether or not you receive it. It is not the material object, situation, or external quest that makes Heart Journey a love affair with God. It is the process and development of the co-creative partnership through an open and loving heart that is essential.

Heart Journey is truly a journey of the heart, a journey into the heart, and the heart of the most important journey anyone can take, the journey to God.

Part One:
The Initiation

Chapter One:
Learning to Ask

Asking as an Initiation into a Spiritual Path

We are not trained in how to ask God for what we want to manifest, know, or experience. In fact, in many religions or spiritual disciplines, the mere thought of asking God for anything material outside of "our daily bread" would be viewed as sacrilegious. Instead, many of us are trained in suffering. We know how to sacrifice and have learned to "offer up" our trials and tribulations. Abundance, and especially *requests* for abundance are inconsistent with this form of spirituality. We have grown to see them as existing separately from our spiritual beliefs, practice, and principles. At times we might view our worldly experiences as an impediment to spiritual development and our connection to God.

> *"And the cares of this world, and the deceitfulness of riches, and the lusts of other things entering in, choke the word and it becometh unfruitful."*
> (Mark 4:19, KJV of The Holy Bible).

This call to separate heaven and earth splits our experience and denies the abundant and beneficial possibilities innate to a loving God. It also negates our ability and birth right to enter into a co-creative partnership.

In a desire to counteract attachment to the physical world and focus on the development of more spiritual qualities, many religious traditions have adopted a nonphysical, nonmaterial, anti-body, other-worldly attitude towards the earth plane experience. This has worked for many religions, seekers, and saints throughout the ages, especially for those professed, cloistered, or tucked away in a spiritual community. But what about those with spouses, children, homes, and jobs? What if the intended spiritual goal arising now for the ordinary lay person working to support and raise a family is not to get through, away from, and out of here as quickly as possible, but to get into fully experiencing physical life from a spiritual perspective? Is the present emerging task one of integrating materialism and spirituality by becoming a co-creative partner with God? Could the next step in human spiritual development be the mastery of manifestation skills aimed at improving conditions for everyone, including ourselves? There are already masters on the planet who can manifest instantaneously from thin air right before your eyes. There are natural laws governing the process. The first and necessary step is to ask, defining clearly what it is you want. The second step involves opening your heart to receiving and giving.

From the Piscean Age to the Age of Aquarius

The spirituality of sacrifice was a product of the Piscean Age, beginning with the Crucifixion of Jesus Christ and continuing to modern times. Life was hard back then when suffering through hunger, illness, oppression, and war was a daily event and way of life. During this period, many religious practiced "corporal mortification," the act of voluntarily punishing one's own body as a spiritual discipline. Suffering as a means to spiritual development is associated with this time period.

As we enter the Age of Aquarius, new insights into spiritual development will blend with what we already know. Aquarian themes are humanistic and holistic with an emphasis on balance and integration of the new and the old, the modern and the traditional, the spiritual and the material, the human and the Divine. The importance of the body, mind, and spirit functioning as a unit on all levels of experience is stressed. We must be aware and multi-conscious in our everyday lives. "Walking your talk," the modern version of "practice what you preach," is the way to becoming a unified and coordinated material-spiritual package. This process of integration is the emerging Aquarian path to spiritual development for the modern layperson.

Unity on all levels is a function of the heart. It is through love and an open heart that the body, mind, and spirit become a whole. The heart hears what the spirit intends, convinces the mind of its importance, and encourages the body to act accordingly. Everything proceeds from heart awareness. The heart is the link, the "Rainbow Bridge," (a phrase first introduced by Alice Bailey, a theosophist), that draws the material and the spiritual together. It is also the open heart which gives, receives, and co-creates abundance.

Co-creating Shared Abundance

Consciousness evolves and new spiritual perspectives arise to suit emerging issues. A spirituality that encompasses the whole human experience including the material and economic side of living is more appropriate to our present time and the challenges that we face, especially if it is used to create not only personal peace, kindness, and well-being, but also to initiate a co-creative shift in consciousness towards sharing with others through the manifestation of abundance. We can do more to emulate God than to think good thoughts and feel compassion for those less fortunate. Through an intimate partnering with God we can actually influence material reality and co-create a climate of abundance, spirituality, and holism that others might partake in either directly or indirectly.

We live in a time when we can individually and collectively increase abundance through sharing. Experience shows that an openness to new options, the circulation of resources, and a commitment to sharing increases abundance beyond perceived limits. When we share, a little can go a long way. For example, the Amish gather to do barn raisings. What one family could not accomplish alone, many can do easily. Also, special interest groups band together to share resources, expertise, and to negotiate for lower costs. We have grown to recognize the power of giving with the donations made to the victims of 9/11, Katrina, and AIDS in Africa. We can accomplish more when we pull together and share.

Furthermore, the more we share openheartedly, the more we are able to receive. Heart openness is a two-way street. The door swings in and out. The capacity is the same either way and there is no difference. The joy in giving is matched by the joy in receiving and vice versa. The amount you receive is either equal to or more than the amount you give. It might not come from the same person, in the same time frame, in the same manner, or be of the same character, but openhearted giving is, has, and always will be returned.

A New Noncompetitive Paradigm

We live in a competitive world, one that sees sharing as having less. Either-or situations abound and vie for our attention. For this reason, if we wish to shift to unlimited shared abundance, we need to incorporate the spiritual dynamic of inclusivity into our perspective on materialism. We need to counteract a mindset that emphasizes competition and leads us to the mistaken conclusion that only one person wins the prize, or only one person has the resources or power. There is an alternate paradigm in Heart Journey of contagious and inclusive success. It states that when one person unselfishly and lovingly helps another be successful by giving exactly what is needed at the right time, a tailwind is created that also draws the giver into a deeper experience of successful and abundant living. When the heart is open, no one is left behind and everyone moves forward.

Abundance is a reality co-created by an open heart from a mindset of unlimited potential. The sharing of abundance expands reality and opens each individual to receiving even more. This is true not only on the personal level, but also on the local, national, and international levels as well. Sharing increases abundance for us all and increases that ability to manifest.

As we enter the Age of Aquarius, we need to incorporate positive and rewarding material attitudes into our spiritual development. A shift in our perspective that would:

1. Focus on a co-creative partnership with God
2. Initiated through the power of a request
3. Implemented by a heart open to giving and receiving

4. For the purpose of manifesting shared abundance

This could bring us to a renewed sense of sacredness that redefines how we live materially as well as how we progress spiritually. This integration of higher and lower can not only expand our experience of God, but also increase our appreciation for the gift of living and the planet we inhabit.

One way to initiate the integration of the material with the spiritual and create abundance is to invite God into a co-creative partnership by stating clearly what it is we would like to manifest. This is a process with little history and it is also something we are not trained to do. Traditional religion has not taught us how to ask, but this is the first step we need to take. It is an initiation into the mystery of co-creative manifestation. To begin to attract what is needed or wanted, we must start on a personal level and we must "ask."

An Example of Abundance through Attraction

To help you understand the potential of a co-creative partnership and manifestation process, let me give you an example from my own experience. In the late 1980's as I was just starting to work with this technique, I asked God for a particular crystal to be sent to me as a sign. The crystal was called a "tantric twin" crystal which is commonly two quartz crystals growing together side by side and fused together to almost look like one. I read about these crystals in a book and wanted one. I had never even seen one, but I made this very specific request to God.

> "Please send me a tantric twin crystal with two points the same height that have a common slope at the top and a rainbow inside. I do not wish to purchase this crystal, or search for it, and I will not ask anyone for one. This is my secret request that only you, God, and I will know about. I know that you will send me this crystal when the time is right and it will be a sign to me."

After making the request, I surrendered to God's timing, manner, and eventual response. Six months later I was with a Cherokee Medicine Woman, Diana Soaring Hawk, who was showing me some feathers she had collected. In mid-sentence she stopped and looked up at the ceiling. She began conversing with a being of the spirit world saying,

> "What?" (pause)
> "Huh?" (pause)
> "Yeah, sure." (pause)
> "No problem!"
> "Okay."

At this point, she reached into her bag, saying, "I was just told that this is for you." Into my hand she placed a tantric twin crystal with the two points the same height and having a common slope. A rainbow was inside. I was stunned. I had told no one of my request, nor had I written it down anywhere or created a formal contract. Once I made the request, I had let it go, placed it in God's hands, and forgotten about it, yet the crystal had come to me. I took it as a sign that God was listening and heard my prayers, even the petty, material ones.

We live in a responsive, co-creative reality. When a request is made by an open heart that is for our highest good and the good of all involved, wishes are honored and granted in the most wondrous and miraculous ways.

The Image of God as Loving

The very act of making a request and initiating a co-creative partnership with the Divine begs the questions, "What is your perception of God? Is God loving or vengeful? Giving or judgmental? Gentle or punishing?" Many of us have been brought up in religions with an exacting, authoritative God. We have inculcated an image of a vengeful Being who smites his enemies and punishes the sinner in hell for all time. This picture instills fear, not love and is not a good basis for a co-creative partnership. Regardless of whether or not this is true for you, you must reassess your beliefs and expectations related to God at this time. More than likely, you will need to undo some indoctrination to experience God as love.

Negative expectations breed negative responses. If you think of God as remote and aloof or untouchable and cannot ever conceive of God as loving, then Heart Journey is not for you. You will never be able to establish a co-creative partnership with a Being you cannot trust as your Partner and do not believe is capable of understanding your situation and the forces you are struggling with. On the other hand, if you believe that co-creation is a possibility and you are open minded and openhearted enough to listen, trust, believe, hope, pray, and change, then read on because for a successful Heart Journey you have to be able to conceive of God as the personification of love. Heart Journey rests on the conviction that God listens to petitions and prayers and responds according to the highest good of all involved, that God can and does perform miracles. This God is a ray of hope, a constant comfort, and a loving presence who would not try to trick you or thwart you. This God wants you to succeed and grow in love and abundance even if your request is not honored.

Many religions refer to God as "father" or "mother." Keeping this in mind, remember, no loving Parent with unlimited resources, seeing a well-meaning son or daughter struggle while doing his or her best to accomplish a goal that is clearly for his or her highest good and the common good of all involved would deny assistance that is so dearly needed and so readily available. What reason would there be to withhold if it were consistent with the child's path? Heart Journey calls you to ask for what is needed or wanted and accept that there is a nurturing, protective, sustaining, and loving God who will support your efforts. Firmly believing that this perspective is true is the beginning of your love affair with God.

Asking for Material Possessions and Money

Traditionally, it is okay to ask God for wisdom, forgiveness, and healing, but not for a new car, especially if you do not truly *need* a new car. Life without a new, mechanically sound car would have to be virtually impossible before you could approach the Almighty with that request! Perhaps it would be okay if you needed the car to commute to work so you could earn money to feed your nine children, or if you would be using the car to travel to a distant hospital for much needed, life-saving medical attention. And even then the promise of several hours of community service might be necessary to escape any guilt. Extreme need is essential in most traditions to qualify for discussion.

This is especially true when it comes to money. Surely, "Thou shall not ask God for dollars" is the eleventh commandment. You do not ask God for money unless, again, it is for much needed medical services, shelter, or basic essentials like food. Traditionally, money and religion have not mixed well, if at all. In some spiritual traditions money is considered the root of all evil. This pronouncement can be made as a blanket statement and has little to do with greed, envy, dishonesty, the inability to share, or fiscal mismanagement. It has been stated that money, in and of itself, and not necessarily the love of money, is a distraction from the spiritual path.

> *"Verily I say to you, that a rich man shall hardly enter into the kingdom of heaven. And again I say to you, it is easier for a camel to pass through the eye of the needle than for a rich man to enter into the kingdom of God."* (Matthew 19;23-24, KJV of The Holy Bible).

> *"No man can serve two masters: for either he will hate the one and love the other; or else he will hold to one, and despise the other. Ye cannot serve God and money."* (Matthew 6:24, KJV of The Holy Bible).

Obviously, in many minds this does not foster an environment conducive to asking God for money or material possessions. The implied message is that if you really care about money, you are starting down the road to hell and you will get there even faster if you start requesting it from God. Does one ask God, the Being set to come in judgment on the final day for money that is clearly the root of all evil? I think not! The same prohibition is true of material possessions and especially anything that might be considered a luxury such as a new home or trip.

The hidden message in this perspective is that God intended life to be hard or held in check. You are expected to make it on your own. God is not concerned with petty wants and will only provide enough of what is really needed. It is only when life is too hard that prayers for relief are appropriate, otherwise you are expected to stick it out and suffer, offer it up, or struggle in silence. After all, God will not give you more than you can handle!

If you believe in a loving God, why would you not consider the possibility that you were meant to be abundant, happy, fulfilled, and rewarded? And shouldn't the descent of grace include material comfort? I believe that we are here to master our earthly and physical experience in the most spiritual way. This includes how we support ourselves materially, and how we view and use our resources. It is possible to create a balance. It is the love of money and possessions and a lack of concern for and attention to spiritual development and a relationship with God that is an impediment, not money and possessions in and of themselves. An openhearted attitude of sharing what is manifested magnifies abundance and the connection to God. In the same way that a spiritually evolved individual instills the God-like qualities of peace, love, and kindness into the environment, a spiritually *and* materially evolved individual can instill abundance, gratitude, and physical well-being into the environment.

I believe that it is okay to ask God for money if you are willing to surrender the results and do your part. "Not my will, but thy Will." Honor the fact that God has the right to say, "No!" My feeling is that money is more likely to come when you are doing exactly what you love to do or what you feel you are meant to do. If you are dedicated to your purpose, you will be supported in your request. Not so if you are just looking for a lottery win.

An Example of Asking for Money

Many years ago I was self-employed with a part-time counseling practice. I was married, raising small children so work was not steady or daily. One day I discovered a mistake in my checkbook. I knew if I did not earn money quickly, I would be overdrawn in a matter of days. So I made this request:

> "Dear God, I need two clients to help me cover my checkbook error. I know you hear me and respond to my prayers, but I am very anxious right now. If you could send me those two clients before this evening, I would feel much better."

I had three new clients call before dinner, something that had never happened before. It is okay to ask for money, but do the work you were meant to do and be responsible with the funds. Wastefulness and financial mismanagement can wear out your welcome. God does not punish or judge, but once you make it clear that you need to learn to handle money wisely, financial limitation and lack can further your spiritual education and be for "your highest good."

When it comes to money, I always thought of it as coming from God. I would look at the bills and say, "Somebody's got to pay these bills! I don't mind doing the work, but you've got to bring the money in." That was my agreement with God. God would send me the clients, speaking engagements, or book orders, and I would do the work I was meant to do, giving it my best effort. And when the checkbook had plenty of money, and the work did not come, I knew to rest and enjoy time with my family.

Asking for Assistance

Then there are the nonmaterialistic desires that nonetheless are still outside of the normal spiritual criteria for Divine requests. "God, please send me a lover, husband, or wife." Or, "God, please help me lose weight." These are intentions that improve your lifestyle. You do not have to be addicted and in an Anonymous support group to qualify for assistance. You do not have to be in dire need to ask for help. On the other hand, you do not have to be perfect or even deserving of assistance. It is a given. You only need to be willing to make a request, believe that it will be heard, even fulfilled if it is for your highest good. Trust enough to remain open to receiving and follow instructions. When you ask God to help you lose weight, but then ignore your queasy stomach or that small voice saying "don't eat that" when you reach for ice cream and cake, you are thwarting the very assistance you requested. It is okay to ask, but then be sure to listen and heed.

An Example of Asking for Information

How frequently do we ask for wisdom or the answer to a specific question? I once asked a burning question about "self." As a professionally trained counselor, I wanted to understand the Western psychological concept of the need for strong boundaries to define "self" in light of the Eastern Buddhist concept of "no-self." These two very different concepts seemed like mutually exclusive systems of thought or perspectives on life until the answer roared in on me. One day, several months after silently asking the question of God, and while driving on the New Jersey Turnpike, the answer became very clear and obvious. There is a graduated integration of needs in response to various circumstances and levels of development. Some individuals need to establish strong boundaries to maintain personal identity and enable self-expression. Others already know who they are at their core and are able to bypass personal preference and self-interest for the sake of service or spiritual development. They are already strong psychologically and spiritually.

In a matter of moments, my thinking shifted as a whole new understanding arose. When this insight occurred, it was not my normal mode of thought, in fact, I do not believe I was doing the thinking, or thinking at all. I was in the midst of pure insight, a state of accelerated understanding that I attribute to Divine presence and response. I would normally access this state in prayer or meditation, but it is also possible to experience it while participating in everyday tasks. Because of the insight received at that time, I am no longer torn between my Western training and my Eastern beliefs. The new combined system makes perfect sense to me.

When you have established a co-creative partnership with God, you can turn to the Divine with all the comings and goings of your life. God becomes ever present in everything you do. You do not just interact during evening prayers or weekly services. It is a twenty-four (hours) seven (days a week) connection. This is a great comfort and strength that is always available, lending insight to your choices and responses. When you are faced with a difficult decision or confused and don't know what to do, ask for wisdom. Ask to see clearly. Beseech! Beg! And then wait patiently for a response. You will be supported.

How Asking can Create Intimacy with God

Many would say that to ask God for anything other than healing, forgiveness, guidance, and what is strictly essential for survival is asking for too much or asking for something inappropriate. To ask for a strictly material item, or worse yet, luxury item would degrade God's image to the level of a benefactor instead of a Being deserving of all our devotion and worship. I am not negating the need to honor God in a sacred and holy way. This is part of Heart Journey. The desire to manifest through a co-creative, Spirit-based exchange fosters great intimacy within one's partnership with God leading to an *increase* in devotion. Regardless of the request, daily interaction enhances awareness, gratitude, humility, and awe. In this way, sacredness and honoring grow along with the desire to surrender, be of service, and do God's work on earth.

The Need for Cleansing

Despite how it might seem at this point, asking does not lead to free handouts. Spiritual development and heart openness are necessary to establish the co-creative partnership and foster manifestation. As your relationship with God deepens, you will be called to cleanse limiting and unloving thought patterns. You will work hard to develop the qualities of compassion and understanding. You must open your heart to God and your neighbor before you can begin to attract and manifest anything. Your experience within the co-creative partnerships does this by repeatedly asking the question:

> Do you wish to be angry, hurt, fearful, vengeful, _____, [insert your own personal favorite counterproductive emotion here], or do you wish to release your negativity and move closer to manifesting your intent? You cannot experience both. They are mutually exclusive and will never exist in the same space at the same time.

This is where the rubber meets the road and spirituality has a direct impact on your material abundance and desired intent. It is a truth and a natural law already stated one way or another in many traditions including "A Course in Miracles" that just as light and darkness cannot exist in the same space, love and fear cannot exist in the same space either. Only love has the power of attraction. If you want to manifest through the power of attraction, you have to mature spiritually. You have to "Love your neighbor as yourself." You have heard this phrase time and time again. You know that this is the ideal, but now you need to consider the possibility that it is also the smartest thing you can do to enhance you own material and spiritual abundance. Heart Journey is not a free ride. You must practice and master lovingness to open you heart to giving as well as receiving.

Heart Journey is a program of spiritual development that the layperson with a family, career, and responsibilities can practice in everyday life, on the job and in the home. It is meant to integrate spirituality and the presence of God into the material and physical aspects of living. All spiritual practices are intended to open the heart to a stronger connection with God and Heart Journey is no exception. Your request and work with the process of manifestation are not the end points of your journey with God and do not represent the totality of your co-creative partnership which is actually unlimited. Your request is only a beginning, an initiation, as all practices are. Eventually, you and God chart your own course which is highly individualistic, mystical, and can barely be spoken of or expressed in words. Heart Journey is much larger than your request. It is simply a beginning to a mystical pilgrimage. Heart Journey concentrates and focuses your attention to help you discover where and how a mystical relationship with God begins.

All that Heart Journey has to offer can occur regardless of whether or not you get what you ask for. The success of your Heart Journey, co-creative partnership with God, spiritual development, and ability to integrate spirituality into your material and mundane experience is not dependent in any way on the successful manifestation and fulfillment of your desire. It is the journey and not the destination that is valuable. In fact, sometimes the reverse is true and you go farther by surrendering your desire than holding on to it. The absence of manifestation can be equally as powerful as fulfillment and can lead you deeper into your relationship with God and your understanding of the integration of spiritual and material worlds. This is a can't lose program in regard to your co-creative relationship with God. Both desire and/or surrender can lead to spiritual maturity.

Asking is only the beginning and an initiation into the co-creative partnership. Surrendering the results of your request is the second necessary step to establishing the co-creative partnership with God.

Chapter Two:
Surrendering the Results

The second element needed to initiate and establish a co-creative partnership with God is to release and surrender the results of your request. You have to accept the possibility at the very outset that what you desire, intend, or wish to manifest might not happen. This does not mean that you are a failure or that God is not listening or refusing to respond. This does not mean that you are unsuccessful in your attempt to establish a co-creative partnership. Nothing is wasted in Heart Journey, and in actuality, you might even get upgraded to something better than what you asked for or even imagined. You must be open to alternatives and know that every request is heard, honored, and responded to, even when the answer is "No!" You and your co-creative Partner are working together for the best possible outcome in keeping with your highest good and the good of all concerned. This can only occur when you are willing to loosen the reins of control and be led.

How Heart Journey is Different

Surrender is a major component of Heart Journey because it is one of the elements that makes the process spiritual. It is every bit as important as asking. Presently there are many self-help manifestation programs available. Most are built on personal power, individual effort, and/or your own will. These programs help you get organized. They teach you how to stay focused on the intended goal through a discussion of successful time management and motivational techniques. The emphasis is on how you can make it happen and push things through against all odds if necessary. The responsibility for your success or failure falls squarely of your shoulders and your ability to master the program. Surrender is not an option. Surrender is not even discussed. While these programs may be successful in their own venue, they are not intended to be spiritual. They are intended to be psychologically uplifting and motivating. Their process is self-mastery. Their purpose is achievement. Manifestation occurs through effort and organization, not through the power of attraction and not in a co-creative partnership with God.

Heart Journey, on the other hand, is not a "do or die trying" program. You do not have a checklist of things to do which you then attack with enthusiasm and resolve. You do not push or force the issue. It is not your individual ego or efforts making something happen. It is the co-creative partnership with God that fosters the power of attraction, drawing to you that which you wish to manifest or experience. Desire and asking initiate the process. An open, loving heart powers the attraction. Surrender allows for Divine guidance.

The Importance of Surrender

Surrender is a necessary element for co-creative partnership. Surrender coupled with a request is an invitation to God to participate as a partner and guide in the manifestation process. If you do not entertain the possibility of surrender to a Higher Authority, then there is no place in your request for co-creation. Surrender, even if only a little in the beginning, is at the very core of Heart Journey. It is innate to the process to "let go and let God." You will not get anywhere without the recognition and acceptance of the need to yield to a Power much wiser and more creative than yourself. In fact, you would be pretty foolish not to do so! God has a different perspective than you do. God sees the past, the future and all the steps and interactions with others in between. God is more imaginative than you when it comes to solutions and rewards. You can have no better co-creative partner than God. It is to your advantage to allow, accept and follow.

Surrender is a major component of many spiritual traditions. In Christianity, one dies to self so that Christ might live through the believer. One of the meanings of the word "Islam" is surrender. The mystic is called to surrender and trust in the journey beyond reason to God. Sooner or later, they all focus on the act of yielding to a greater, more intelligent, and loving Force. Yielding is what makes Heart Journey spirit-based. Surrender is what makes asking a spiritual practice. The relinquishing of control opens the heart to receiving. When you enter into the co-creative experience with God you have to trust. You have to accept the possibility that what you wish for might not happen when you want it to happen, might not happen in the manner of your choosing, or might not happen at all if it is not for your highest good and the highest good of all those involved. Something better could be available, or perhaps it is better that nothing change or occur. There are always events and influences beyond your awareness. Surrender allows you to entertain other possibilities.

For this reason, all requests and contracts are to be qualified with the statement, "Not my will, but Thy Will and for the highest good of all concerned." Even if you forget to include this in your request, it is still implied. In Heart Journey, all intentions are subject to change within the co-creative dynamic which is never static. Conditions can change moment to moment and you must be willing to adapt. You have to be able to follow your Partner's lead and flow in the direction of ease, so stay alert. Be prepared to yield when the opportunity for Divine creative intervention arises.

An Example of Surrender to Divine Creativity

One very hot summer day, I helped to build a sweat lodge. The temperature was over a hundred degrees and the humidity was 100 percent. I was in the sun most of the day, and just as the sun set, we went into the lodge for a sweat. By the end of the day, I was feeling sick from the heat.

The next day, I was to take visitors to an open, above ground mine for a day of hunting for crystals. I had never been to this mine or any mine before. Driving on the interstate at 9:30 in the morning, it was already ninety-five degrees. I did not think I could physically handle another day in the sun and heat. In particular, I did not want to be in a hot, glaring, windless, gravel pit searching for tiny crystals, so I made a request to God for a cloudy day. In my small mind and with my limited ability to create, this was the best that I could do.

The instance I made my request, a truck passed pulling a boat on a trailer. The name of the boat was "Afternoon Delight." I understood that this could be a message that my request had been heard and answered. Perhaps an upgrade was in the future, something better than clouds. This was great play for me and I yielded immediately, saying, "I accept! Show me!"

An hour or so later, we arrived at the mine. The sun was still shining, but this was no windless, glaring, gravel pit. The mine was nestled deep in a cool pine forest and along the side of a bubbling brook. The temperature was around eighty-five degrees. We sat in the shade of the trees by the running water and spent a wonderful day sifting through dirt and stones finding garnet, amazonite, unakite, and rough opal crystals.

In my judgment, cloudiness was the only option for the gravel pit, heat, and humidity I was doomed to face. My thinking was very limited, and my solution to the problem was, frankly, boring. God on the other hand, dwells in unlimited potential and is a much better Creator than I am. I was very grateful for the communication and a delightful day.

How the Process of Surrender Begins

This example illustrates the obvious and nonthreatening choice when it comes to surrendering and yielding. It is, and I chose it specifically for that reason. This is how the process of surrender can start. It does not have to involve a major life issue. It can be a very simple process like listening to offers and saying "yes" to what's behind door number two. As with learning to ask, you can begin with small surrenders. Practice yielding to little, everyday, ordinary miracles. Over time, you will see the value in yielding and grow less resistant to surrendering control.

The "afternoon delight" story is a good example of the early days in a co-creative partnership with God when you never know what will happen or what is possible. You are continually surprised, amazed, and grateful. You begin to see how limited your own thinking is and how much you need to let go and open in order to receive the full creative benefit from God. Small blessings arise in the most ordinary circumstances. You might not even notice or be aware of these events unless you are paying attention.

Some will discount this story as pure coincidence though the timing of the trailer and boat was instantaneous to the request. Some will claim that the weather for an outing is far too petty for God to be concerned with and I was irreverent to make such a request. Still others will say that reality is fixed. The mine was always cool and shaded, and everything that happened was totally blown out of proportion and misinterpreted by my own imagination.

I don't apologize for my experiences. I don't try to explain them to others. And even more importantly, I do not try to explain them away or discount them. My experiences simply are, as illogical and irrational as they may sound to some. To me they are God whispers and part of the playful co-creative dynamic with God that I have experienced and prospered by. You do not have to believe them. You should not expect to have the same experiences. But I trust that you will have your own experiences within your own co-creative partnership with God. I retell my stories here to clarify the concepts I present and open you to the possibility of your own exchange with the Divine.

As you move on to the next chapter and seek to discover your heart's desire, remember that surrender can be a positive experience with beneficial results. It does not necessarily involve suffering, but can instead involve great play. Within this play, ordinary everyday miracles do occur. You do not have to see fireworks in the sky spelling out God's name or witness the lame rising to walk to be touched by God's presence. God is right here, right now, in this very moment. When you surrender, you open to small, everyday miracles occurring in your own life. With time, the miracles can become unbelievable. But then later, even the most difficult to believe events will become ordinary and common place, something to be expected, just a natural part of living and co-creating with God. Others will doubt or dispute your experiences, but your experiences are authentic no matter how miraculous.

Chapter Three:
Heart's Desire

Desire as the Basis for Asking

Once you have decided that you wish to enter into a co-creative partnership with God and understand the need to both ask for what you want and surrender the results of your request, you must determine what it is that you truly want. You can start out with something small and make a simple statement if you like, but you can do a formal contract requesting what you wish to manifest. Composing a contract in words or symbols is extremely powerful and requires careful consideration. It should not be done lightly or quickly. You have to determine what should be included in your contract and what should be left unsaid. In the best of circumstances you get to the very root of your intention and ascertain your true and present heart's desire.

Heart's Desire

Desire fuels the co-creative relationship with the Divine and the manifestation process. It is as essential as water is to a plant. The stronger the desire, the more energy fueling the process. The truer the intention, the less friction and fewer impediments you will experience along the way. The strongest and truest desired intention is found in your heart and is known as your heart's desire.

How do you determine your heart's desire? It has distinctive characteristics. You have to *really* want it. It has to be something you are passionate and excited about. It should bring a smile to your face and joy to your heart just to think about it becoming real. It should get your juices flowing early in the morning, keep you going all day, and dreaming all night. It should not be a passing fancy. It is better if you know in your heart you were born to do something meaningful, be an agent for change, or experience the fulfillment of your desire. At its best, your heart's desire should be something you have wanted to do all your life, something you were born to manifest from the very beginning. A less formative desire or less lofty material intention will still suffice. Your heart's desire does not have to be spiritual in nature for manifestation to occur as long as you stay with it. However, it is those individuals who eat, drink, breathe, and ache with desire and commitment who manifest the highest levels of attainment.

False Desire

If desire is the fuel and energy for the co-creative partnership and manifestation, false desire is empty calories. It will get you nowhere. It does not have power or potential. You cannot want it, whatever "it" might be because it is the correct thing to request. Your intention cannot be something that your parents would expect you to do, your spouse needs you to do, or is in keeping with your traditions. It can't be the right thing, the rational thing, the acceptable thing, or even the spiritual thing. It cannot be chosen for the purpose of other's approval or regard. It has to be your own, your heart's desire. Any second-rate, half-baked wish will become becalmed and go nowhere. For manifestation to occur, your vision should be backed by strong and steady focused intent fueled by passionate desire.

The Ineffectiveness of What You Don't Want

Do not get derailed by focusing on what you do not want. This might be a good beginning, a jumping off point, but it is a lousy finish. Negative visions are not co-creative and lack potential because they do not make a visionary statement regarding where you wish to go or what you wish to do, have, or be. Positive desires are co-creative because they channel the energy of desire and Divine potential into a perceivable outcome. Energy will follow thought and foster a magnetic or attractive impulse. What you do not want to have in your life does not have this kind of power because there is no goal in mind. There is nothing at the end of the tunnel other than the absence of a difficult or unpleasant situation. Your vision is void and therefore lacks strength. At the same time you run the risk of attracting more of what you do not want. Energy has been known to follow negative thoughts and attract negative results. For example, "I hate my job," might lead to unemployment. It would be more powerful and attractive to state the positive characteristics you want for your next career move.

Dream higher and dream well. If there is a situation in your life that needs improvement or closure, pray the solution and not the problem. Translate all negative situations into clearly defined positive outcomes. Focus on the potential for transformation. Seek the highest good for all involved by expanding your thinking and visionary potential beyond any limiting feelings of woundedness, anger, fear, or victimization.

Victimization Versus Co-creation

I have a saying that I keep in mind whenever I get upset or feel victimized. "Don't get angry, don't get even, get enlightened!" We all have situations that seem unfair and beyond our control, but it is important to separate the external situation of being a victim from the internal mindset of feeling, behaving, and responding as a victim. Do not get stuck. Do not dwell on your woundedness. Thinking like a victim will only intensify or prolong the victimization. Energy will follow thought! Instead, think like the co-creator you are. God may be your Partner, but God is not the only co-creator in the partnership. You also have potential. Pick yourself up and begin to dream, desire, and manifest! What would God do in your situation? What would God create? (That's a loving God, by the way. Smiting your enemies is not an option!) Heart Journey is about open-heartedness.

You have two choices, you can get trapped in the victim mode whenever something hurtful happens to you or you can create something better. The two points of view and options for action are mutually exclusive. You cannot create as long as you are wallowing. In fact, you cannot see options while wallowing. You have to let go of the victim mentality completely before a paradigm shift to creative alternatives can occur.

Example of Victimization Versus Co-creation

Fred had a very unreliable car. It was constantly failing him at the most inopportune times and costing him a lot of money for repairs. He kept thinking, "I need a new car." Day by day, his need increased! Energy follows thought and this is bad wording because it emphasizes need more than new car. A better statement might be, "I can afford a new car." Finally, Fred's car died completely and he was totally without transportation to work and school. There was an unused, good car in the immediate family that would have helped him out at least temporarily until a new car could be purchased, but it was never offered to him to buy or even to borrow. Fred did not feel comfortable asking for it. For two days Fred felt victimized by his situation, family, and even God. He was wallowing. How could God let this happen when he was at such a low ebb financially and at such a difficult time in his life? Why didn't his family come to his rescue and give him the unused car, or at least let him use it temporarily?

Fortunately, Fred only wallowed for two days. Knowing a victim mentality negates the co-creative potential, he decided to shift his thinking. He began to think creatively with the understanding that if this seeming misfortune had befallen him, it might be for his highest good, and if he dealt with it directly it would be with the full support of God. A few days after adopting this new, braver, co-creative style of responding to this situation, Fred bought a brand new car. The down payment was made with money he got from trading in his old car. The monthly payments were less than the monthly repairs on the old car, and to make matters sweeter, he had been able to negotiate a much lower price for features he had always wanted in a car. Now he had a sunroof and automatic door locks and windows. The endpoint of Fred's car problem was a cheaper, new, nicer, mechanically sound car with better gas mileage. This was not just a better alternative to the old car, it was also a much better alternative to the "woe is me" attitude that initially consumed him.

Your vision should never rest in victimization. You cannot create what you truly want from this position or any negative position. As long as you think, feel, and behave like a victim, you will continue to experience life as a victim to any number of people and forces. This mindset weakens you and drains away your ability to desire, hope, and co-create. It defocuses your energy. Without the energy and focus innate to desire and a positive intention, there is nothing to fuel the co-creative process. When you get in this state - stop! Think! Remember that co-creative manifestation is only a paradigm shift away. Take a deep breath and then shift. Begin to desire, refocus your attention, redefine your intention, and co-create.

Styles of Discernment

People fall into three separate categories in regard to determining heart's desire. There are individuals with an already chosen desire, individuals who wish to surrender completely to God's desire, and those who are virtually clueless.

Strong Desire

Some people know exactly what they want right from the start. Though they may use the information in this chapter to hone their request, they already know where their passion lies and what to ask for. For them, any techniques for determining desire would seem to state the obvious and simply confirm what they are already thinking. Determining your desire does not have to be a difficult process. I recommend that you not be impulsive even if you know what you want. Once you open yourself up to the possibility of asking, your request will evolve over a period of time and the format or wording of your request might change. If you can, stay with this process for at least a month. Take time for reflection, prayer, meditation, and greater clarity. This will make your request more powerful and to the point.

Be forewarned that if your desire is very strong and clear, your surrender will need to be equally strong during your Heart Journey. Desire and surrender need to be an equally matched pair.

Confusion and Uncertainty

There are some people who are clueless right from the beginning as to what they might desire. They are totally lost. Not only is the process of asking foreign for them, but the inward search for passion also seems without precedence. They would like to feel passionate and discover their heart's desire, but they honestly do not know what they might be passionate about. Many of these individuals have been caregivers for long periods of time. The question, "What do *I* want?" has not come up. For others, their upbringing centered more on external cues such as the perceptions of others, peer pressure, and the need for approval than internal cues. The ability to recognize personal preference, likes, dislikes, and the possibility of self-determination is undeveloped.

While the information in this chapter will be helpful, these people can still feel confused and uncertain. That is not unexpected. Remember, few of us have been taught to ask or trained how to do it. It is a learning process for everyone. Don't be afraid. God is kind and loving. If you ask for something that is not for your highest good and the good of all those involved, God will simply say, "No." Take time to test the waters and slowly feel your way.

The important thing is this: if you find yourself feeling uncertain and confused do not fall victim to someone else's input. Do not ask for outside help. Do not reinforce the attention to external cues. This is counterproductive. Instead, use this time to turn to God for insight and direction. Meditate, pray, sit on a beach, or walk in the park. This is your opportunity to get closer to God. This is the start of your Heart Journey. You do not have to have a clearly defined, specific goal, though that is the ideal. Have a sense of the direction you wish to head. You can improvise and make adjustments as you go, but take the time to reflect and contemplate until you have something to start with.

For you, Heart Journey will involve constant reassessment until your heart's desire becomes clear. With each step you may need to adjust the wording or symbolism in your contract. Determining desire and learning to ask will be an ongoing process.

Strong Surrender to God's Desire
There are some who truly do not have a strong desire either because they are in an unworkable situation that requires surrender and/or they feel more comfortable with total surrender. God's desire is their desire which is eventually the point we all reach in Heart Journey, this life time or beyond.

There is a clear distinction between these people and those just mentioned above. The people in strong surrender are neither confused nor uncertain. They are as clear as those in the category of strong desire only they are in the opposite pole of strong surrender. They are ready to relinquish control completely or at least over some area of their lives and they have a very trusting relationship with God. Spiritual development is essential with this contract choice. It is a position of strength and not weakness. The contract is built around the "desire to surrender" rather than desire in and of itself.

What does a surrender contract look like? I have seen simple, "I accept" contracts, or those that included only one word or theme, i.e., "Surrender," or "Yes!" "Use me," is another. These contracts are extremely powerful. The individuals who wrote and signed these contracts all had amazing Heart Journeys, as powerful as those with strong desire.

This kind of contract is particularly transforming when there is a situation in your life that you cannot solve, cannot control, and need to turn over to God. By surrendering and accepting God's desire, you are placing people, situations, issues, or feelings in God's hands, letting God decide and direct the outcome. What might seem scary and foolhardy to some, is actually very comforting to those who trust and are confident of God's love.

The Heart Journey for those individuals who focus on surrender can be a continuing set of releases that require higher and higher degrees of faith and trust. Some eventually come to a crossroads that only complete surrender can bridge. Even the desire for union with God must be surrendered for union to occur. Others come to a crossroads that finally requires making a choice, a personal choice based on desire.

Methods for Determining Heart's Desire or Surrender

Listening within and the Inner Voice

There are a number of ways to discern the appropriate intention for your Heart Journey, but the best ones all involve the ability to listen within. This is done through meditation, prayer, journaling, art, poetry, walking, or sitting communing with nature. Set time aside daily and don't be rushed. You want the process of determining your heart's desire to stabilize before you actually make your request. As long as there are daily shifts going on and your desire statement is changing repeatedly, you are not ready. Stay with it until there is some consistency or at least a common theme. Then look for refinement. Hone and focus your desire. Remember, you are growing spiritually. If your desire is changing it can be a signal that your thinking is being uplifted to higher and higher levels of intention, lovingness, and clarity. Allow time for this to happen before forming your contract into words and symbols.

If you have never listened internally before, when you first turn inward there might be a flood of information that needs to be processed before you get down to the realization of a desire. Anger or fear can arise as part of a cleansing reaction. If listening to these emotions is long overdue it could take time to get some clarity on a positive vision. Remember, it is not enough just to know what you do not want. It can be the beginning of awareness, but it is not the end product because what you don't want doesn't have co-creative, magnetic power. It cannot foster positive attraction. Continue to reflect until a productive vision arises.

You will know you are not ready if all your desires seem to be solely the product of negative emotions born of difficult situations you wish to free yourself from. Journaling or artistic rendering will help you bring the issues to the surface more quickly. Some thoughts you will need to let go of, but others might lead you to necessary components of your desire. Do not be in a hurry to get on with it. You are not just working on the endpoint of determining your desire, you are also strengthening you intuitive abilities by learning to listen, reflect, know, accept, and process information regardless of whether its purpose is to cleanse, to transform, or to identify intention. Stay with the evolution until a visionary perspective arises around freedom, what you wish to do, where you wish to go, or how you wish to proceed. You must have a positive desire or surrender statement to move toward.

Recognizing Passion

Knowing what brings you great joy is a blessing and helps with your Heart Journey discernment. God intends for you to be happy, and therefore, that which brings a smile to your face, joy to your heart, excites you, relieves all sadness, and gives you a sense of fulfillment is closely connected to your heart's desire. Passion is a powerful force and a twin sister to desire. Many times they go hand in hand. If you feel this kind of emotional pull towards a situation or activity, it is important to follow up on it even if it is not the most logical or financially lucrative idea you ever had. When you state your intention you do not have to know or understand how everything will fall into place or come about, but you do have to know what turns you on, draws you, fulfills and nurtures you on an emotional level. This is a vital piece of information and not to be ignored.

Some people want to pick an intention that is safe and secure, such as financial security. You might get side tracked into what makes the most sense and will be financially lucrative. Heart Journey is not about logic or security. It is about desire and passion. If these elements are not present, you will not have the energy to attract. Don't be distracted by what you think you should do, what feels safest, or even what is most logical and within your grasp to manifest. You have missed the point if you choose something you know you can do successfully on your own. You will not need a co-creative Partner in that case. Instead aim higher; aim for your heart's desire.

Personal Symbolism

Symbols can be very important as you prepare to compose your Heart Journey contract. In the best sense, they can be indications of what is and is not important. Be observant of everything that goes on around you, particularly repetitive sightings. In the Native American tradition, animals, birds, and signs that occur in nature are pieces of information. This is a form of communication. Native Americans believe that Mother Earth and Great Spirit are talking all the time through the happenings in nature. There are books that describe the meaning and power associated with each animal. If a symbol or comment comes to you several times and in several different ways, it might be significant to your discernment process. Pay attention and do a little research into the meaning or meanings of that symbol. If it has import and seems to apply, reflect on what it means generally as well as what it means to you personally. If it does not seem to apply or make sense to you, let it go.

Example of Personal Symbolism

I go walking at a local park most days. There are deer, fox, Canadian geese, turtles, heron, bluebirds, and various other birds in the park, but I do not see any of them with great consistency. So I pay attention when I do see something. To me, the deer always means gentleness. I immediately backtrack to what I was thinking when I first noticed the deer. Do I need to gentle my stance on a particular topic? When I see a turtle, I consider the need to be more protective or to move slowly. The fox signals the need to be smarter about the way I handle things. These might not be the interpretations others would use, but they are the ones that work for me at this time.

Each summer I note what weeds, or "volunteer medicinal herbs" (as some people prefer to call them), grow in my garden. They are clues to my own physical and psychological health. I had lots of thistle springing up in the garden though I pulled it up many times. It was several years before I discovered that what I was not able to pull up were the rhizomes 12 inches down in the ground. These spread, even in winter. To me this was a sign that I needed to look below the surface into what was going on in my life and what I was feeling at a deeper level. And, I should adjust my response. What I was doing was not working. The weeds kept growing back and I was constantly pulling up thistle. Once I understood that my actions were ineffective I knew to try a different response in regard to other areas of my life besides the weeds in the garden. What goes on around you can be directly important to Heart Journey and the discernment of your heart's desire.

Moving Ahead Regardless

What if you have done your reflecting and are still confused? What if you are unable to listen inwardly, but you know what you want? What if your desire keeps shifting on a daily basis? If you have spent a month trying to daily discern your desire and you feel you have done all you can do, it may be time to move on. You are not meant to get stuck in reflection permanently. Do your homework and then start to compose your contact or intention as best you can. Heart Journey is a learning process and you do not have to be perfect. Conditions do not have to be ideal. Getting clear of confusion is part of your journey both before and after you activate your intention. The lenses will continue to align and come into focus. Learning to reflect is a continuing part of Heart Journey and you will come back to this process again and again as further shifts occur. With time you will grow to hear the inner voice more clearly. For now, be as open and insightful as you can and then move on.

Gather all the information you have and begin to create a vision that is an integration of what you have come to realize or understand along the way. The end product should be a culmination of all the insights you have had. Your desire might exist on only one level, the physical, emotional, mental or spiritual plane, or it might be a multidimensional request. It can be singular or complex. It does not matter as long as you are comfortable with your intention and it truly reflects your heart's desire.

Final Steps and Confirmation

Once you have a vision in your mind, close your eyes, relax, and picture the outcome you want. Walk through it step by step. Does it feel right to you? Are you comfortable with the goal you are setting? Can you see yourself completing the tasks at hand and arriving at the destination? Are you able to hold to your desire over time? Can you hold it loosely and yield when and if need be? It is important to be open to all possibilities and possible ways of manifestation. Are you comfortable with allowing God to modify the results or choose the method of fulfillment?

If all of this seems relaxed and natural, or as close to natural as you can get at this time, then you are ready to compose your contract and on your way to forming a co-creative partnership intent on manifesting your dream.

Chapter Four:
Negating the "Gimme God" Image

It is not the intention of Heart Journey to foster a gimme God image, a God whose purpose is to fulfill human desires. God is not a fairy godmother in the sky and cannot be reduced to that within Heart Journey. Though it is true that you are to form a contract based on your heart's desire, the level of interaction, cooperation, and personal integrity you need to maintain your Heart Journey precludes anything other than sacredness. What sounds simple in the beginning is actually a spiritual path demanding surrender, discipline, patience, and open-hearted lovingness. You will need to do your part within the co-creative partnership and develop spiritually by releasing limiting thought patterns, cleansing negativity, and becoming more loving. Heart Journey is not a free ride and your co-creative Partner is not a gimme God. There are several aspects of Heart Journey that specifically negate the gimme God image.

Surrender

The first major challenge to the gimme God image is surrender. All intentions are to be qualified with the statement, "Not my will, but Thy Will and for the highest good of all concerned." This statement is innate to Heart Journey. It is part of the program even if you forget to include this in your contract. The process of manifestation through attraction and receptivity depends on open-heartedness. It depends on yielding to a higher authority. This is non-negotiable.

In order to communicate with your co-creative Partner and follow God's lead you must be willing to surrender to guidance and insight. When working cooperatively with God there is great ease. Everything falls into place and flows. This is a great indication that you go with God. When on your own ego-driven trip forcing things to happen, there is stress, difficulty and delay. Nothing seems to be working and you create your own problems. This is a strong indication that you do not walk with God on this project. You might be magnifying problems by trying to run ahead of schedule when the time is not ripe. On the other hand, you might be procrastinating until you miss important deadlines or run out of time. Even worse, if you are really out of step with Divine guidance, you could be going the wrong way, doing the wrong thing, with the wrong people. Ease and correct timing are by-products of close cooperation with your co-creative Partner. When you walk with God, even though you are delayed or somehow arrive head of schedule, your timing is still perfect, and you show up at the best possible time. Actions become effortless.

There is a subtlety to the whole process of manifestation when you do your part in allowing things to happen rather than imposing your small but tenacious personal will to force things. You act as the gentle midwife who uses all her skills and knowledge to assist the baby and mother with the birthing process. The midwife is never intrusive or invasive. She does not force the baby to be born according to an external schedule. The midwife simply helps the mother focus while guiding the child into this world.

On your Heart Journey you will do the same. You will lend your skills, efforts, and expertise to the manifestation process. You will not force or rush the process. You will not delay or impede. Like the midwife you will gently guide your intention into this world by yielding to the guidance of your co-creative Partner. Though your intention and request are the beginning of the manifestation process, the co-creative partnership is built around your ability to yield and surrender.

No Guarantees

The second challenge to the gimme God image is that there are no guarantees in Heart Journey that your wish will be fulfilled. What you want to happen may or may not occur in the manner of your choosing, within the time frame that you expect, or with the desired results. If your contract is not for your highest good and the good of all involved, nothing will manifest until you reflect, reassess, and reorient yourself accordingly. You must stay open and improvise as necessary. You could be looking east with expectancy, when actually your ship is coming in from the west. When one door closes (or does not open at all), another door opens. Stay alert! Alternatives and options will arise.

An Example of Acceptance and Reorientation

Barbara wished to experience a Native American vision quest with all the trimmings. She wanted to experience a sweat lodge before a silent retreat of five days. She planned to camp out on the beach in a remote area of a national park. Everything was carefully planned down to the smallest detail over a period of months. When the day came, the trek to the backpacking site was very difficult. Everything had to be carried in over a distance. The weather was unusually hot and humid. A five-day supply of water was extremely heavy and all the attempts to lighten the load failed. Having never backpacked before, Barbara and her companion brought much more than was needed. All the authentic Native American paraphernalia and creature comforts weighed them down and required several trips. Moving everything to the site and setting up camp took all day and was exhausting.

In Barbara's mind, she really wanted to get back to nature and experience it in its rawest form. Ultimately, she did experience nature, but not as she expected. By the end of the first day after struggling to set up camp, she wanted to "rape the land and put up a high rise with a shower." Nature in its rawest form had not been kind or supportive. Her encounters with the unyielding forces did not stop with the difficulties getting in and setting up on a remote beach. The next morning, just as the vision quest was beginning, Barbara and her companion were informed by the park ranger that they must evacuate the island immediately as a newly formed, fast moving hurricane was approaching. This meant packing out everything that had just been packed in, a task requiring much coordination. So much for silence! Things were not going according to plan!

Barbara and her friend retreated to a hotel as the storm blew over during the night. Surprisingly, the room came with a steam bath, i.e., sweat lodge! The next noon they were back at the park, but by this time all vision quest plans were cast aside. They trimmed down their packs and only carried the essentials back into the site. There were no plans for silence and no sweat lodge.

What happened over the next few days almost broke Barbara in two. With nothing to do, nothing to read, and not much to say, Barbara sat and watched the sand crabs, gulls, foxes, and ponies. Their antics and idiosyncrasies made them appear almost human. They had distinct personalities and displayed understandable emotions. Barbara watched them clearly communicate with one another. Their command of the area and their ability to survive and thrive in the wild back country was amazing.

But none of them lived in the more populated areas of the park or the public beach. None of them could survive among humans, let alone thrive. The all-terrain vehicles, cars, trash, noise, boats, and the people who brought them devastated the very land wildlife depended on. One could not find a single crab on that stretch of public park beach. In the back country, hundreds of baby sand crabs could be found in a cup of water scooped from the surf's edge.

That is when Barbara broke down and cried, touched by raw nature in a way she had not expected. The very act of her walking on the beach and camping out made her a part of the problem. She was one more human encroaching on a natural environment, stepping on crab dens in the sand, hoping for a high rise and hot shower. She stood looking east and her ship came in from the west.

When you make your request, there are no guarantees regarding what or how things will happen. The manner in which your request might be fulfilled can be totally outside of your realm of thinking. God is better at determining what is needed to get you where you want to go or need to be. The underlying purpose behind your request is more important to God than your chosen or anticipated experience as in the example given. Barbara wanted a silent, Native American vision quest to be touched by nature. In the end, everything fell away except for the raw interaction with nature that touched Barbara deeply.

Simple is Best

The third challenge to the gimme God image is that the simplest intentions or contracts seem to work best. I have seen one-word contracts, six-page contracts, and everything in between. I have seen gardens, altars, collages, scrapbooks, and mobiles used as a contract. The more you ask for and the more complicated your request, the more dilute your focus becomes and the longer manifestation will take, assuming it occurs at all. When your request is complex, your attention is scattered and your statement is less powerful. Energy follows thought, or in this case, energy follows several or many thoughts, dividing your attention, and undermining your ability to attract any one desire.

Focus is essential for manifestation to occur. God is unlimited, but you only have so many brain cells. A simple contract or intention you can carry in your head and heart will get you farther, faster. It has greater co-creative potential because it becomes a point of reference for all that you do. The truth is that simple contracts have profound and far-reaching implications and effects. In a complex or multifaceted request, one item might become contingent on another and this might delay the whole process.

An Example of a Simple Contract

Rick had a one-word contract that he worked with for several years. The word was, "unlimited." He chose this contract at a time in his life when he felt limited by his own fears, lack of confidence, and situations beyond his control. Rick believed in the possibility of unlimited potential, but he did not practice this and he was not sure how to begin. The purpose of the word unlimited was to open him up to new and better ways of thinking, being, and loving that were spacious and freeing. The word unlimited was not qualified or defined in anyway. It stood alone. The contract was as stated, one word and one word only. It was Rick's desire to explore its meaning and to go wherever it and God took him.

As various life situations would arise, Rick would ask himself, "Is this leading me towards my goal of being unlimited? Am I open and courageous, stepping outside of my comfort zone? Or, am I limiting my options and choices based on fear?" Every decision, movement, action, and feeling had to pass inspection given this criteria and new belief system. This might sound mostly like a psychological shift, but changes also took place on the material and spiritual levels as well. The impact of this one word was multidimensional, far-reaching, and profound.

Part of Rick's attention was focused on applying the word unlimited to financial resources and business practices. He started to work smarter, not harder. He thought of ways he could earn money repeatedly while only having to do the work once. In this way,

Rick would not be limited by time. He studied time management issues, becoming more efficient while cutting costs. He began to save and invest, letting his money work for him.

But most importantly, from a spiritual perspective, Rick integrated his financial and professional habits with his philosophy and dedication to the Divine partnership. He began to work co-creatively with God by calling forth work as needed, but trusting that he should create or rest when business was slow. When he needed more money, the phone would ring off the hook and work would pour in. When he needed time off for family and friends the phone might not ring all week. Rick learned to yield control of his work schedule. His job was not to complete this or that task. His job was to walk in balance with his purpose everyday and in every way, both in his personal life as well as in his professional life.

In following God's lead and yielding, perfect timing arose. This adherence to the ebb and flow of business made for greater efficiency and ease because Rick was in tune with the co-creative process.

> *To everything there is a season, and a time for every purpose under Heaven.* (Ecclesiastes 3:1, KJV of The Holy Bible).

By recognizing the pace, there was less stress with greater productivity and more free time. Financial anxiety diminished. Rick grew more relaxed. Meditations were more insightful. All this brought Rick closer to his goal of feeling unlimited while at the same time deepening his intimacy and communication with God. A single word or symbol can have many different interpretations and applications, while at the same time being extremely powerful and life transforming.

A True Partnership

The fourth challenge to the gimme God image is that Heart Journey is a true partnership between you and God. It is not a free ride. For this reason, your intention or desire should be something that you are willing and able to contribute to. If you do not have the necessary skills, then you will need to acquire them and do your part when, and if, you are called upon to do so. Sometimes miracles happen without any input from you, but most of the time your effort is required. Be prepared! God generally does not do it all. The ball will be in your court at some point. You need to be an active, equal, and willing participant to benefit spiritually.

There is so much more to Heart Journey than receiving what you want, but you have to do your part to see those other aspects. If you don't see the need to contribute to the co-creative partnership and become a full participant, you will not understand what Heart Journey is about or experience the co-creative potential of a partnership with God. You will miss out all around.

The Untrue Partnership

Asking to purchase a winning lottery ticket is not doing your fair share of the agreement even if you promise to give some percentage to charity. What co-creative contribution would you be making other than purchasing a ticket? What leap in consciousness is likely to occur with that request? Or surrender? None! You would not be growing spiritually. You would not be co-creating with God heart-felt abundance for others. You are simply attempting to cash in on a "get rich quick" scheme. The money would have nothing to do with your sense of spiritual purpose. You would not have made any effort to love better. Without greater lovingness, there is no heart openness which is key to Heart Journey and the attraction process. If you cannot commit to anything more visionary than a free ride, Heart Journey is not for you and your request will fall on barren ground. Don't waste your time trying.

Manifestation Takes Time

The fifth challenge to the gimme God image is that intentions take time to manifest. They are not generally fulfilled swiftly. You should not be too quick to abandon one contract for another. Normally, I recommend that you spend at least one year with your intention, though two to three years per contract is more likely. Sometimes it can take many years. Manifestation through the co-creative process involves attracting and receiving what you desire and this takes time. The bigger your request, the longer the process can take. The farther you are from the goal, or the greater the distance between your starting point and your final destination, the longer the time period and process also. It is not possible to load up the wish list and move quickly. Some people might spend a life time with one major co-creative project in mind and this is okay.

The process of manifestation through attraction and receptivity requires a period of development and level of experience that grows over time. The co-creative partnership, once established, evolves as you mature spiritually. You learn to communicate and activate spiritual muscles different from the ones you are used to using. Heart Journey is a practice, a spiritual practice that raises your consciousness. Take small steps every day as this is the best way to practice.

It is important to stay with your intention for a period of time even if nothing is happening. Do not rush the process or abandon one intention for another until the initial request is completed or it becomes obvious that manifestation is unlikely ever. The longer you stay with your intention, the stronger your co-creative partnership with God will become.

Heart Openness

The sixth challenge to the gimme God image is that, in general, we all tend to be lousy at receiving. Receiving abundance is a learning process directed at opening the heart to both giving and accepting. One would think that receiving abundance would be an easy task, but it is not. "Attracting and receiving" is not the same as "going and getting." Many people thwart receiving. How many times have you thought of yourself and your life in terms of limitations rather than abundance? You don't have enough money. There is not enough time. You have not done enough or been enough. Is this the thinking that you reinforce? Is the glass half empty rather than half full? Your interpretation is not just a matter of perspective. It has power and affects your ability to receive.

How many times have you complimented someone on their looks or clothes, only to have the compliment negated. "Oh, this old thing! I just threw something on!" How many times have you, yourself, negated a compliment? The first step in attracting and receiving abundance according to your heart's desire is to rework your thinking and change what you say. Be positive. Accept all compliments with a simple, "Thank you!" This is where it all starts.

Opening to attracting and receiving is a skill you will need to master and continue to practice as you open more and more. Each step might bring a new wave of vulnerability as many people equate openness with the likelihood of being hurt or disappointed. Others view it as a loss of control. Some feel the pressure to return in kind everything they receive. This is not true acceptance. Regardless of how sure you might be of what you want, you may not be as ready to receive as you think you are.

Spiritual Development

The seventh challenge to the gimme God image is the need to develop and progress spiritually. By its very nature, a heart opening cleanses negative emotions by bringing them into your awareness. Fears, doubts, anger, a lack of faith, or an inability to surrender must be addressed for you to open your heart and stay open. If painful memories associated with old wounds arise, you need to get beyond these barriers and shift limiting thought patterns to more positive inner states and external responses.

Though other factors are also important, your ability to co-create, attract, and manifest can be proportional to your ability to address your own fears and cleanse negative thoughts. You must stay openhearted and progress spiritually to receive. The strongest attractions occur in those who are able to sustain an attitude of trust and lovingness even in the face of adversity. As you develop and mature spiritually and emotionally, you are better able to achieve this level of trust and lovingness.

Sharing

And finally, the last challenge to the gimme God image is that your ability to receive is fostered and enhanced by your ability to share. What comes to you needs to flow through you and out to others. The buck cannot stop with you. The abundance you receive is meant to go on to generate abundance for others. Abundance is based on continuous movement and flow.

Conclusion

For all these reasons, Heart Journey is a spiritual practice that enriches your relationship with God and heightens your sense of sacredness. It is not intended to foster a gimme God image. Quite the contrary, the co-creative partnership with God leads to spiritual development through surrender, cleansing of negative emotions, and open-heartedness.

Chapter Five:
Pre-contract Considerations

The Purpose of the Heart Journey Contract

The Heart Journey contract, no matter what physical form it eventually takes is meant to reinforce and support what you have learned about yourself and your heart's desire during the reflection and discernment process. Your request at this point could be simple or complex. It could be highly spiritual or mundane. Even mundane requests require spiritual growth and a co-creative partnership with God. In the broadest and highest sense, the focus of your intention might be on your spiritual purpose and on the spiritual development needed to fulfill that destiny. We all have a purpose while here on the planet. The closer we are to our heart's desire, the closer we are to knowing and fulfilling our purpose.

Spiritual Diet

There is an ecological system on the universal plane just as there is an ecological system here on earth. Here we have learned that every seed, plant, animal, and environment is important to the balance and consciousness of Mother Nature. The same is true on the universal plane which is the realm of invisible, spiritual forces. Although all souls are created equal, we are all in different learning stages, moving through dissimilar processes and times. These variations create a diversity necessary for the balance and consciousness of "Mother Universe." Each one of us is important on the universal plane and has a role or purpose to fulfill within the whole.

Here on earth, if you take a seed, plant it in the ground, and give it the right amount of light, water, nutrients, and climate, that seed will sprout, form roots, shoot up, flower, and bear fruit. Under ideal conditions, it will become the very best that it can be and nothing less. It has been programmed for this by God from the beginning of time. As soon as the conditions are right, the seed will glorify its nature.

The same is true of the soul as it manifests through the personality. When given the right amount of light (which is spirit), the right amount of water (which is emotional fulfillment), the right kind of nutrients (which is knowledge), and the right climate (which is the physical environment), you will bloom and glorify your nature too. As soon as the conditions are right, you can become all that you were intended to be by God from the beginning of time. You are programmed for this.

As you prepare to compose your Heart Journey contract, reflect on whether or not you are being fed correctly. Do you set aside time daily for spiritual development? Are your connections to others emotionally satisfying and nourishing? Do you expose your mind to quality insights and creative, artistic, inventive, and enlightened ideas? Does your physical environment facilitate or thwart your efforts? Do you maintain your body? Will the Heart Journey intention you plan to set is motion improve on less than desirable conditions, or support and enhance what is needed for your potential to manifest? The best contracts, no matter how simple or complex, will be a step forward.

Heart Journey Participation

As you reflect on your contract, remember that you do not have to know how your heart's desire will come about. Nor do you have to take full responsibility for making it happen. You will not be following a checklist or to do list that must be accomplished through your own skills and efforts. You are entering into a co-creative partnership. Allow God to assist you and envision this occurring. Expect miracles to happen!

On the flip side, do not expect God to do all the work for you. Heart Journey is a participatory spiritual path and you will need to contribute in a manner that is consistent with your skills, talents, and desires. Keep this in mind since intentions have to be believable. For this reason, your vision should be reasonably achievable with your participation. Being successful with a project you have always wanted to complete is doable. Being financially supported in what you do best is reasonably achievable. Your participation should be whole-hearted and in keeping with who you are. Consider what you excel at, wish to excel at, or are passionate about. Your contract should reflect your love of God and love of co-creating. Do not expect God to carry the load entirely and do not expect to do it all yourself.

It is essential that you believe that your vision can be achieved some day, some how with Divine collaboration and co-creation. You have to be able to see your vision as real and know with certainty that it can be accomplished eventually. Make adjustments accordingly. For example, a seventy-year-old woman is not likely to become a biological mother. This is not doable without medical intervention. But this same woman could become a grandmother, a mentor to an older child, or a sponsor to a child in need. A man who is paralyzed will not be running a marathon, but he can participate in the wheelchair division. If you cannot be an astronaut because of eyesight, age, or medical condition, become a rocket scientist or build rockets in your backyard. There are doable and believable alternatives to every situation. Just look at "Team Hoyt" (www.teamhoyt.com). The father, Dick Hoyt runs, bikes, and swims marathons and triathlons pushing and pulling his son Rick who wants to compete and is wheelchair bound.

For every unattainable or unbelievable option there is an alternative that is doable. Your desire should be something dear to your heart that you believe can happen. If you cannot believe it or see it happening, it won't. The common expression, "Seeing is believing," is rewritten in Heart Journey. "You will see it when you believe it!"

Be Positive

Energy follows thought, and it follows a positive thought faster and more productively than a negative one. God is abundant and the vibratory rate of a hopeful, trusting, loving, and creative thought is more synchronous with Divine intent and potential than the vibratory rate of an angry, fearful, negative one. Like the song says, "Nothing from nothing leaves nothing, you gotta have something if you wanna be with me." It is difficult to co-create around a "don't like" or "don't want" intent. There is little to work with other than the lack of what already exists. You are asking for a "void." Do not waste your energy and time on a negative thought or request. It will go nowhere or cause more harm than good to you as well as to others.

A positive vision based on your heart's desire has potential. It has power. It is alive! Growing! Attractive! Your vision has an immediate vibratory compatibility with abundance. When there is a positive goal, the intention becomes attractive and funnels energy in a directive manner. Make it a better world; take the time to frame your request in the most positive manner. Move through any negativity to ascertain a positive alternative. See yourself in the best of circumstances and shift your intentions to the most rewarding outcome.

Translating Desire into Thought

Your thought is your translation of your desire into concrete, physical terms. It defines the application and implementation of desire into form. For example, someone might be restless for a change. Perhaps s/he realizes the desire is for a career change. Restlessness (negative emotion) has now shifted into a positive intention (new job). Suppose this person wishes to do something more rewarding and fulfilling. This is a valuable piece of information that must be investigated and translated fully into thought. Exactly what does "more rewarding and fulfilling" mean? What are the job characteristics associated with these words? There could be a hundred different meanings. This is where application comes in. Thought is the refined, grounded, measurable definition of your desire. It is the translation into a perceivable outcome with recognizable indicators of attainment or forward movement. Taking our example one step further:

Desire: I want to change my career to something more rewarding and fulfilling.
Translation: I wish to become a doctor to help people heal.

Here we can see that the energy of desire has been funneled into a specific profession directed at fulfilling a particular purpose. Desire is now defined in terms of application and results. This is a crucial step in composing your contract. You must progress from the emotional arena of desire to an accurate mental representation in words or symbols that clearly defines your desire in terms of a perceivable goal or intention. Your translation should not only be true to your originating desire, it should also be focused and concrete.

Be Concrete and Specific

Your request, intention or contract must be specific and not nebulous. Do not say only, "I want peace and love." Define your terms. What is your conception of peace? What form or forms of love you are seeking? Do you want a good friend, a lover, a mate, or someone who fits the bill for all three? Whatever your love interest, you might wish to list some of the qualities you are looking for in another, or what you hope the relationship will look like over time. You do not need a narrow and limiting definition of what you want, but your request must be specific enough to clearly signify progress or some degree of attainment. You should also be able to tell when you are off track or not making any progress. If your goal is specific enough, it acts as a measuring tool or gauge by which you can ascertain the effectiveness of your efforts.

Concrete and Specific Examples

Let's use a few concrete examples. If you ask for money without any qualification, don't be surprised to discover that a dime on the street is money. Is this or is this not the fulfillment of your request? Stating the purpose of the funds broadens your intention, and perhaps what you need will come to you without money. Stranger things have happened and you need to be open to Divine upgrades. If money will be used for a specific purpose, state the purpose, not the amount of money desired. It is the experience you are after. Get to the bottom line.

If you ask for a home, and you are living with your parents, realize that you already have a home. Perhaps you would prefer to say your "own" home and maybe list some desired characteristics, e.g., in a rural area and by a lake or stream.

If you are interested in employment, describe your ideal job. You might get a new job, but unless you have a model, you will not know if this job is in any way connected to your Heart Journey contract and your co-creative relationship with God. Assuming your contract is in effect for several years, and you change jobs a couple of times, a good job description will help you discern your progress towards getting closer and closer to the ideal with each change.

If you are interested in healing, describe what the healed state will look like. You might have multiple problems on the physical, emotional, mental and even spiritual level. What would indicate to you that you are being healed? Contemplate the various forms healing might take.

If you wish to progress spiritually, describe the area of development. Do you wish to be of service to the poor, the infirmed, the young, or the old? Do you wish to teach, preach, or just set a good example? Do you want to be part of a spiritual community? What practice would you like to follow to deepen your spirituality? What vision of your relationship with God do you have in mind?

Definitions need not be narrow or limiting, but some specificity is beneficial. Progress is frequently slow, especially in the beginning. Signs of progress in the present help to guide you in the future and give you valuable feedback regarding the hands-on, daily work involved in Heart Journey. If you have specific items in your contract and can see small changes taking place, this will not only encourage you along the way, but also clue you in on which internal attraction muscles are working and which ones are not. Milestones are also good indicators of effective communication with your co-creative Partner. You will be able to gauge if you are intuiting correctly, choosing wisely, and proceeding in agreement with God. Knowing that progress is occurring in cooperation with God builds and sustains trust.

Any form of positive feedback is encouraging and instructive. You are more likely to be aware of progress occurring, even subtle changes, if your intention is clearly defined with a perceivable outcome. It will also be easier to ascertain when you are becalmed or all progress has stopped.

But Don't be Too Specific

While it is important to be specific, at the same time do not be too specific. Do not request a particular person for a lover, or a certain job with a particular company. Limiting yourself to one person, job, situation, or option as a stated intention narrows your focus and thwarts interest in a co-creative partnership. There is no sharing of information or ideas, no brainstorming with God, no feedback. There is no room to maneuver. When you are this specific, you are not willing to "let go and let God." This is a blatant attempt on your part to control another person or situation. You want what you want and God is expected to deliver. You have flipped through your limited agenda catalogue and now you think you know best. You don't. Requests like this are not only limiting and controlling, they are also not in your best interest because they negate the possibility of a Divine upgrade.

Divine Upgrades

I have always been amazed at God's ability to creatively upgrade my limited thinking. A Divine upgrade is when you get something better than what you asked for. Sometimes you get more than you could have imagined. God substitutes and compensates for your limited wishing as long as you remain open-hearted and loving, and the upgrade is in your best interest. You only need to be upgraded once or twice to get it, how beneficent and abundant a responsive, loving God can be.

Example of an Upgrade

I was headed for a convention and I needed a new pair of shoes. This was in the olden days when shoes were cheap and I was poor. I needed $25 for the shoes and I made my request to the Divine because I did not have the money. Within several days, I started receiving checks from people I had written off as bad debts two years before. For reasons unknown to me, they had never paid my bill or responded to my phone calls. I had since let it go and forgotten about them. Within a week I had $375 even though I only asked for $25. At first I did not get it. I did not understand what was going on. It was not until the third check came in within a week that I saw the pattern and knew what was happening. I had been upgraded. My vision was small at the time. I only needed and only asked for $25 for one pair of shoes, but fortunately I was not taken at my word and the God saw fit to make my whole trip easier financially.

A Focused, Sustained Thought

Your intention needs to be specific and concrete. This will result in a focused thought when translated from desire. Both your desire and focused thought need to be sustained over time. You do not know how long manifestation will take. There is no guarantee regarding if or when it might occur. You must be able to "hold that thought" for as long as necessary. Consequently, you will also need to "hold that desire" as the sustaining force behind the thought for as long as necessary.

During the discernment process, you are advised to continue reflecting until your desire becomes stable. There is a very good reason for this. A desire that is stable will translate into a thought that is stable. The two go hand in hand into the future. When you first begin to reflect, desire can easily fluctuate from day to day. After a month or so, desire becomes more stabilized. It needs to be clear and steady as you begin to translate your desire into a focused, sustained thought. When there is consistency at the point of origination, stability is easier to maintain.

It is important to desire the same thing day after day and not shift to other intentions that either impede or distract from your original contract. Refinement and development of your intention is expected, but mutually exclusive or highly unstable desires will never amount to anything. There is no staying power. This is one of the reasons why people fail to attract what they want. Their request changes frequently. The more stable and desirous you are, the more focused and sustained your thought will be, and the more likely you are to manifest. Stability is crucial to the co-creative process.

The Role of Emotion

Passion increases the effect of desire and adds to its attractive power. Desire tends to be time dependent as some desires come and go, changing over time. But when an individual is passionate about something, the intensity is usually channeled into a life-long quest or character trait. One might say, "I desire a new career or a home," but the same person can be passionate about singing, art, dancing, writing, foreign culture, ethnic food, or spiritual beliefs. A passion can start when you are young and last into old age. Passion magnifies desire by extending and stabilizing its life over time. The two are different, but can work hand in hand.

The emotional dynamic is very important not only for manifestation, but also for the co-creative relationship with God. Heart Journey is a love affair with the Divine and the emotional component is necessary for this connection to be made and maintained. As you open your heart to giving, receiving and loving well, you are also opening your heart to receiving Divine love and guidance. The longer you can sustain a higher and higher level of love and trust, the greater your opportunities for receiving.

On the other hand, the more fear, doubt, or anxiety you experience, the more likely you are to resist receiving. It sounds absurd to be anxious about receiving abundance or your heart's desire, but the truth is that many requests are intended to stretch the individual into new territory. This is where the rubber meets the road. With each intention will come a growth process. You will not be the same person after starting your Heart Journey. It is intended to foster spiritual growth. For this reason, do not state an intention that is far beyond what you can handle emotionally unless you are really ready to step up to the plate. Excitement, anxiety, and nervousness might be expected, but not fear. If you are terribly afraid before you even begin, developing trust in God, your co-creative partner will be difficult.

Emotional investment in your intention is good, even intense emotional investment, but do not become attached to the timing, method, or outcome. Surrender is still essential if you are to work co-creatively with God. The two poles (desire and surrender) work together to foster a creative tension. Always hold your request in open hands, remembering the phrase, "Not my will, but Thy Will, and for the highest good of all involved." As much as you want your vision to manifest, you must still let go and let God.

Necessary Components for Manifestation

A co-creative mind with a focused, sustained thought backed by strong desire and an open heart is powerful. The focused, sustained thought defines the parameters of what is needed or wanted. It directs abundance into form by working co-creatively with God. Desire facilitates consolidation and also attraction. The more desire you have laced with surrender, the greater the dynamic tension between these two poles and the stronger your ability to attract. The more stable your desire, the more sustained your focused thought. It is the open heart which receives abundance. It is love that allows the heart to open and stay receptive. As long as the heart is steeped in positive emotion and not subject to fear, anger, or doubt, receptivity is maintained. This is the process of attraction and manifestation.

Surrender Contracts

Your desire might be to forego personal desire and surrender to God's desire. This is an act of faith and trust in God. If you are writing a surrender contract, the translated thought might not be as specific as that of a desire contract, but it will still need to be sustained. It is also helpful to have guidelines in regard to assessing progress.

For example, assuming you have a one word contract "surrender", you should heighten your awareness of those times and situations wherein you are able to release and let go, and also those times when it is difficult. In the ideal situation you would consciously turn people, places, possessions, and situations over to God for resolution or care. Your intention will be to do nothing and allow God's plan to move forward unimpeded.

You must be a watchdog to catch any tendency to resist letting go. If this occurs, stop and assess the situation. What is there about this situation that is different? Why are you holding on? What do you hope to gain? Prevent? Not lose? What needs to take place for you to move through this resistance? These are questions you would need to address with the help of your co-creative partner.

Make This Journey Your Own

Heart Journey is about you and not about what another should or should not be doing. Mandates, agendas, or an emphasis on others is inappropriate. It will dilute the power of your contract, divert your attention from your true heart's desire, and leave you without a means for a co-creative partnership with God. Heart Journey is your journey, not someone else's. It is about your personal vision and communication with the Divine. This is your chance to ask for the highest and the best you can conceive of, spiritually, mentally, emotionally, and/or physically. You do not have, should not have, and will not have control over how others act now or in the future. If anything, Heart Journey is about letting go of control and placing others in God's care. When you write contracts about expectations you have of others you set yourself up for failure. Also, it is not okay to compose a contract for someone else to sign.

There is a gray area in regard to contracts that involve relationships. It is all right to request better, more loving relationships. It is all right to seek to honor your spouse, children, friends, or parents. It is all right to ask for relationship healing or to wish to be a better lover. These situations might be within your power to transform, if and when you change your attitude and behavior. Use wording similar to, "I am now having a loving and committed relationship with an intimate partner that benefits us both," or, "I am committed to loving well," or, "I ask God to bless and guide our union."

On the other hand, it is not all right to request that a specific person begin to respond in a particular way, even if you think it is for his or her own good. For example, "My spouse has given up philandering and is totally committed to me," is not an appropriate Heart Journey relationship intention. Nor is, "I have a better relationship with my spouse because s/he has stopped drinking." When others are involved, be general, compassionate, and loving, not controlling or judgmental.

Love as a Remedy

One reason individuals end up with long and involved contracts is that they want to have a perfect life. Their multifaceted intentions attempt to cover all the bases and fix everything. That's a lot of healing! Life after Heart Journey can be better, but it will never be picture perfect. There are too many people and situations you must learn to accept, not change, for perfection to be possible. Life is constantly evolving and changing. As old problems are solved, new ones arise. You have a greater chance of internal evolution than external perfection. It is not so much what goes on in your life as how you handle it. Your responses will need to change before your life can change. Control is incompatible with an open heart. Anger blocks receptivity. Negativity of any kind thwarts attraction. How can you co-create the life you want when you are controlling, angry, or negative? You can't! What alternatives do you have for creating a better life? Only one! Love.

The greatest remedy you can foster for any situation comes from an open heart that maintains a high level of compassion, understanding, and lovingness. We have all met highly evolved spiritual individuals who seem to exude love. We just want to be with them. Their energy is contagious. They make us and everyone else feel loved. When we are in their presence, all our problems seem to fade. We see things in a new light: the light of love. Our ability to understand increases and sometimes solutions spontaneously arise. Our whole stance softens. We no longer want to criticize; we want to help. We refuse to contribute to the problem and instead embody the solution, love.

Becoming one of those highly evolved loving beings is the goal of a successful Heart Journey. For this reason, a simple intention held like a meditative focal point in the mind and heart is a more powerful tool towards greater lovingness, manifestation, and abundance than a long, involved, and highly corrective contract. Single intentions are best because they foster both progress and lovingness. They also simplify the co-creative process allowing for greater intimacy with God and clarity around all Divine communications.

Retaining What you Already Have

As you begin to ascertain what your intention or contract might include, you do not need to ask for things that you already have or situations that are already going well. You will not be losing anything by entering into a co-creative partnership with God. What you have, you will most likely keep. The only limits to abundance in your life are those that you personally set. God is not going to remove some of the good things in your life to compensate for the new items you are requesting. There is not a limit on God's grace and goodness.

"Be Careful of What you Ask for" and Other Fears

You may hear, "Be careful what you ask for," (at least once while preparing your intention) from a well-meaning friend who doesn't think you should make a request, or is fearful of the process. There are those who will see the Heart Journey contract as demeaning to God or devoid of spirituality regardless of your request. You might doubt that God has time for your intention. The God I know was, is, and always shall be all knowing, all seeing, everywhere, at all times and omnipotent. Multi-tasking is God's forte. There is nothing too small for God. There is nothing too big. There is nothing impossible.

Those who have a fear-based image of God as the avenger or supreme judge would not risk trusting God with a request. They would be afraid that calling attention to themselves by asking could generate negative consequences. Consider this: do you really think that a loving God is standing ready with a thunderbolt in hand in hopes that you might foolishly ask for something inappropriate or otherwise? Do you think God might take advantage of your inexperience with the Heart Journey request process to trick you? Do you think God's response might be to punish you just for asking? Or humiliate you by granting your wish in a manner that is inappropriate, or at an inconvenient time? If you believe that God is truly loving, wouldn't it be more feasible for God to just say "No!" if your request was not in your best interests or for the good of all concerned? You have to determine for yourself what is God's commitment to you, your spiritual purpose, and your life while on earth.

If you believe that God is loving and write a Heart Journey contract to invite God into the co-creative process, you will be on your way to manifesting your potential. This is not a quick process. It takes time, maybe even a lifetime. You begin your Heart Journey by writing a contract that truly reflects your heart's desire.

Chapter Six:
Composing Your Contract

After you have completed your period of reflection and discernment, lived with the information and symbolism until it became stabilized and coherent, you are ready to compose your formal contract. There are still options to consider as you create your contract. There are many different ways to convey your request and also several different types of contracts you can use.

Contract Media

The first step in creating your formal contract is to decide which avenue of expression you wish to use; verbal, visual, or symbolic. Your contract can be in words, pictures, or actual objects with either single or multiple meanings. Some people are more comfortable with left-brain verbal processes. Their internal mode is thought-based and it is easier for them to express themselves through words. Others are more comfortable with right-brain artistic forms of expression. They see and think in pictures. Words do not capture all they wish to express. For these people, a visual media more accurately reflects what they wish to convey. Those who wish to leave their request open to evolving interpretations might choose a symbolic media consisting of words or pictures, or some combination of both. Choose the media which best corresponds to your internal process and reflects your translation of your vision and request.

Contract Formats

Format and media go hand-in-hand. Once you have decided on the media, choose an appropriate and corresponding format. Verbal formats include, but are not limited to, a contract, letter, affirmation, poem, agreement, song, phrase, or single word. Visual formats include, but are not limited to, a painting, mural, collage, mobile, carving, video, or multimedia artpiece of any design. Symbolic formats might include any of those mentioned above or perhaps a Heart Journey garden, altar, prayer shawl, or meditation room. I have seen some very creative contracts represented by a collection of symbolic objects. Use your imagination. Be as creative as you wish. Know what you relate to best. There is no right or wrong in this. There are no limits to what you can choose or how you may wish to express your request or intention. It is only important that whatever you create has meaning and impact for you. Choose that which inspires you most before the activation, knowing that it is a work in progress and you can continue to refine it.

Regardless of the media or format you pick, you will need to create a physical, emotional, mental, and/or spiritual representation of your heart's desire that is significant and meaningful to you. Take the time to make it special. It is your dedication to your partnership with God. While creating your request or intention remember to be positive, concrete, and specific. Most of all, you must be emotionally invested in your request to sustain a focused thought over time.

Types of Contracts

So far we have discussed the individual request or contract, but other kinds of contracts exist and may seem more appropriate once you have completed your discernment and know what you wish to intend. Depending on the people involved and the nature of the request, a relationship, group, business, professional, or healing contract might seem in order. For example, it is possible for a couple to write a relationship contract to strengthen their bond regardless of whether or not they are married. A business, company, or partnership might compose a contract similar to a mission statement with an emphasis on spirituality and partnering with God. A professional, especially those involved in healing practices might wish to work with spiritual input or guides to enhance the potential for benefiting clientele. It is also possible to write a contract to work co-creatively towards your own healing. There are many different kinds of contracts one can use besides the individual contract. Choose the type which best fits your heart's desire or be creative and adapt the contract guidelines to fit another, more suitable type of Heart Journey contract.

Individual Contracts

The personal and individual contract is meant to only include your own dreams and goals. It is for you and you alone. You will be working with the process of manifestation within the co-creative partnership. If you are using verbal media, the individual contract is a simple handwritten or typed contract that you leave unsigned until the appropriate time. For the best results, write it, wait a day, then reflect on it, and rewrite it if necessary. Repeat this process until the contract says exactly what you wish it to say and you are happy with the result.

If you are creating a visual or symbolic contract the process is similar. Assemble the things you need and then work on it over several days. Reflect on the meaning and then rework the fine points. Repeat this process until the final product feels complete and true to your intention. You will need to consider how you might sign your creation or set your request in motion.

Relationship and Group Contracts

The personal relationship contract might focus on the nature of the bond between two or more people, their commitment to one another for the future, and/or each individual's contribution to the relationship. Composing your contract with your spouse can be like going to a marriage encounter. It fosters a sense of renewal. Group contracts are also possible, perhaps for those living together or working towards a common goal. To utilize this type of contract you must look at the present state of your involvement in either the relationship or group and then envision how you wish to grow spiritually with the co-creative assistance of God. Contracts can be written, visual or symbolic. Once you figure out how to sign or activate your contract, you will need everyone present for the ceremony. If the contract is verbal, everyone should have a copy. If the contract is visual, perhaps everyone can have a replica or color xerox copy. If your contract is highly visual and symbolic, everyone can have a snap shot of the piece.

Business or Professional Contracts

For those individuals who wish to bring greater spirituality into the business world, a business or company contract might be appropriate. God is very much a part of this intention or spiritual mission statement. This type of contract can be written for a sole proprietorship (as an individual contract), partnership (relationship contract), small company, or large corporation (group contract). The purpose of this contract would be to ask for guidance for the business and extend an invitation to God to participate in a co-creative partnership.

Creating a Heart Journey professional contract is particularly helpful to healers such as massage therapists, acupuncturists, counselors, and those who use Reiki or Sekhem healing energy on their clients and wish to invite Divine co-creative assistance into their practice. Healers can also ask for assistance in benefiting others from spirit guides, saints, angels, dakinis, power animals, buddhas, avatars, gurus, and Christ.

Health and Healing Contracts

If you are dealing with a health issue or illness, you can gear your contract toward finding ways to relieve your symptoms, pain and suffering, or learn to function without limitations by adapting techniques to circumvent a disability. You can even write a contract seeking to cure a persistent problem. A remission is more likely than a cure, but miracles do happen especially if you are committed to doing the inner work necessary. Healing can take time and persistence, but can be permanent.

Abundance comes in many forms and the co-creative partnership with God can take on many different tasks. Use the Heart Journey contract to focus on the one or ones that are foremost in your mind. Do not try to address every issue in your life. Stay with what is most important and pick the options that are most suited to your individual needs and situation.

Prioritizing, Evaluating and Organizing Your Intentions

Once you have settled on the media (verbal, visual, or symbolic), and the type of contract you are interested in (individual, relationship, business, professional, or healing), begin to sort through the material gleaned from the reflection and discernment process. Your contract might be very simple with one and only one request in mind. This is good. Composition should be easy. Even a single word or symbol can be very powerful and convey all that you wish to convey. If your contract is a surrender contract most likely it will be simple to compose also. The problem is that many people arrive at this stage with multiple requests. If you are one of them you need to do more work to get your request polished before composing your contract.

Prioritize

If you have a number of requests, your tendency might be to list all of them. Resist this temptation. It will not serve you. Simple is best. Begin by prioritizing your wish list. Put those items you want to work with the most at the top of the list. Continue listing. Let go of what is less important or not necessary. These items will be found at the bottom of your list. Narrow your focus and commit to sticking with what is essential. Trimming away the extras is important since a multifaceted contract is more difficult to compose and sustain over time. The more complex your contract, the longer the time period required to affect manifestation and the greater the possibility that you will lose interest. It is sometimes better to have a short term single intent contract than a long term multifaceted one. You can always write sequential contracts as items are achieved.

Evaluate Desire

Once you have prioritized your intentions and dropped items off your list, evaluate each remaining request for the associated desire quotient. What does not truly move you or have emotional impact will not serve you. Strong desire is essential to the attraction, surrender, and manifestation processes so you do not want to dilute your true intent with weaker, less desirable add-ons. Stay with the true passion and heart's desire. The goal is to compose a simple, focused contract that is steeped in desire.

Organize

After you pare down as much as possible and feel you can go no further, you might still have a number of intentions. Organize the remaining information into themes or main areas of concern if you can. Look for commonalities. Combine smaller requests into broader categories. You do not have to write everything down. Find words, phrases, or a sentence that says it all. Sometimes a single word captures the essence. If so, use it. A lot can be simply understood or implied without being blatant. God will know what you mean.

Life can and will improve simply because you are opening your heart to God and the co-creative process. You don't have to address every issue. An improvement in one area of your life will most likely have a positive effect on other areas. Don't focus on little things. It is the bigger, innermost desires that matter.

Once signed, you will need to carry your contract with you wherever you go and whatever you do. Simplicity allows you to do this easily. Keeping your contract in the forefront of your mind and heart activates and sustains the co-creative process. The more heart-centered your contract, the stronger the imprinting will be. The simpler your contract, the easier it will be to remember in reference to everyday life situations that your face. This is where the process of application comes in. The Heart Journey contract becomes a part of daily living and decisions will be made with it in mind.

Multifaceted Requests

When all is said and done, your intention might still be multifaceted and complex. While a simple contract is best, this is not to say that an intention cannot be longer than one word, or focus on more than one area of life. I have seen successful contracts that contained two, three, four, or even six points or more. Since a lengthy contract is too difficult to retain in your mind and heart you will need to structure a bigger contract in a way that is memorable. Use a single word or symbol as a umbrella with subcategories or various forms of application associated with it. Package your ideas. A longer contract gains strength when the items are interconnected, thematic, or pictured forming a geometric pattern.

For example, a contract with three points can be viewed as a triangle. Suppose a young mother wanted to write the following intentions:

1. I am the best mother I could be to my children.
2. I am a devoted wife. I love my husband. Our marriage is a bond that strengths our family.
3. God walks with me as I develop spiritually.

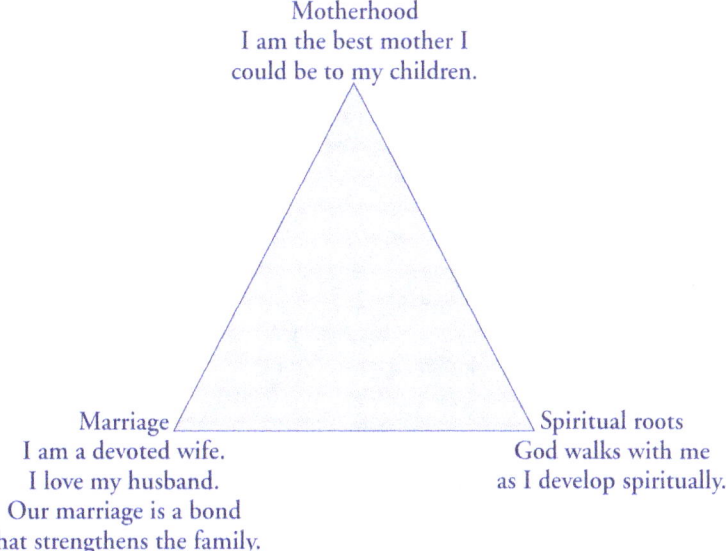

A central theme of giving and receiving love might be the unifying element in this contract and help this mother focus on one intention within several different areas of manifestation. If so, the diagram might now be adjusted to simplify the request by focusing attention on one chosen overriding theme, but still maintaining several areas of interest. This strengthens the focus of the contract, making it easier to remember.

Suppose this mother and family needed new housing. In addition to spiritual and relationship concerns there are pressing problems that also needed to be addressed. The family has outgrown their two bedroom apartment. With the children now in school all day, the mother wishes to return to work. She is not sure exactly what job she wants

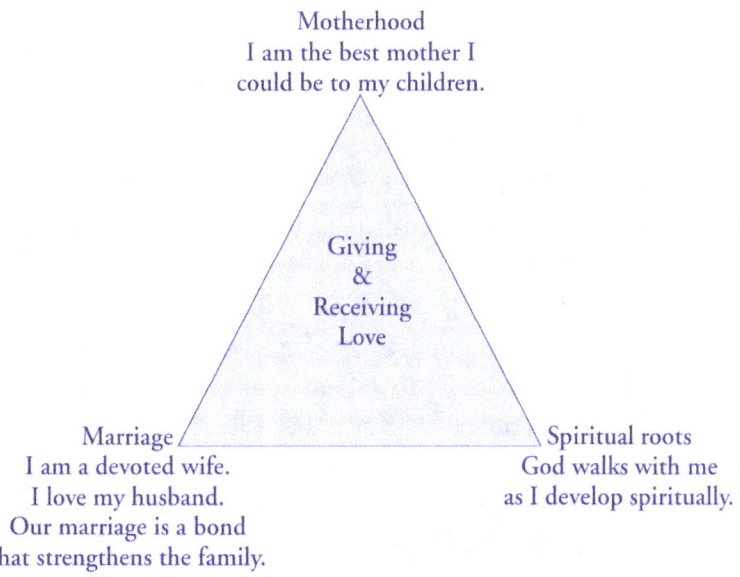

to do or has the skills for. She is just beginning her search and is open to suggestion. Becoming part of the work force will greatly relieve the financial burden on her husband and enable them to pay off all of their debts. Having a job, new home and becoming debt-free is a very important part of her co-creative intention. The additions to the contract could now look like this:

4. We are in the home of our dreams.
5. My career is fulfilling and financially rewarding.
6. We are debt free.

Here we see the six points of the co-creative contract which all revolve around the desire to give and receive love more fully than has been done in the past. Although this is a broad contract that touches on many areas, the woman need only search her heart whenever a situation arises or as she goes through her day and ask, "Am I being as loving and giving as I can be in this situation?" If not, then "Please God, help me to be more loving and create a better situation for myself, my family and all involved." Or, "Am I open to receiving love in this situation?" If not, then "Please God, help me to be more open to receiving your love and abundance for my own sake and for the sake of my family and all involved." A multifaceted contract has been made simple. It is now easy to carry it in the heart and mind while going about the day.

Here is another example of a contract that has several points, but does not necessarily have a separate central focus such as "giving and receiving love" to unify them. Instead the overall task integrates the various points.

You wish to start you own business as a free-lance playground architect. You want to make playgrounds more interesting and beautiful, but also safer for children. As you transition from your present job with a private corporation to self-employment, you need to be able to support yourself financially. You might be able to consult part-time for your old business, but hopefully the process of acquiring clients will be easier than expected. You are not sure how this will all play out, but you need to move forward. Financial support is essential because you also need to take a specialized training or certification program to really advance in your new field. The three interwoven intentions:

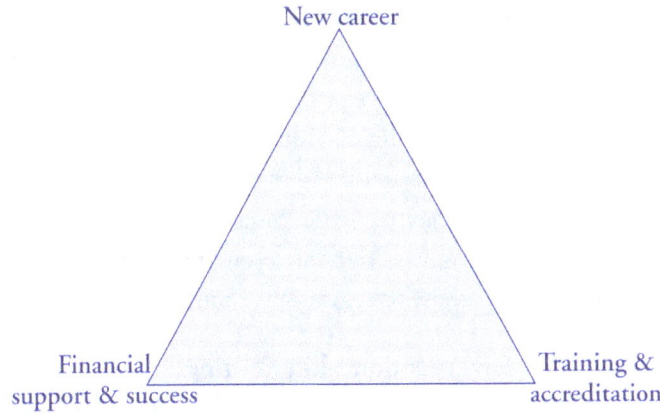

1. New career
2. Financial support and success in this new career
3. Training and accreditation

now appear to be a package deal and therefore are easier to remember and adhere to because they are all part of the same goal, i.e., a new self-employment career as a playground architect. Each item supports, and in turn, is supported by the other two items listed. The ability to focus is very important to the co-creative process and anything you can do to concentrate your attention is not only helpful, but also highly effective.

With this new career focus in mind, you would then begin to work co-creatively with God on the timing, manner, and sequential steps necessary for your career shift. In the first example, the mother, wife and newest member of the work force would do the same. She might study childrearing techniques, endeavor to spend quality time with her husband, and set aside time for prayers and meditation each day. When she walks in balance in this way it will be easier for her to sense the best way to proceed to secure employment. Even though an intention might appear to be very materialistic, the underlining process is always spiritual. You walk with God, paying attention to what *is* and what *is not* working, discussing your progress along the way with your Divine partner and praying for guidance. It is a joint effort and the task is made easier because of the co-creative process.

We have seen how a three item contract might be viewed as a triangle and a six item contract as the Star of David. A four item contract might be viewed as a square, five points as a pentagram. The intentions can take on any shape you wish. The result does not have to be geometric. It can be artistic and free-form. The greater the number of points in your contract, the more important it is to have an underlying unifying principle that helps to narrow your attention. This then becomes the focus of your desire though there may be several areas of manifestation linked or affected by this primary intent.

Before Writing or Composing Your Contract

Before you begin to compose your contract, close your eyes and once again picture your honed and refined request coming to fruition. You should still feel excited and fulfilled. Perhaps it is the climax of a life-long dream. Spend time in this space. Wear the cloak of success. Walk around the envisioned manifestation. View it from all angles. Feel comfortable. Commit to participating in the co-creative plan. Note any reservations you might have. When everything feels right and you are at peace with your request, open your eyes and begin to compose or create your contract.

Pay Attention while Writing

Be very aware of what goes on during the composition stage of your Heart Journey contract. Frequently, the co-creative partnership begins even before the contract is signed or activated. (God reads your mind and knows where you are headed.) This can be a time of major input as you learn to open and receive, so pay attention. Note anything unusual happening. If you live in the city and see a falcon for the first time outside your window, this is important. Record the event. You might not know the meaning of the falcon or any other event at that moment, but still note it. Symbols evolve and become clearer with time. Interpretations can be literal, cultural, or personal. They can have more than one meaning. You do not have to understand any of the possible meanings now as you write your contract. Trust that they will be discovered along the way if they are important. The more you open your heart, the more is revealed.

Another important thing to note at this point is what tasks are the easiest to accomplish or those that are most troublesome. From the moment you feel drawn to Heart Journey and the creation of an intention, what you need to guide you and sustain you throughout the process will begin to flow to you. Your training starts here and is furthered by your personal request and initiation into the heart.

Technical Writing Tips

When writing the contract, there are certain key elements and grammatical considerations to keep in mind. Certain phrases have more power than others. Though the following suggestions might sound simple, they can have dramatic effects. Since energy follows thought, you will want to magnify the potential for manifestation and eliminate any hidden self-sabotage.

Make "I" Statements

Wherever possible use "I" statements in word or symbol, not "we" and not "you." After all this is your Heart Journey, so personalize it. Claim the process as your own. For example: "I open my heart to greater love by practicing forgiveness." Or, "I am forgiving and my heart is open wide." Only use "we" when you and a partner agree to write a personal or business relationship contract, or a company has agreed to do this. Never use "you" as it is inappropriate to write about others or even mention changes you might be expecting others to make. Focusing on others or distancing yourself from your own intentions by using the pronoun "you" weakens your contract.

Use Present Tense

Phrase or visualize your contact in the present moment rather than in the future. You want it as close as possible to your reality. Do not distance yourself time-wise from your intention. Do not write, "I want to become more loving," when "I am more loving," is more immediate and powerful. Do not write, "I want to be more loved," but "I am loved." Instead of "I do want to make a career change," try, "I am in a career that rewards, excites, and fulfills me." If you use future terms, your vision might stay in the future, perpetually out of reach. It could always be tomorrow and not today. If you use, "I want to," rather than "I am," you might also distance yourself from an immediate or present moment improvement. It sounds too much like you are getting ready "to do" something rather than doing it. How much better and more powerful it is to stay in the present tense and make "I" statements so your contract becomes an affirmation in the immediate moment.

Do Not Use Negatives

As stated before, Heart Journey is about what you do wish to co-create in your life, not about what you don't want or wish to eliminate. Don't use negatives like "no," "not," "no longer," etc. Do not include words, symbols, or pictures of what you do not want. For example: "I am no longer working at that horrible company." These are reactionary words rather than co-creative endeavors. If it is important for you to address a problem in your life, envision a positive and beneficial resolution. See yourself in an improved situation. "I have my dream job" Then go on to describe the job in greater detail. Define what makes it a dream situation. Trust that God will help you move on to a better scenario if you put in the effort and do your part. Anger, hate, and negative reactions have no place in Heart Journey and will only impede your ability to receive abundantly because they close the heart rather than open it.

Use Positive Language

Say or symbolize what you want in a way that emphasizes the solution and not the problem. For example, "I am driving a new car." Not, "I need a new car." If you use "need" or even "want" in your contract, you will be emphasizing your deficient automobile more than an improved mode of transportation. "I need a new car," will go a long way to increase your need, rather than fulfill your request. You will watch your old car go right down the tubes with this statement. Negative reiteration steadily increases need or want. Instead try, "I am enjoying my new, safe, affordable, and mechanically sound car."

Intentions, Not Vows

Your personal vision statement or contact should be an intention, not a vow. Do not commit yourself to deadlines or difficult to adhere to schedules. Do not paint yourself into a corner or set yourself up with criteria for failure. No one is perfect. For example: "I have a regular meditation practice" is a life affirming goal. "I will sit one hour each day regardless of how I am feeling or what is going on in my life," becomes limiting and binding. Remember the goal is to establish a loving and intimate co-creative relationship with God. Do not set God up as the enforcer or watchdog for a new habit you are trying to establish, no matter what that habit might be. By being gentle with yourself you will foster a more loving and supportive co-creative relationship with God.

Be Flexible

Your vision is not set in stone. You can make adjustments after the signing without having to write a completely new contract. You have not been trained in how to ask. Learning to ask is a growth process in itself so it is okay to rewrite portions of your contract at any time. Your vision should be open rather than limiting, flexible rather than fixed. Allow yourself as much freedom as possible to make corrections or adjustments. As you do so, you will be learning to refine, co-create, and grow in love and trust. Your co-creative Partner understands there is a learning curve to the Heart Journey process, so rewrite as needed. Just make sure you go through the discernment process again and don't be too quick to revise.

I remember one friend who wrote in her contract that she want to go to Africa. She meant for vacation, but being in the foreign service, she received orders for a reassignment overseas in, you guessed it, Africa. Because she was planning to leave the service and relocate to the western United States, she quickly rewrote that portion of her contract and turned down the position.

Leave Plenty of Room For Upgrades

Commit to a process, not a rigid and immutable goal. God may have something better planned for you. Remember, Divine upgrades are possible. Wouldn't you want a higher, more loving intelligence to make substitutions when available? Allow for that process by holding your personal vision loosely and giving yourself room to shift around. For example: do not request a particular house that you wish to live in. Give the Divine plenty of room to bestow something more beneficial than what you have chosen for yourself.

Qualify Your Contract

Always think of your contract within the context of, "Not my will, but Thy Will and for the Highest Good of all involved." You must hold your vision loosely while at the same time surrendering it to God. This is to your advantage since it allows you to receive bigger and better dreams than the ones you are aware of or have thought of. Co-creative partnerships are not fifty-fifty exchanges. God is a more powerful creator. God is not only already way ahead of you, God also sees farther down the road. If you have requested something that obviously (to God) is not in your highest interest, substitutions will immediately start to move into position. Learn to honor and trust God's expertise right from the beginning by accepting and including the spoken or unspoken, written or unwritten understanding, "Not my will, but Thy Will and for the highest good of all involved."

Gratitude

Another written or unwritten part of your contract should be an expression of gratitude. We all have a lot of be thankful for. Express it openly and clearly. Gratitude uplifts the spirit and should become a part of your daily Heart Journey process. By being grateful, you are creating a stronger bond with God and synchronizing your emotional energy with that of abundance. Start out on the right foot at the very beginning by incorporating your appreciation into your Heart Journey contract.

Offering

If you feel it is appropriate, you can make an offering in your Heart Journey contract. Your offering can be either general or specific, a one-time event or a continuing promise, but make it heartfelt and sincere. Take the time to think about what you might gift to the world to make it a better place. Do your part, then take your promises seriously. Sometimes your offering is directly tied to your request, sometimes not. Give or offer what feels right to you. Be generous. Remember, you need to give as well as receive. Heart openness is a two-way street or doorway that opens both ways. Sharing your abundance increases your ability to receive now and also in the future. Expanding your doorway through giving is the beneficial thing to do.

Reflection and finalization

Once you have written, drawn, or created your contract, meditate with it and live with it for several days before signing or activating. This is not to be a rushed process. Take your time. As you try your contract on, see how it sits with you emotionally as well as intellectually and spiritually. Discuss the contract with your co-creative Partner. If you are part of a Heart Journey group, have each member share his or her contract. This will enable everyone in the group to see the diversity and creative differences, not only in what is asked for, but also in regard to style of presentation. Use this time for feedback from the other group members. After careful reflection, make any necessary additions, revisions, or deletions. Stay with it until you are comfortable with the final result and ready to make a commitment.

Examples

Here are examples of three very different Heart Journey contracts. One is written while the others are almost totally symbolic.

The Written Contract:

my prayer:
  may all my relationships be win-win
  grant me emotional protection
  family caring and wisdom
  physical well-being
  and abundance.
my humble offering:
  two hands in service
  one heart for total lovingness
  a mind open to receiving and sharing
  the ability to bear or bare Light
i surrender to Love
i surrender to the Void
i surrender to Divine Passion and Guidance.
  thank you for:
    the Light,
    the shadow,
    and the dance in between,
    for sight, foresight, insight, and knowledge.

This written contract has many of the elements already presented here in this chapter. There are both specific and general items, gratitude and surrender, and an offering. There is a play on words which expands the meaning of some of the terms beyond what is written.

The Symbolic Visual Contract

The symbolic contract below has only two words in it. The words are "totally unlimited" and appear written in a foreign alphabet to down play the verbal content. This contract was artistically put together in a digital media. The symbols around the mandala were hand-picked and everything had meaning to the person who created this contract. The Sun and the Moon are indicative of the Divine marriage and the lotus on top of the mandala reflects a desire for enlightenment.

A Garden Contract

Another contract revolved around a garden that included a heart shaped path. As the individual walked the path each day, she would reaffirm her intention to always respond in a loving manner to daily problems and situations that would arise. It was not enough for her to be loving, she wanted to grow daily in her lovingness and sought new ways to demonstrate this as she walked in the garden. The garden was not large or demanding. The dimensions were only 20 by 20 feet. Her father helped her lay the framework for this garden and while they were working, they talked a lot about abundance and opening to receive. When it was time to sign the garden, the woman suggested to her father that he write the simple statement, "I will receive," on the garden boards and sign it. This then became his Heart Journey and over the next few years he did open to receiving assistance from his children.

Empowering the Heart Journey Contract

Once your contract is complete, create a ritual or ceremony to bless, dedicate, and sign your contract. This will activate your thoughts and the energy within your personal Heart Journey vision. This is a special time and ideas for ritualizing your contract are given in the next chapter.

Empower your Heart Journey contract with an attractive display in words, pictures, or symbols. Make it appealing and memorable. If it is written, think about framing it and hanging it on the wall where you can see it. Or take a copy with you wherever you go. Thereafter, continue to empower your contract by referring to it often. Keep it foremost in your mind. Expect that it will manifest. Know that it will happen or that you will understand why something else is more appropriate. Look for signs and let things develop naturally. The contract is your heart's desire. May you receive according to your heart's desire.

Chapter Seven:
Creating a Ritual

Instructions

Once you have written or created a symbolic representation of your contract, you will need to create a ritual and pick a time and location to activate your contract. You will be committing to your vision for manifestation through attraction and receptivity and also officially inviting God into a co-creative partnership. The birth of this new venture should be planned as a significant event. It is intended to be a special celebration, permeated with sacredness and ceremony. Activating your Heart Journey contract is an initiation and should be treated as such. It is an initiation into:

1. Opening your heart to receive and giving more love
2. Attracting and manifesting abundance for yourself and others
3. Your co-creative partnership with God

Think of it as a marriage, a union of individual desire with Divine intent for the purpose of manifesting beneficial forms of Divinity on earth. This includes, but is not limited to lovingness, kindness, mercy, compassion, peace, receptivity, sharing, and abundance through human representation. This opportunity is yours despite your past, regardless of your faults, and without any criteria associated with worthiness. You don't earn it; it is your right, and perhaps even your responsibility. The only requirement at this point is that you are willing to ask, willing to try, to listen, accept, and surrender to a better plan. Like any turning point in your life, this is an event of great importance and should be celebrated with a ceremony of that magnitude. Be as creative with your ritual as you are with your contract. Be as joyous with your ritual as you would be for any major life transition. It is a sacred passage. There are a few guidelines you might wish to consider, but you are free to create a ritual of your choosing.

Considerations when Planning Your Ritual

Location, Location, Location

The location you choose for the signing of your contract can be as simple or as lavish as you wish. First, decide whether you wish to do the ritual inside or outside, in your home or away from home. You may wish to travel a distance to a special or sacred location for a few days, or at least overnight. It all depends on what feels right to you and where you are apt to feel the most connected.

If nature calls you, then outside is better, either on your own land, on public property, or at a park. An outdoor ceremony can incorporate fire, air, water, and earth by having a small campfire in the open air by a lake, stream, or the ocean. You can sign your contract under the stars in a night sky. This can be especially nice if the moon is up. Or sign your contract while in a boat on the water, or in a tree house.

You may prefer an inside location. Inside your own home is fine or any other place that draws you. Consider the options in your area. For example, there might be a local monument, famous landmark, or place of worship which would suit your purposes. Sometimes the very ritual itself that you are in the process of creating dictates a particular environment.

The most important criteria for picking a location is that you feel connected to the surroundings you choose, and you are able to relate with depth and sacredness while there. You want your intentions supported by the visual, olfactory, tactile, and/or auditory elements. Temperature, sound, smell, and a level of comfort are all important to the sensory appeal. Choose a location that will magnify your emotional connection to the spiritual context of the moment and will support your plans for the ceremony.

Timing

The time of day is as important as the time of the month and the time of the year. The high points of the day tend to be around sunrise, sunset, or high noon. Those who favor the night might prefer midnight or the quiet hours before dawn. If a particular time of the day is special to you, either because it is your birth time or the exact time of a memorable moment in your life, you might consider it for your ritual. There is no best time, only what feels right for you.

To some, the time of the month is important. Those who follow certain earth-based religions and traditions such as the Celtic and Native American traditions might be drawn to a particular phase of the moon, especially either the dark of the moon or the full moon phase. Those women who follow a Native American tradition may wish to consider signing their contracts during their moon time. This is the time when a woman is menstruating and at the height of her flow. Native Americans considered a woman in her moon time to be at her most creative and insightful. The tribe would count on wisdom gained during these times.

Holidays, whether religious or secular can have special meaning when choosing a day or time of year for the signing. The actual day when the changing of the seasons occurs, either solstice or equinox, signals an energy shift and may be the appropriate time for your ceremony.

For those who are open to astrological considerations, you can choose a time that resonates with your sunsign or birth horoscope. There are also times of great astrological significance like the Harmonic Convergence and whenever a Star of David is formed in the sky by the planets. The Star of David is created when the planets line up to create two interlocking triangles. This configuration is highly significant. It is symbolic of the integration of heaven and earth, or Divinity with humanity. The symbolism is particularly apropos to the Heart Journey and important to several religions besides the Jewish faith. The Star of David is also found in the Buddhist Vajrayogini empowerment mandala, and in the theosophical movement. The Theosophists believe the Rainbow Bridge within the heart and the Star of David connects and unites two levels of experience, Divine and human.

Participation

You need to consider if you wish to have a private ceremony on your own or a ceremony with other participants or attendees. Group or shared participation can be wonderful, especially if everyone in the group has a Heart Journey contract. In this case, create a shared ritual. The group that activates together can evolve into a wonderful, supportive community after the signing if you decide to meet regularly and discuss progress and experiences. If no one else has a contract, friends and family can still witness your signing. Or you can decide to have your ritual alone, and then have a shared celebration afterward.

Preparation

In the days or hours before your ceremony consider a fast or cleanse. This is a time of letting go. You may wish to abstain from alcohol. If you can, clean up your diet and eat wholesome foods. You might do a symbolic cleanse with an actual shower or ritualized bath. As you venture forth, you will need to leave some attitudes behind. This is a good time to make amends or avoid conflict. Pay attention to what is arising and be willing to release what no longer serves you now and might impede your contract and progress in the future.

Sensory Elements in Your Ritual

Sight

If the visual element is important to you, consider a costume, headdress or mask. Put things together from your closet. A flowing dress might be important for a woman who wants to create movement in her life. Arrange the area in which your ceremony is to take place. Bring in candles, statues, lights, and flowers. I have seen some individuals create temporary or permanent altars with sacred objects and a Star of David formed from ribbons. Set the mood for your signing.

Sound

Think about the music or sounds that could add to your ceremony. Pick out a CD or tape to play. If you have musician friends, ask them to participate. Live music and/or drums and rattles add to the ceremony. If you are outdoors, the sounds of nature might be the only music you wish to hear. Feel free to sing. Sing with abandon and really belt it out, or lullaby your signing. Those who are feeling particularly creative might compose their own tune for the ceremony or spontaneously improvise. An affirmation that is directly related to the intention of your contract is very motivating, especially when it is a memorable phrase sung with a catchy melody.

Smell

We don't always think about the importance of smell, but it does enhance the ceremony and our experience. You can light incense or scented candles. Fragrant flowers or petals might perfume the air. If you have essential oils, use them for anointing.

Touch

The feel of certain fabrics on your skin can add to the moment. Consider the texture of objects to be used in your ceremony. The location also has a texture whether it is a sandy beach, a desert, or forest.

Taste

Taste is also a consideration if you are eating during your ceremony in addition to sharing a meal with friends and family following the ritual. You may choose traditional foods that are celebratory or have others bring shared dishes.

During the Ceremony

There is no right or wrong way to do the ceremony of signing your contract or activating your symbolic intention. It can be whatever you want and as simple or complex as you need it to be. The important thing is to create a moment of sacredness that has meaning and emotional impact for you.

Following the Ceremony

Now the fun begins. After your ceremony, have a party. Make it a real celebration with food, music, dancing, and great joy. Celebrate your passage to beginning of a new era in your life.

Part Two:
The Co-creative Partnership
and Manifestation Process

Chapter Eight: Communicating with God

Introduction

You have an intention. You have meditated and prayed, gathered your thoughts and feelings in regard to your heart's desire, and written a co-creative contract with God. You have activated your contract and celebrated. Now what? Perhaps you are hoping that the manifestation process would automatically kick into high gear and your heart's desire will instantly materialize. Possible, but unlikely! You are just beginning your Heart Journey and co-creative partnership with God. There is still much to be done before manifestation through attraction and receptivity can occur easily and on a regular basis. Your goal is not just to realize your heart's desire, but to establish a stable and productive co-creative partnership that enlightens and fosters spiritual development. For this to occur, you must learn to communicate with God. This involves both talking to God and listening.

It is important to remember that we live in a responsive environment. There is an exchange going on all the time. God listens. God hears. God responds. It makes no difference to the response process what you call God. You can be more general and use spirit, source, energy, higher self, soul, primordial mind, or super consciousness. The name does not matter anymore than the location. God is out there, or in here, or everywhere. For the purposes of consistency, simplicity, and sacredness throughout the text, I have been calling this Force and Being, God, and will continue to do so. Now that you have officially begun your Heart Journey, I again invite you to use whatever name suits your own personal practice or religion. Call the name which is nearest and dearest to your heart. Heart Journey does not compete with or exist outside of any religion or belief system that is based in love. Heart Journey complements and seeks to increase your sense of communion with God and all life. Make the necessary individualized adjustments to proceed in a sacred and meaningful manner.

What is important is that you accept the possibility that something exists outside of your sensory awareness, and that you have just asked this Being or Force to join with you in a co-creative endeavor. Whether you come to the process a believer or skeptic, you have just entered into a mystery. Now you must begin to discover and assemble the puzzle of your own personal Heart Journey. I can tell you of my experience, but each journey is highly individualistic and unique. It will be up to you to establish a meaningful exchange and piece together a coherent understanding of your experiences with your co-creative Partner.

The Importance of Communication

You now have a Partner, a sacred Partner, and you are one-half of a co-creative team. As in any collaborative effort, partners need to talk, get to know each other, and grow in their ability to work together. That is your job description at this stage of the journey. The co-creative process cannot begin until you learn to communicate. Divine feedback is essential. If you are not talking with your co-creative Partner, you are on your own will-based trip. If you are not listening to your co-creative Partner, you are on your own will-based trip. Co-creation is God-based and it takes two to tango, hence the need to communicate.

It would be helpful if there were clear cut means for communication with God. There aren't. Few of us are prepared for a one-on-one conversation with God. Think of the Bill Cosby comedy sketch when God contacts Noah about the coming flood and the need to build an ark in his driveway.

> "Noah, it's the Lord", says God.
> "Right," responds Noah.

We are as enlightened as our fears allow us to be and no more. Unfortunately, in many traditions God has a judging and frightening reputation. This does little to allay our fears in regard to direct communication. We have little history with Divine communication because we were not trained in how to proceed or what to expect any more than we were taught how to ask for our heart's desire. Religion might teach us to pray and talk *to* God, but when it comes to listening for answers we may be referred to scripture and sacred text. The implication is that God speaks to us only indirectly through the words and experiences of others more saintly or enlightened, those professed, those behind cloistered walls. In reality you can be a mother, father, child, in any profession, of any age, any religion, or nationality, and experience direct communication with God. The only requirement is a willingness to listen.

In Part One of this book, you were taught how to ask for your heart's desire. This you have done with the formulation and activation of your contract. In this section of the book, you will be taught how to communicate and collaborate with God in a co-creative manner. Information will be presented to sensitize you to the various forms Divine communication might take. Guidelines for interpretation and evaluation will be established so you can distinguish between subconscious chatter or fears and higher input. Direct communication is central to the co-creative partnership and the success of your Heart Journey. Learning to communicate is every bit as important as learning to ask. It is the next logical step.

Communication tends to be subtle, consisting of symbols, signs, coincidences, ease, God whispers in either your ears or head, lucid dreams, and visions. Sometimes communication is illogical and unbelievable. Exchanges can be incredible. Still there are distinguishing characteristics to Divine communication that clearly indicate higher input. Three of these distinguishing characteristics are wisdom, spiritual insight, and love. God speaks in the language of wisdom and love, and the messages instill spiritual insight.

So, how do you begin to develop and hone your conversational abilities? Here are three essential steps;

1. Sharpen your ability to listen
2. Develop a common, meaningful language
3. Establish guidelines for communication

Sharpen Your Ability to Listen

Listening

The first and most important step you can take in fostering communication with your co-creative Partner is to turn down the mental distractions in your life so you can hear and then endeavor to listen. This is absolutely essential. Most Divine communications are subtle. If you cannot hear your own heartbeat over the roar of life's activities, you will not be able to hear God. You have got to step out of external events of your life and into your inner experience, if only for a short period. The best way to develop and enhance your ability to listen is to create regular, daily, listening time. Set aside time to meditate, journal, reflect, commune with nature, or participate in any other quiet, introspective activity that opens you to receiving guidance. Of those activities mentioned, meditation is, by far, the most powerful. The particular form of meditation you practice or the particular tradition you follow does not matter as long as it is not guided meditation. Guided meditation is appropriate for relaxation. It is highly directive and frequently focuses on a location such as a beach, lake, or mountain retreat. You need to be free to focus on communication with God and whatever is arising in the co-creative partnership. I prefer Buddhist Vipassana meditation, also known as following the breath. It is the silent inner experience that is key. It is in the quiet that you foster receptivity by freeing your mind and senses from distractions. Learn how to shut down and turn off. Daily practice is essential. As little as ten minutes a day can get you started.

There are numerous meditation courses in every locality, many of them free. If you decide to meditate but have never done so, take an introductory course. Many people think that meditation involves silencing the mind completely. This is very difficult to do and frustrating for the beginner. It is probably more appropriate to say that meditation is the repeated attempt to train the mind to be still. As in any endeavor, practice is the key.

Within the co-creative partnership, communication on a daily basis is essential. Imagine that you and your best friend run a company together. Each day brings opportunities, problems, and decisions that must be discussed. Could you run a business together without conferring with each other? Is ten minutes too much to ask? Would you not spend much more time than that with your business partner? A co-creative Divine partnership demands the same attention. Ten minutes is not the ideal, but it is a beginning. Forty-five minutes to an hour daily would be ideal. You can take more time, as much as you need, but allow for at least ten minutes.

With time and practice, you might be able to perceive in the midst of work, play, or daily activities, but this is unlikely in the beginning, not having become sensitized to the subtlety of Divine communication. To become open to the process you must quiet your mind and must be open to listening. Once communication is established, it is important to continue with your listening time. The daily practice strengthens and maintains communication and the co-creative partnership.

Talking to God

The second most important thing you can do to awaken your ability to listen is to talk to God. Have a running conversation. Ask questions. Ask for guidance and ask for wisdom. In the same way that your contract creates an invitation, your questions are a petition for answers and open communication. You do not have to ask a series of questions. One heart felt question and request for advice, insight, or wisdom will do it. Answers may come almost immediately or take months. Learn to be patient and take your problems to God.

Example of Listening

Years ago my father had open heart surgery. One valve was weak, needing replacement, and he also had a congenital defect. A major artery for the left side of the heart was missing, and consequently, half of the heart was smaller than the other. While he was in surgery, I sat at home in meditation and prayer, sending healing Reiki energy. At some point I felt that he was out of danger and got up from my meditation mat, but I still wondered how he was doing. Shortly thereafter, the plumber arrived to fix a leak in the well pump in the basement of my house. He was finished in under ten minutes.

He was so quick I thought maybe the problem was too difficult to repair and he needed to come back with extra parts, but the pump was fixed.

He said, "It was a simple valve replacement job, in and out."

When I made out the check to pay him, he told me his first name was Kenneth. This is also my father's first name. At the time, I knew my question was answered and my father was all right. As always, I was open to listening. In my mind this was not a coincidence, but a coincidental communication.

Some answers have taken months. Insight might come in the middle of the night, while driving the car, cooking dinner, or watching children play. There is no knowing when the answer will come, but I believe that all questions are answered eventually.

Develop a Common, Meaningful Language

There are some people who hear God, see God manifesting, or simply know what is being communicated. The vast majority of us do not get that strong a signal. The more common language of God is spoken in symbols, signs, coincidences, (like the example just given), ease, God whispers, lucid dreams, and visions. For most people and for most of the journey there are no broadcast responses or letters from heaven, only subtleties. This is part of the mystery of Heart Journey and your co-creative partnership with God. For this reason fostering the ability to listen with all of your senses is important. A heightened awareness on the physical, emotional, and mental levels is key. You are searching for clues, gathering evidence, and piecing together the information you receive into a cohesive and understandable communication.

Symbols

God is everywhere, omnipresent, and therefore in matter. There is no difference between God above (or wherever you envision God to be), and God, here, right now, in matter. It is all connected, all the same energy, but at different vibrational rates. You can learn to see God in matter through symbolism. Symbols are tools of awareness that can appear at any time and in any area of life. Symbols can lift your consciousness out of ordinary, mundane perceptions into an energetic transformational process that leads to spiritual insight.

Once you sign your contract, invite God in as a Co-creator, and become involved in Heart Journey, you begin a symbolic journey. Be observant of all that you see, hear, feel, think, and know. Remember the symbolism that appeared to you as you wrote your contract. Remember the form your contract took. What are these symbols and what do they mean to you now? If you saw roses at that time, then roses might be a significant symbol while on the Heart Journey. What symbols do you normally relate to? Do you have a power animal? Reflect on what comprises your current symbolic language. If you do not have any symbols now, it just means that you are starting fresh.

You do not have to be meditating to recognize symbols. Events in science, psychology, religion, and the mundane world are symbols that can guide and teach you as everyone's consciousness moves forward. Cloning and stem cell research raised ethical questions. How we treat mentally ill individuals reflects on who we are and are ability to be compassionate. Respect for other beliefs and traditions challenge us when fanaticism is present. Observe what is happening around you in your daily life and what comes to you nationally and internationally pushes you to refine your thinking and character.

God has a natural inclination to move to creation and manifestation. It is constantly occurring, somewhere, sometime, in someone, but I tend to think of it more as occurring everywhere, all the time, in everything, and in everyone. The more God moves through you and inspires you, the more God will move silently on to others and inspire them also. The more beneficial changes you make, the more others around you will be inspired to make their own positive changes. Misery may love company, but company loves success. Raise your own consciousness, and the consciousness of the world begins to shift too. God becomes manifest in the world.

You are not in a vacuum. World and local news events can be significant on a personal level. Scientific breakthroughs can be symbolic. The reactions of the media, people, and governments to the events in other countries, environmental concerns, and even political and social events might be important symbols as well as personal, everyday events. When the Berlin Wall came down, it was a symbol of freedom for everyone, not just for East Germans. As you begin to catch the symbolism arising, you begin to understand the process of communication with God.

Symbols are all around us and God is talking to us all the time. If only we would learn to pay attention to what we are being shown. Note any significant world or national events that occur within thirty days of your contract signing. You can also write down important personal events during this time period. If you have any insights, note them also, but do not be concerned if you cannot relate to the events as symbols at this time or ever. It is all right to simply note or record the information. You can refer back to your records from time to time, and eventually, correspondences between you, your Heart Journey contract, and the events might arise. The important thing is to be observant and train your awareness to stay open to arising symbolism.

Example of Symbolism

The rainbow symbolizes happiness and wealth. It is over the rainbow that "troubles melt like lemon drops." If you search for and find the end of the rainbow, you will discover a pot of gold. It is a beautiful symbol of hope and encouragement. Whenever we see a rainbow in the sky, we smile knowing the storm will pass and the sun is beginning to shine again.

Many years ago, my son asked me how to find the end of the rainbow. We were driving home at the time and it was beginning to storm. I told him, wrongly, that the end of the rainbow was a myth. Because of the way the light fell on the rain drops, the end of the rainbow would always be shifting and never be found. Shortly after arriving home, the storm caught up with us. The sun came out while it was still raining and I called my son out onto the front porch to see the rainbow and continue our discussion about how impossible it was to find the end of the rainbow.

To my surprise, the rainbow descended from the sky, past my neighbor's yard, crossed the street, and ended at the foot of my driveway. There was no mistaking this vision. All the colors were clearly seen on the black asphalt. This symbol came at a turning point in my life, a time when I was unsure of the future and what it would bring. The end of the rainbow at the end of my driveway gave me hope.

I mentioned this occurrence to a friend. She replied that the same event had happened to her at one point in her life. She had gone out in the rain, cast her umbrella aside, and danced in the rainbow. I was intrigued. It had never occurred to me that you could get this close. I resolved to dance when the next rainbow showed up. I did not have to wait long. In a matter of months a second "end of the rainbow" appeared at the end of my driveway. I hurried to the spot and danced with the colors on my skin. That was years ago and the event has never occurred again. It was there when I needed encouragement and then it was gone.

Signs

Native Americans use signs from nature in their daily spiritual communication and I have great respect for their beliefs and practices. They see Mother Earth as alive, supportive, and constantly in communication. They not only use power animals, but all occurrences in nature, all sightings of animals, and environmental shifts. Signs are everywhere. If you spend some of your listening time in nature or walking, be observant of what goes on around you, and what you find along the way. God is communicating with you.

Example of a Sign

Years ago when I was running workshops at a small center, the co-presenter and I would go out for daily morning walks and return with various items we had found along the road. When we would display the morning catch to the attendees, we would invariably find someone with a direct connection to each item. One morning we found a Ken doll head, as in "Ken and Barbie." We could not imagine who would relate to this item, but one woman certainly did. At the time we were creating Native American prayer sticks both for intention and cleansing to burn in a sacred fire. While at the seminar, this woman was deciding to end her affair with a married man. She immediately saw the Ken doll head as a sign, confirming her intention. The doll head went on the top of her prayer stick. Her prayer stick was the last one into the fire and she paced back and forth until it was completely melted. We all supported her decision. Her life was entering a new era. She had new insight into her sexuality. The Ken doll head, recovered from a rural country roadside was a sign and key to her transformation.

Coincidence

Sometimes it is the timing of the event that calls to you and not the symbolism itself. You ask a question or ponder an option and suddenly the phone rings. The message in the call obviously applies to your question. Remember the boat called "Afternoon Delight" mentioned in Chapter 2: Surrendering the Results. It appeared instantaneously to my request for a cloudy day. The timing of the event made the communication obvious. License plates, billboards, and what's on the radio can all be important, but they must have one outstanding characteristic; they must immediately follow the thought or question by only seconds.

One of the tasks in Heart Journey is to establish guidelines for communication and this is a determining guideline for coincidence; it must be instantaneous or so obviously connected in a very apparent manner as to not be questionable, but almost unbelievable. How many boats named "Afternoon Delight" travel Interstate 95 in Virginia just as I am requesting a cloudy day? Not many! The odds are probably a million to one that this boat would appear the instant of my request. So, be aware of the sequence of events and the timing in which things happen. This can tip you off as to a subtle form of communication. Occurrences can be unbelievable. Honestly, I do not know how or why this works, but it is my experience that it does.

Ease

One of the most important avenues for communication comes through ease and flow, as opposed to difficulty and a lack of success. Frustration can be God's way of telling you that certain things are not meant to be, or you are going about it in the wrong way, or at the wrong time. In Heart Journey, ease, as well as hardship, is meant to be a sign.

Let me be very clear here about what I am saying. Ease versus difficult as a form of Divine communication specifically applies to Heart Journey and your contract. I am not addressing difficult life situations outside of Heart Journey. Within Heart Journey and the requests made in your contract, progress through ease versus frustration and failure is a form of Divine communication. It is something to pay attention to and heed. There are some things in life that are not meant to be difficult. By the very nature of the process, attracting what you want and opening to receiving is one of them.

In Heart Journey you certainly pull your share of the tasks and responsibilities, but you should not have to force things to happen and it is probably to your detriment to do so. Force is indicative of self-will. Ease is indicative of co-creation with Divine Will. When you are working with your Partner and using the process of attraction and receptivity, things should flow. Doors should open when you need them to open. If the going is extremely difficult, it is a sign that something is off regarding:

1. Intention (what you are attempting to do)
2. Timing (too fast, too slow, too early, etc.)
3. Technique (too little, too much, wrong approach, etc.)
4. Company (who you are working with or depending on)
5. Expectation (process and manner of unfolding)
6. Use of power (seeking to control others)

Pay attention! A "no" or "stop" response is every bit as important as a green light. This is where meditation and entering into the silence can be crucial. When the going gets tough, it is time to reassess. Check in with your co-creative Divine Partner. What needs to happen next? Do you need to make an adjustment? Wait? Let go?

The way you ascertain if everything is correct is by the ease with which opportunities and progress occurs. When there is ease, everything is unfolding as it should, your timing is perfect, and your life is in balance. You are not too rushed for time with family, friends, and health. However, if you set matters in motion, make inquiries, do your part, but then doors slam in your face, it is time to call home and check in with God, to ask if this is the path you need to proceed on and at this time. Perhaps you should be patient, or instead take corrective action.

Example of Difficulties and the Lack of Success

At one point in my life I wanted a guru or teacher and I set out to find one. On my first attempt I took a meditation course in a well-known tradition of heart-centered yoga. It was a four week introductory course held in a room with posts and support beams in the middle of the floor. On the final night of the course, the presenters showed a video about the guru and his many acts of compassion. I shifted my chair around a post in order to see the video. We were then instructed to close our eyes and meditate as we had been taught to do. After ten minutes, we were told to open our eyes. A picture of the guru was on the altar. By looking at the picture we would know whether or not this man was our teacher, our guru. I opened my eyes and almost burst out laughing. I could not see the picture at all. The post was in my way!

My next attempt occurred while flipping through a local new-age paper. There was an article about a female lama in the area. I thought to myself, "Perhaps she is to be my guru." Immediately the God whisper in my head replied, "You will call no man nor woman master in this life time!" I was so shocked, I actually wondered, "Who thought that?" It wasn't me, of that I was sure!

But, undaunted and willful, I decided to try one more time. A local center was teaching a workshop on, "How to find your guru and master in this life." I signed up. I thought, "This will answer all my questions and lead me to my teacher." I went to the talk and once we were all seated this announcement was made. "The talk on finding your guru and master in this life has been cancelled. You will have to wait until the next lifetime for that! Instead the topic for tonight is _____."

I almost fell off my chair laughing, but I got the message. There was no ease in this search. Everything seemed to be going wrong. I was blocked at every turn. The God whisper had been very clear, but I persisted. In the end, my search was unsuccessful and would surely continue to be so. The announcement about the cancelled talk confirmed the future and my path. I ended my search.

God Whispers

God whispers are those voices in your head that don't seem to be yours. They do not have to be audible sounds, though they can be. For most people, they are similar to other thoughts except that they are totally out of character, self-generating, and a non sequitur to what you were thinking. They stand out as something you, yourself, did not think. In the example just given, the God whisper in my head, "You will call no man nor woman master in this life time!" came out of the blue. I was shocked. There was no doubt in my mind that I did not think this. It was as if someone else broke into my thought patterns and implanted this statement.

Example of God Whispers

Another form of God whisper is the gut feeling many have and label as intuition. I remember a woman on television talking about an accident she was involved in that was not her fault. She was driving home and making a left hand turn when from out of nowhere a woman on a bicycle rode right into her path. The cyclist was a young mother and died from her injuries. What haunted the driver was that she had ignored repeated God whispers and intuitive gut feelings that urged her to delay her return home or take a different route. She had discounted all the messages. She regretted having failed to listen and heed the guidance God was giving her.

Lucid Dreaming

Another form of communication with God is lucid dreaming. This type of dream is very different from "normal" dreaming which is generally a by-product of the unconscious. Lucid dreams are more vivid. They stand out as distinct from other dreams. To begin with, the dreamer is a conscious participant in the lucid dream and fully awake though the body sleeps. Actions and events tend to make sense in comparison to the hazy craziness of common dreams. The lucid dreamer may be able to interact in the dream, ask questions, and direct movements. Many times there is a message, an insight, or "Ah-hah! moment," revealed in a lucid dream that has great personal significance.

Example of Lucid Dream Communication

I have a Medicine Wheel garden in my back yard that I built under the guidance of a Cherokee Medicine Woman. At the time of its construction, I had a large pointed stone with a flat, slanted top in my side yard. Most mornings in the warmer months I would meditate sitting on this stone. It weighed hundreds of pounds, but I choose it to be the central or "creator stone" in the Medicine Wheel. I wanted it to be positioned on its end with the point sticking up in the middle of the Wheel.

One night during a lucid dream, as I watched the stone in the center of the Wheel, it fell over, and rotated on the ground until the point was aimed directly at my home office and the window where I sit and write. The new position made perfect sense to me. Even in the dream I immediately understood. Every Medicine Wheel is a power point connected to every other Medicine Wheel in the world. Seeing that creator stone directed my way while sitting at my computer was very encouraging. It gave me strength as I worked and wrote.

The lucid dream or vision of the stone in the Medicine Wheel also gave me the conviction to move that enormous rock. It was so heavy I thought it must be bolted to the ground. I tried a number of different techniques before I finally found one that worked. I somehow got the stone on an old American Flyer sled and tied the sled to the back of my car. As I began to drive the stone around back to the appropriate location, the old sled creaked, groaned, and nearly shook apart, but finally it moved. That the sled held together is a miracle! The one thing that kept me trying different techniques for moving the stone was that I saw it, so clearly, in the center of the Medicine Wheel aimed at my office window in the lucid dream.

Visions

There are several ways to see. Some people see visions in midair as clearly as anything else in the room. Some see visions with their eyes closed, the pictures playing in their head, or dancing across the inside of their eyelids. Others see as in a dream during twilight sleep or meditation. Occasionally, visions are only evident when photographs are developed. There is a well-known picture in the Baltimore area of the Pope's plane landing at the airport with a huge angel of light over the plane. The angel is over a hundred feet tall and dwarfs the plane as it taxis to the gate.

One mode of transmission is not necessarily more important than the other. As with the other forms of communication, the quality of the message itself is the defining trait. The play of pictures might be a form of daydreaming, a release from the unconscious. On the other hand, it could be highly significant. The proof is in the pudding, or in this case, in the quality and intention of the message. In the next chapter I will discuss the necessary characteristics associated with Divine communications. Equally important, I will also discuss those traits which are never a part of Divine communication. But for now, remember this; visions, no matter how real they might appear to be, may or may not be significant. It all depends on the level of insight and understanding that arises from them and the quality of the message being conveyed, which is a distinguishing factor in communications from God.

Example of a Vision without Significance

After coming in from a walk, I went upstairs to my bedroom to kick off my shoes and prepare for a shower. Suddenly, a window of light opened in midair before my open eyes. I stopped to watch a light show that I can only describe as the beginning of life. It was like looking into a womb approximately twelve inches round and seeing the first cell divide and then continue to divide again and again. It was a magnificent vision that lasted several minutes, but to this day I am not sure it had any significant meaning, though it was, and still is, unusual for me to see a vision clearly with my eyes open. I am more likely to see pictures inside my head.

The ability to see anything at all, either externally or internally was a learning process for me. It was not an innate ability I was born with. It grew over time with my ability to "allow." In the beginning, I would get so excited about seeing, the vision would immediately disappear. I had to master a quiet acceptance, without fear, without excitation. Imagine yourself sitting in nature when a bird or butterfly lands on your hand. If you want the visitor to remain, you will not jump for joy or make a sudden move. You will continue to observe from a place of calmness and peace. This is what I needed to learn.

Stranger than Fiction Communication

I read "The Politics of Experience," by R. D. Laing, when I was in graduate school. It had a profound effect on me. One of the points he makes in this insightful book is that there is little difference between the actual experiences of the mystic and those of the schizophrenic. He draws direct parallels between the two, step by step, with only one major distinction. The mystic returns to reality as we know it; the mentally disturbed person does not. This book sustained me through some of my strangest experiences. As long as I came back from wherever my mind led me to cook dinner, run carpool, and change diapers, I was confident that my awareness was fleeting, not a permanent mental disability, no matter how weird it got.

Heart Journey is a highly individualistic program. Divine communication is unique and can come in ways that are totally unexpected and difficult to comprehend. The "Ballad of Mildred" is one such story, hard to imagine, impossible to believe by anyone not experiencing it directly, but true as best as I can convey it.

The Ballad of Mildred

I had a 386 CompuAdd computer that died one day. I had not backed up my hard drive and was very upset. As I drove my computer to the CompuAdd store I pleaded with

God. "Please don't let it be my hard drive! Let it be my mother board. I will upgrade to a 486 motherboard if the cost is $1000 or less."

After the technician at the CompuAdd store checked out my computer, it was confirmed that my motherboard had died. The replacement cost was $2200, more than I could afford at the time. The CompuAdd technician suggested I take it to someone new in town who was cheaper. After this second repairman checked out my computer, he quoted me a price of exactly $1000. It was a deal, or so I thought. My computer spent the better part of the next month in and out of the repair shop. Nothing went right. I lost my modem, the computer would not boot or crashed repeatedly, and every return to the repair shop stretched into a week.

In desperation and frustration, I went back to the CompuAdd store. It was the CompuAdd technician's last day and last hour as an employee when I arrived. (Perfect timing!) Normal procedure was to charge for all consultation time, but after hearing my tale of woe and knowing he had referred me to someone incompetent, the CompuAdd technician checked out my computer for free. After all, what was the store manager going to do, fire him? He explained the new problems to me and what needed to be done. I bought a new modem, took the computer home, made all the technical corrections to the interrupt codes, and booted up my computer successfully for the first time in a month. I was so happy, I bent over, kissed the monitor screen and said, "I love you, honey."

> In my head I heard, "My name is not honey, it's Mildred!"
> "Mildred!" I was shocked, and not fond of that name.
> The inner voice said, "Yes, Mildred. It has special meaning."
> I was speechless. I could not believe I was having a conversation with my computer!
> The voice continued, "Look it up in the dictionary."
> I replied, "They don't put proper names in the dictionary!"
> The response came, "This one is there. Look it up yourself."

So I looked it up in the dictionary. It was there and it meant "gentle power and strength!"

Thus began my strange collaboration with a conscious computer. Mildred had a mind of her own. She would become unstable or shut down when I was tired. I learned to just give up and go to bed. She was always fine in the morning. She would occasionally refuse to perform certain functions for no apparent reason. I remember one time in particular, I was working with a program I had been using for ten years and I could not get the information I needed for one client. I repeated the task. No response. I deleted the information and input it again. No response. I entered a new client and the program ran perfectly. I tried the first client again, no luck. I deleted the client, rebooted the computer, entered a new client, then the one causing me problems, and a third new client. I ran the batch. The first and the last came out. The problem client was lost again.

By this time in our relationship, I was used to Mildred refusing to do work and signaling me that something needed to change. It was her way of saying I was not paying attention and doing what needed to be done. Commonly, at this point I would stop work and meditate. While sitting in the silence I would see what special handling the client needed. Immediately, the program would begin to run perfectly without any corrective action.

This type of situation happened a number of times with Mildred, but always with different software programs. In each case the problems were incomprehensible and impossible to correct, but solved with meditation. Though I was used to this bizarre interaction, nothing prepared me for what Mildred did next. She began to yodel.

I cannot begin to describe this sound coming from my computer other than to call it a warbling, yodeling sound. Mildred did not do it all the time, but frequently enough to be very annoying. Eventually, she did it off and on for three weeks straight. I was writing at the time, in fact, I was writing about the process of manifestation through attraction and receptivity presented in this book. One day, Mildred was really wailing. I could not stand it any longer and decided to open the computer case and investigate where the sound was coming from. There was a small speaker in the computer with an electrical connection. When I removed the connection from the speaker, the sound stopped instantly. Silence ensued. How sweet it was! I put the case back on the computer and proceeded to write.

Several hours passed and I had not backed up my writing when the power went out and I lost everything. I knew this was a sign that I should go and meditate. Thirty minutes of silence brought great insight and I knew where I was off. What I had been writing was not totally correct and the power outage stopped me in my tracks. When I returned to the computer, I was distraught and crying.

I said to God, "You cannot do this to me. This is too hard on my system. Don't let me type for several hours when I am off base and then turn everything off. Give me some warning."

The thought voice reply came, "Well, you turned off the yodel!"

I was amazed! I never expected this response. Suddenly I realized that Mildred would yodel whenever my writing and energy were off! I immediately hooked the little speaker back up.

I realize that this story strains belief, but it happened consistently and repeatedly over a year's time while Mildred and I worked closely together. I would hit the backspace button whenever Mildred would start to sing. I would continue to press it until she stopped. I would go meditate until a new insight would shift my thinking and then return to the keyboard with a fresh perspective. If I had done my homework and was now on track, Mildred would remain quiet. If not, she would instantly act up. She only did this when I was writing spiritual material and never when I was doing normal work like accounting. Once the text was written correctly, Mildred's singing ceased completely. I eventually passed the computer to my son, and six months later Mildred crashed and died. I now meditate regularly before sitting down to write.

It is my karma to convey truth as best I know it. I have done so. It is the reader's karma to determine what to believe and what to be open to.

The moral of this story is that weird, yet wonderful things can happen on your Heart Journey. The trip is highly individualistic when it comes to communication with God as your co-creative Partner. I have mentioned but a few communication processes here. I am sure you will discover your own.

Chapter Nine:
The Nature of Communications

Introduction

Regardless of the mode used for communication, whether symbols, signs, coincidence, ease, God whispers, lucid dreams, or visions, there are certain qualities associated with all Divine communications and these are important to note. There are also qualities that are not in keeping with communications from God and are more likely to reflect unconscious material. Learning and remembering the distinguishing characteristics for communications presented here will assist you with recognition, discernment, and comprehension when interacting with your co-creative Partner.

Distinguishing Characteristics

Divine communications within Heart Journey have loving, supportive, and encouraging traits that clearly differentiate this kind of exchange from unconscious material generated by your own fears, desires, anger, and negativity. When dealing with symbols, signs, coincidences, and ease it is easy to misinterpret the meaning of an event or place great emphasis on something that has no meaning at all. When it comes to God whispers and the thought voice, it is easy to substitute personal preferences and longings for the real thing. Lucid dreams and visions are sometimes subject to distortion because they occur during altered states of consciousness when the mind and memory are less clear. Because of the subtlety normally associated with Divine communications, there is room for error, *unless* you pay close attention to the *quality* and *intention* of the message that is being conveyed. Although both Divine communications and those experiences arising from emotional debris and individual agendas might appear similar on the surface because of their modes of transmission and subtlety, there is a world of difference in their quality and intent.

What Divine Communications Are Not Like

Never Meant to Control

Divine communications are never controlling, demanding, or manipulative. God gave you free will from the very beginning and involvement in Heart Journey and a co-creative partnership is not going to take that away. Though suggestions and guidance might be offered at times, communications are never directive. Nor will God ever encourage you to control or manipulate others. God gave free will to everyone.

Not About Others

Communications are never judgmental of others. In fact, they are never about others at all. This is your Heart Journey. It is about you, not them. Because the contract is your statement concerning intended goals and your invitation to God regarding the co-creative process, Divine communications will focus on your growth, purpose, well-being, and progress.

Never Critical

Within this dynamic, criticism of you, even constructive criticism, is rare. Anger is nonexistent. God does not know this language and does not communicate at this level. You will never be chastised for what you do or don't do, say or don't say, feel or don't feel. If you are off the mark, you will be gently shown this. Your performance is not graded. Even if your intentions and efforts fall away completely and you put your contract in a drawer and forget about it, nothing will happen except that your goals and co-creative partnership will lie dormant. You get out what you put into Heart Journey. Nothing in, nothing out. This is true no matter how grandiose, humanitarian, or crucial you think your plan is. God will let you go without a negative response and without judgment.

Will not Flatter Your Ego

God will not flatter you with praise and treat you as special. You are no more special than the next person. In God's eyes everyone is special; equally special, and comparisons will not be drawn. Though every life has purpose, God will not give you a "mission" that only you can accomplish. You will not be told that you are crucial to the success of God's plan or only you can save the world. Millions of people are advancing in consciousness and you will not be chosen to corner the market on insight. The truth is you are expendable. Spirituality will proceed with or without you. You simply choose to grow or not. Ego traps are not part of your communications with God.

No Fear-based Messages

Your fears will not be confirmed. Fear is counterproductive to your goals, process, and the co-creative partnership. The purpose of Heart Journey is to lift you beyond fear to become a more loving person. Love and fear cannot exist in the same space and it is essential that you grow in love if you are to receive. Your openness, receptivity, and ability to attract what you desire is directly related to your ability to love others, God, and yourself. A giving heart is an open heart capable of receiving. Only love fosters heart openness.

Fear also counteracts trust in God which is necessary for a strong co-creative partnership. Though you surrender to your Partner's expertise for guidance and advice, you still function as an equal participant in the manifestation process. You are not without skills, knowledge, or strengths. You bring a lot to the table and your efforts contribute to your success. Fear-based messages undermine confidence in your ability to contribute, and raise barriers to trust. Are you doing something wrong to warrant a fearful message? Is the Divine communication meant to "put the fear of God in you?" No! There is no reason for God to communicate a fear-based message. Corrections are made gently and impartially, in a matter of fact manner.

All your efforts are honored as brave attempts, even when they fail, even when they are misguided. You are a student of the co-creative process and partnership. You are learning. Communications from God will support you in your studies. Consider all fear-based messages products of your own unconscious.

Rarely Predictive

It has been my experience that when certain individuals initially open to listening within, the first thing they think they hear or perceive is the death or injury of a loved one. God is loving and not waiting with baited breath for you to sit in the silence long enough to be informed of all the bad things that will happen to you or those you care about. These predictions are products of your own unconscious fears coming to the surface to be cleansed.

The lines of communication you are seeking to open in Heart Journey will not help you predict the future, nor should they. They are meant to convey wisdom, insight, and guidance within the co-creative process. You are on this journey to grow in love, not fear. Predictions not only raise fears, many times they are fears masquerading as warnings. There is a cleansing process innate to Heart Journey and every meditation practice. When you first listen within, and especially in the silence, you may witness you own mind creating drama, hardship, anger, hurt, and pain. This is where a good meditation teacher can make the difference between a negative experience and a positive perspective. In Heart Journey, your fears will be coming to the surface to be cleansed and released. They may look like predictions to you. The best advice is to avoid prediction completely, especially early on, and seek a good meditation teacher.

Predictions that indicate an outcome, whether positive or negative, should also be avoided for other reasons. In God's eyes, possibilities are unlimited. In ways that you cannot see or imagine, you have unlimited potential regardless of the stumbling blocks you perceive. Options for unlimited potential are always present though not as you envision. Predictions deny that potential by setting a fixed outcome. They can either guarantee success without effort or portend failure despite a major contribution. Neither is good for your spiritual growth or the co-creative partnership. Do not abandon your God-given right to choose or progress for a fatalistic prediction. Any prediction is only an assessment of where you are right now, and where you are headed given present and past choices. Nothing is written in stone. You have free will. It is a muscle that grows stronger with use. The way you exercise it is by being proactive in addressing issues in your life and making good choices. The more free will you exercise, the more free will you have, and the harder it will be to anticipate what you will do. Learn to see beyond the present into new possibilities and do not fall into fear.

Won't Condone Your Anger

Anger will not serve you or your purpose, but instead delay your Heart Journey progress. For a multitude of reasons, anger will never be sanctioned by God and God will never lead you to hate, (despite what some think). Harmful or hurtful actions will not be promoted, supported, or condoned. Others will never be condemned for their actions *no matter what they do.* Revenge is out of the question. Forget the "eye for an eye" Bible justice. You only poison yourself in the process. Revenge drags you down, but forgiveness lifts you up. For this reason, it is more likely that God will be asking you to put aside your anger and its justification and see with the eyes of compassion. Heart Journey is about opening your heart and loving well. Once you sign your contract and invite God in, you will be encouraged to always do just that.

On the other hand, you are not expected to be or continue to be a victim. Nonviolent protection is encouraged and conducive to spiritual growth, while retaliation is not. An ounce of prevention is worth a pound of cure both for the intended victim and the perpetrator.

There is an old story of a snake that terrorized a town. One day a saint visited the village and the town's people told him of the problems with the dangerous snake. The saint went and spoke with the snake and the snake's attitude was completely transformed by the meeting. He vowed never again to harass the town's people. Many months later the saint returned to the town. He found the snake in terrible shape, abused by the very same town's people he had once terrorized. The saint, realizing what was happening and seeing the snake so beaten and demoralized, bent over and whispered, "I never told you not to hiss!"

What Divine Communications are Like

The communications you receive during Heart Journey are consistent with a loving and gentle God. They are meant to encourage and support you as you learn, progress, and grow spiritually. Keeping the following positive qualities in mind as well as those eliminators just mentioned will help you clearly distinguish between what is a communication from God and what is a product of your own unconscious.

Loving

Heart Journey, by its very nature is heart-centered and all communications flow from love. You will be informed, guided, and sometimes even asked your permission as situations arise and progress is made. Your particular needs and personality quirks will be taken into account. Communications can be highly individualistic, whether mundane or spiritual. Lessons for personal growth tend to be custom made and to the point. In fact, this is one of the more difficult aspects of Heart Journey. God is loving and not just to you. God is loving to those you are in conflict with or those who have done you wrong. God is loving to your boss, your relatives, your wayward teenaged kids, and even your enemies. You know you are dealing with a loving Divine communication when you are asked to love a difficult person and you want to shout in disbelief, "You want me to what? Are you crazy?" It is immediately clear that no unconscious of yours would have ever come up with that idea. Welcome to Heart Journey!

Uplifting and Challenging

When you sign that contract and you enter into this spiritual path so you can learn to open yourself to receiving, God is going to help you get there by challenging your human frailties and shortcomings. Wherever and whenever you are not loving, God will point it out in a most gentle and impartial manner. You will not be shown your faults necessarily, (you know what they are). Rather you will be shown your potential to be more loving, forgiving, and compassionate. The beauty of the system is that if you are patient and willing to listen, you will also understand *why* you need to respond in a more loving manner than in the past, not just for the sake of others, but for your own sake as well. To receive openheartedly, you have to grow beyond your own present heart limitations. If you did not need an opening, if you had everything you ever wanted, you would not have signed up. This is where the rubber meets the road and it is difficult for everyone. God is more loving than you can imagine or sometimes accept. You will be called upon to lift up your sights and grow in your ability to be loving in all areas of your life and to all people.

Encouraging and Supportive

The good news is that God will not only encourage you to become more loving, but God will also support you every step of the way. You do not have to make grandiose displays of love or become a martyr. You need only let go and see with the eyes of compassion. Begin to see through God's eyes and you will open to a new level of understanding. Choose to be mentored. Ask to be shown. Say, "Yes!" Once you do this, everything changes. It is like having x-ray vision that allows you to see past the obvious to what is really going on. Suddenly, the mighty have weaknesses, the hurtful are in pain. And the saddest ones of all are those incapable of giving and receiving love, and don't even know it. It is not your job to tell them. You need only be an example.

There are great benefits and rewards for opening your heart and loving more fully. You will be healthier mentally and physically, less stressed and happier. With time, you will begin to develop an immunity to what others say or do. Their stuff is their stuff. You will maintain your balance and not be affected negatively.

I have a saying, "There are no unloving people on the planet, but the vast majority of us are incredibly inept!" Keep this in mind when you are asked to be more understanding than you thought possible. Communications from God will encourage you to see and grow beyond your personal perspective and limitations, whatever they might be.

Insightful and Wise

Your paradigm shift in regard to lovingness will come about through Divine communications that convey insight and wisdom. The more truth you request, the more you strive to know, the more open you are to suggestion, the less fearful you are of the response, the greater the insights granted to you. With time and practice, you may be privy to the "whys" and "wherefores" of many events in your life while receiving guidance on important matters. After all, things do go better with God! Depend on it.

In your practice, as you begin to quiet your mind and sit in the silence, mention your concerns, ask your questions, and then lay them down before God knowing that when the time is right all your concerns will be addressed and all your questions will be answered. It is in the silence, when the mind is resting in a "gap" of not thinking, in between breaths, that insight arises. It might come slowly with minimal awareness on your part, or burst into your consciousness. It does not matter the manner in which it happens. The distinguishing characteristic of this communication is the resulting paradigm shift occurring in your own thinking, born of new insight that came to you, (and was not thought by you), and the inherent wisdom in that insight that was initially beyond you. God grants insights that speak loudly in the language of wisdom.

Example of Insight and Wisdom

At one point in my life I had to make a difficult decision, one I would rather not have had to make. At the time I was not clear. My thinking was emotionally charged. I felt more reactionary than rational and considered. I could have easily made a poor choice. When I sat down for my morning meditation, I placed my options before God and asked for insight and guidance. I then let everything go and proceeded to quiet my mind and still my thoughts. As I meditated, I became aware of fears that arose as impediments to my understanding. I addressed each courageously and then let it go. I would not allow my fears to limit my ability to see and comprehend. With each fear I faced and released, it seemed like a veil would fall until suddenly there were no more veils. In an instant I knew and understood all the forces that would both impact my decision and result from my choice. I was finally seeing purely, clear of my own emotional debris. I made a wise decision based on that knowing and to this day it is one of the best decisions I have ever made.

This is not to say that information will always be forthcoming, quickly, easily, or at all. There are times in every spiritual journey when fog descends and the traveler is clueless. Insight does not come. At these times, there is nothing left to do but trust in God and put one foot in front of the other following the wisdom previously comprehended through prayer or meditation. Insight is not always associated with communications from God, but when it is present, and especially when it is accompanied by wisdom, it is highly indicative.

Protective

After a while, you will get the sense that you are being watched over, guided and protected. This is another aspect of Divine communications that boggles the mind. That any Being would be so concerned with your comfort and safety is surprising.

Example of Protection

When I was visiting Maui, friends and I drove to Hana, a small town on the rainy side of the island. There are numerous waterfalls along the way and the scenery is exactly what you would expect from a tropical paradise. The distance from Kihei to Hana is not great, but the road is so narrow and winding it takes several hours to complete the journey traveling at speeds of 20-35 miles per hour. While packing, the thought voice said, "Take scissors." I had a tiny pair of nail scissors among my things that I was not planning to take. But the voice insisted, repeating again, "Take scissors." So, I packed them without knowing why.

We stayed at a remote state park outside of Hana and we were really roughing it. We packed carefully, but only took what we thought we needed for two days. There wasn't a supermarket in the area to supply us with things we had forgotten or needed unexpectedly. We either had it with us or we had to do without.

No sooner had we arrived when the screw in my sunglasses came loose and fell out. Two days in the Hawaiian sun by the ocean without good sunglasses was not my idea of fun. I found the screw, but then there was the problem of how to screw it back in. Nothing had a narrow enough edge to turn the tiny screw. Nothing, but the nail scissors I had been instructed to take!

This is how specific, loving, and protective communications can become as your relationship with God grows stronger.

Humorous Example

In my communications with God, God is rarely serious and has a wonderful sense of humor. Even when I am at my lowest, I might laugh out loud at some of the responses. I remember working intensely with God on a difficult relationship problem I was having. I was very sad at the time. The thought voice queried me with, "Where are you?" I was so low I replied, "In the gutter!" A second later I chuckled when the response came, "Good eye, good eye!"

For those of you who are parents of children who play in Little League, the phrase is probably familiar. When your child is up at bat and hits the pitched ball you scream and cheer. But when your child doesn't swing at a bad pitch or ball, you say, "Good eye!" Your comments praise your kid for accurately assessing the situation and recognizing a bad pitch.

Energetic Example

You will discover, probably much to your surprise, that not all communications are verbal or visual. Some are energetic, purely energetic. I have several posters of beautiful Tibetan mandalas in my home. For years I have meditated in front of them. In the beginning I made a serious attempt to unlock their secrets. I would study the mandala noting the variations in colors and forms, counting how many this and thats were here or there. One day the mandala zapped me. An energy bolt came out of the poster and hit me between the eyes. I instantly recognized my folly. My investigative mind games had gotten me nowhere, but in that instant I understood that certain aspects of the spiritual journey are beyond the intellect to experience or comprehend. I immediately surrendered to the current and for several years the mandalas and I played energy games. When the energy tapered off, I would purchase a new mandala poster with a different theme and the games would begin again. I cannot tell you exactly what I learned or how I grew spiritually during this time. I can only say that I did grow spiritually from the exchanges.

Energetic exchanges can occur at any time and during any activity. You do not have to be meditating to feel charged. For many people a lot goes on in the night, in the dream state, during lucid dreaming while asleep, or in the twilight hours of early morning. The energy might be felt in your head, heart, or anywhere in your body. Do not be afraid of this kind of communication as long as it is soothing, comforting, and blissful. Set aside your fears, and relax into it. In all likelihood, the cells of your body are being healed.

Rational Versus Irrational

This story about energetic transmissions and comprehension without the intellect's involvement brings us to a discussion of rationalism in regard to Divine communications. In many traditions, as one enters the Holy of Holies, experiences tend to be irrational or even impossible given reality as we know it. Another word that might be more appealing and familiar to you is "miraculous." This is the domain of miracles, where prayer heals, seas are parted, and Lazarus rises from the dead. God is not always rational which is not to say that God is always irrational. Communications can take many forms and are not limited to what you think things should look, sound, or be like.

At some point in the Heart Journey you have to let go of the need for rational experiences and intellectual explanations. Demanding logic from mysticism will only delay or stall your progress. And you are on a mystical journey. There will be situations that you cannot comprehend intellectually or explain rationally. I have given some examples here. No one would claim that the "Ballad of Mildred" makes sense. I certainly won't! It is also wise to remember that others are not likely to believe or accept your experiences as real. It is not their place to confirm or deny. Rather, it is your job to distinguish what are Divine communications. Cull wisdom and insight from those communications that are inspired, and then continue living. The clearest indication of your sanity is the return to everyday productive living.

Heart Journey is about opening your heart to attracting and receiving what you want in an effortless manner, and your mind must be open to not understanding how that might happen. If you discount miracles they will never happen. There may be many unsolved mysteries in your Heart Journey. Check your logical, rational mind at the door, stop expecting scientific proof, and simply remain receptive to communications from God in whatever forms they might take.

Chapter Ten:
Communication Guidelines

Establishing Guidelines for Communication

Your working relationship with God is pliable, not static or formulaic. You can personalize your interactions by establishing communication guidelines that make it easier for you to perceive and comprehend exchanges as long as you do not seek to restrict or control the flow of ideas and feedback. You are a co-creative partner in all aspects of Heart Journey and in every sense of the word. You have free will. Though you signed a Heart Journey contract, it is amendable at any time. It is also true that your path and process are open to any modifications you need to make that assist you on your journey. Furthermore, it is correct and even advisable that you define and state what you think you need in order to understand exchanges and establish effective, insightful communication with your co-creative Partner. This can be done at any point in the journey, and repeatedly, but is particularly helpful early on when you are unsure as to the nature of communications. There are any number of guidelines you could use. Here are only a few suggestions.

Choose a Specific Symbol with a Specific Meaning

You can establish specific symbolism and criteria for understanding that symbolism. You may not always need this, especially later in your Heart Journey, but it is a good starting point if you are just a communication beginner. Later on, clearly defined symbols and criteria fall away as you become more centered and trusting, capable of receiving and understanding the most subtle communication. Even silence can speak volumes. You will grow to recognize and comprehend the most unique experience and distinguish between Divine input and unconscious debris. At that point, specific interpretations will not be needed at all. But, in the beginning, specific symbols and criteria can be crucial to the initial contact with your co-creative Partner and the early success of your communication.

If there was a specific symbol that arose repeatedly as you were formulating your contract, or a symbol that you have always been drawn to, you might ascertain its meaning and use it as a sign of Divine communication. Spiritual, religious, or Native American power animals or sightings in nature are appropriate. A rose was highly significant as a symbol for me early in my Heart Journey. The symbol or symbols that you choose should be something that you might see, but will not necessarily see on a regular basis.

Examples of Symbolism

Deer have always meant gentleness to me. Though I live in a rural area, I only see deer once every few months. Each time, I immediately retrace my mental steps to what I had been thinking, feeling, or saying. Where did I need to be gentle? Were my thoughts willful or accepting?

The same is true when I see a bluebird, especially when the bluebird is on my property which is not so common. The bluebird is a very gentle bird that will allow itself to be pecked to death in an attempt to protect and shield its young. Who do I need to defend? When I see a bluebird I also think of it as the "bluebird of happiness." What joy is entering my life? Bluebirds generally fly with a mate in the spring and summer months. There is a message here to review what is going on in regard to male-female relationships.

Sometimes I see a fox which has very different energy. Foxes tend to be crafty. Do I need to be smarter in regard to a challenge I am facing? I see turtles in the pond all the time, but only once has one come on land and crossed my path. Turtles have a protective shell and hibernate in the winter. Do I need to be more protective? Should I withdraw? Occasionally I hear an owl hooting at night. What wisdom do I need to be in touch with and follow?

When you have a symbol like the deer or a rose that you are drawn to for any reason, pay attention. What does the symbol mean to you? What does its appearance confirm, convey, or deny?. What is the context of this symbol at the time of its appearance? How does the meaning apply to your present situation? Is the symbol animated in any way and are the actions significant?

If you are not familiar with communications with God, symbolism is a good place to start. Choose and establish a specific symbol that has special meaning for you. Indicate to God that its appearance will be noted by you as significant.

The Rule of Three

The rule of three is used in psychological counseling and also in spiritual discernment. If during a session, a client mentions something with a deeper meaning, but does not seem aware of the implications, the counselor might allow the oversight rather than challenge the client and his or her reasoning. The counselor will wait for the comment or topic to appear again because he or she knows that anything important arises more than once. The counselor will simply make a mental note of what was said. If the comment or topic arises again and is again passed over or brushed aside by the client, the counselor will add the second piece of information to the first. But when it is brought up the third time, the counselor will most likely confront the client with what has been said and either push for more information and a deeper understanding, or challenge the client with an interpretation. At that point the counselor has three solid pieces of information to go on and this is more powerful than one single piece of information by itself.

The same is true in spirituality; three is a magic number. In some traditions, the student must beg for the teachings three times before the teacher is convinced of the student's sincerity and will agree to instruct him or her. Three elements are associated with many religions: Father, Son and Holy Spirit form the Blessed Trinity in many Christian religions; Dharmakaya, Sambhogakaya and Nirmakaya in Buddhism are three states of awareness and manifestation; Brahma, Vishnu and Shiva are the Gods of building, sustaining and destroying in Hinduism.

The rule of three is an important criterion to use in the communication process. It implies that important pieces of information will be conveyed to you three times and in most instances in three different ways. If you are new to communication with God or ever unsure, ask for confirmation, i.e., three signs.

For example, if you ask for specific guidance on a particular course of action, you might wait for three meaningful responses that confirm or imply "yes, this is the best course of action at this time." On the other hand, you might receive three pieces of information that indicate "no, this is not the best course of action at this time." It is preferable that the three signs come to you in different media within a relatively short period of time, unless the signs are both significant and obvious. It would not be as significant or significant at all if you saw three deer together in a field or even separately on the same drive home, unless this was highly unusual. It would be more significant if one day you were seeking guidance and saw a deer on your lawn, were given a pin with a deer on it, and received a call from a friend saying she was gifting you with a weekend at her new vacation home on Deer Lake. The proximity in time with the three different modes of communication would be important, especially if your concerns could be related to the symbolism or your interpretation of "deer." Different spellings and meanings can be contributory, such as "dear" or "John Deere."

In Chapter 8: Example of Difficulties and Lack of Success, I related the story of my unsuccessful search for a guru or master. As soon as I had three clear "no's" I gave up my search and moved on. I did not waste more time on a futile task. These indications were not close together time-wise, (stretching over a year), but they stood out as a complete set, each event conveying the same guidance, but in three very different manners.

It is also appropriate to use the rule of three is regard to ease versus difficulty. If progress is tough and you get three very clear "no" responses to your inquiries or efforts, reconsider. Reflect on the situation or do a meditation session. Perhaps there is another way to accomplish the task at hand. Maybe your timing is off. The rule of three can save you a lot of time and effort by indicating when to move on, when to make an adjustment, when to wait patiently, or when to quit entirely.

The rule of three is a very powerful tool for discernment. Look for three separate instances, occurring at three different times, and arising through three various forms of communication. Remember though, there may be times when no discernible information is available. In that case, it is best to be patient.

Milestones of Success

Perceivable milestones are good indicators for the effectiveness of communication and the co-creative process. They also help to break large projects down into more manageable stages and mini success stories. It is advantageous to build these markers into your Heart Journey process.

For example, if your overall intent is to open a shared-profit store that specializes in selling the handiwork of indigenous people from around the world, you need to get organized and think in terms of the necessary steps. Tasks will include forming your organization, finding a good location for your store, hiring good help, importing wares, establishing credit, handling taxes, advertising, and other tasks too numerous to mention. If your only milestone is completion, you might wait a long time before there is definitive proof of your success and the effectiveness of your communication with God. However, if you break down the tasks and focus on one step at a time, constantly reassessing progress and asking for feedback, the co-creative process is with you everyday and every step of the way.

Communication with God needs to be a daily ongoing event. If you are a photographer, review the situation, setting, and task, then meditate before a shoot. If you are a parent, reflect on the difficult choices you are making for your children. If you are a healer, ask for guidance in helping your clients before you see them or during the session. Inspiration happens when you pay attention inwardly and it can make any task or process easier and more powerful. Even if you do not get any insight or feedback, still keep the lines of communication open. Your invitation is always out there if you practice meditation or look inward daily.

As you begin to work with the milestones and stages that you set, listen carefully for your co-creative Partner's feedback. Communications may be subtle. You might only have a gut feeling, but the result of following that feedback can be so stark and powerful that there can be no misunderstanding or misinterpretation. The proof is in the pudding! When you feel drawn to a particular situation that helps you along your way and doors seem to open automatically, your ability to hear and sense correctly and then respond appropriately is sharpened by your easy success, even if this success is only a small part of what you hope to accomplish. Ease many times indicates you are going in the right direction. It is an important piece of information and an obvious guidepost on the path. Following gut feelings that lead to ease and then immediate success speaks volumes though each factor taken independently is subtle, minor, and seemingly insignificant. It is the united group dynamic (subtle communication, leading to ease, and immediate success) that stands out. Many small, sequential steps followed by immediate successes are more empowering than one huge step take over a longer period of time, even though successful in the end. Therefore, breaking your Heart Journey intention down into small steps and setting milestones along the way increases your opportunities for communication including accurate interpretation of feedback, and confirmation of that interpretation through minor successes.

On the other hand, if you get the feeling that you should not engage in a certain situation, you withdraw, and the direction ultimately turns out to be a dead-end, you have saved yourself a lot of time by listening instead of trying to force through an unworkable option. You have successfully heeded discouraging guidance. This is also indicative of your listening skills and a valuable piece of information, especially when your rational mind was telling you to proceed.

The reverse is also true when you continue down a path while ignoring contradictory feedback from your co-creative Partner. You learn as much from uninformed, independent, willful failure as you do from listening, heeding, and succeeding. When you ignore subtle messages and proceed in a contrary manner, either doing what you should not be doing, or not doing what you know needs to be done, your lack of progress or failure becomes very obvious and offers insight into how you are, or are not, communicating and interacting with God. Specificity in the form of milestones and stages brings clarity to communication and to the co-creative process, both when you succeed and when you fail.

Being specific and setting milestones also fosters trust. In your partnership with God there will be times when you must take action and put in the effort to move things forward. The ball will be in your court. At other times, you will not and should not be doing much of anything. You must shift gears and wait it out patiently, trusting that everything will continue within its own Divine manner and timing. Your project might come to a complete halt during this period, but if the ball is in God's court matters need to develop without your effort, input, or interference. Daily communication and milestones help you to see these shifts in the need for your active or passive response as they occur. Regular feedback gives you the confidence to step in, or the faith to step back, and the wisdom to know the difference. Everything is as it should be.

It is not necessary to be detail oriented regarding milestones and stages when you write your contract. Most contracts tend to be broad and this is good. To be highly specific while composing your contract can be limiting later on. It is like putting the cart before the horse, or the manner in which things shall proceed before Divine communication is established. Milestones and stages are more appropriate to the working out of the contract once the Heart Journey process has begun and the co-creative partnership is established. It is something that can and should be reassessed daily, like the running of any business project.

Asking for Wisdom

It is best to focus on wisdom, creativity, guidance, and spiritual growth in your communications with God. Set parameters in regard to the type of information you wish to discuss and receive. Well-defined areas of interest foster clarity. By narrowing the field, you will be able to maintain your focus and limit confusion. You do not need to know extraneous information that does not directly concern you or your contract. You neighbor's business will not help you to grow spiritually and may actually thwart your ability to receive abundance. Do not fall prey to these derailments. Clearly, God is not bent on giving you privileged information about others anyway. Psychic impressions are not what Heart Journey is about.

Guidance is for you, to assist you in patterning your own thinking and spiritual growth. If you make it a habit not to ask questions about people and situations that do not directly involve you, your contract, or your Heart Journey process, your thinking will be free of distractions and unconscious agendas. The most creative minds are those that are not cluttered with irrelevant information.

The guidelines presented here are simply examples of what has worked for others. Numerous other possibilities exist, so use what works for you.

Chapter Eleven:
The Process of Manifestation

Introduction

Manifestation through the power of attraction and receptivity does not just happen. It is the end product of a series of steps that you take internally and externally, either consciously or unconsciously, in partnership with God. Results may occur instantaneously or slowly over time. The technique is not foreign and not without precedent. Everyone has received something he or she wished or prayed for, even if it was only something small or insignificant. In some cases, fulfillment was spontaneous with the individual never really understanding what occurred or exactly how manifestation happened. Attempts to replicate the process generally produced inconsistent results.

It is a goal of Heart Journey to bring the process of manifestation through attraction and receptivity into the light of awareness through:

1. The contract you have already written,
2. The co-creative partnership with God you've initiated,
3. And spiritual development.

Although an explanation of the process will be given and guidance offered, this will never supersede the miraculous aspect of manifestation arising through attraction and receptivity. Because of God's intimate involvement and contribution to the process, mystery will always remain and miracles will still happen. Manifestation through attraction and receptivity is truly a co-creative endeavor dependent on God's blessing. You will never be in the position of control, forcing manifestation to occur. It is only within your power to provide the ideal conditions and heart openness needed for receiving openhandedly. The miraculous result of the process remains in God's hands and is always attributed to God's grace within the highest good for everyone involved. Technically, you are not the one manifesting at all. Learning and practicing the principles of manifestation through attraction and receptivity will increase your chances of witnessing and experiencing a miracle, but you are only setting the stage for the Master of Ceremonies and the events that might occur. Remember, there are no guarantees!

What is presented here is not the only pathway to manifestation through attraction and receptivity. It is simply the easiest to understand and practice at this stage of the Heart Journey. Other pathways exist and may or may not be part of your walk. Also, the processes of manifestation, attraction, and receptivity are not the only processes you might experience while on your Heart Journey. The possibilities for spiritual growth when co-creative partnering with God are unlimited.

The Four Elements Needed for Manifestation

The process of manifestation through attraction and receptivity complements co-creation with your co-creative Partner and your Heart Journey path. This is not a will-based process, but one built on the balance of desire and surrender, attraction and receptivity, ease and effort. You have already been introduced to the first elements, desire tempered by surrender, during the formation and signing of your contract. You had to state your desire, but then surrender the results. You might remember, "Not my will, but Thy Will and for the highest good of all involved." The balance of desire and surrender is central to your ability to attract and receive, and it is the first subtle skill you must master.

The process of manifestation through attraction and receptivity is a mystery of the highest order and an understanding of the process only comes through careful study, observation, and integration of the key elements and forces on a personal level. Although an overview will be presented here, little more can be said because the process of manifestation through attraction and receptivity is highly individualistic for each person and each situation. Once read and understood, you will have to feel your way along toward manifestation within your co-creative partnership. Heart Journey is a mystical path that you and God travel together. God is your guide and tutor, filling in the blanks that cannot be spoken or written here or anywhere else. The knowing, the "Ah-hah!" and essence of manifestation through attraction and receptivity is beyond words and teaching. It resides within the co-creative partnership. I could say it resides within the descent of grace or Divine miracles, but that would imply outcomes unattainable by all but a few individuals, which is not true. I believe any and every one can have the experience of manifestation through attraction and receptivity, even on a regular basis. Does this make it any less miraculous? No! It will always be a great mystery, one that originates and evolves directly from your co-creative cooperation with God.

This is why communication within the co-creative partnership is so important. This is why the information on Divine communication and the co-creative partnership comes before the process of manifestation through attraction and receptivity. This is why your belief in a loving and supportive God is so crucial to your Heart Journey. This is why

Heart Journey is truly a mystical path fostering spiritual growth even though the initial intention is purely desire based. Your relationship with God is the key that unlocks the mystery of what is presented here.

There is little known about the process of manifestation through attraction and receptivity, but in almost every case, the four elements mentioned below will be included and stand out as the initiating elements.

1. Desire tempered by surrender
2. Focused and sustained potent thought
3. Flow
4. Avenue for manifestation

Desire Tempered by Surrender

Desire is the starting point for manifestation through attraction and receptivity as it is the energy that fuels the process for however long it takes, even during stressful periods and setbacks. The strength of your desire at the outset and throughout your Heart Journey is closely related to your ability to manifest. In the first part of this book, you were instructed to ascertain your desire before composing your contract. It was important that it be your desire, not someone else's wish for you. It had to be something that you truly wanted. The more passionate you were about your desire, the better.

Ascertaining your desire at the start of your Heart Journey prepared you for the process of manifestation through attraction and receptivity. The same desire that went into the writing of your contract is the desire and energy needed to fuel the manifestation process. No desire, no formation.

This is true regardless of which pathway to desire you took, whether active or passive. Some actively chose or determined their personal desire and goal. Others perceived intuitively what God might wish and surrendered to that desire. In the process of manifestation through attraction and receptivity, you can be the initiator (or the one with the burning desire), or you can be the perceiver (the one burning with the desire to perceive, experience, and transmit Divine intention). Both stances integrate and balance desire and surrender thereby fostering the ability to attract and receive. It is the strength of the desire and not the pathway to desire that is important.

Equally important to desire, is surrender. It is fair to say that these two seemingly opposite poles are actually working together as a team in the process of manifestation through attraction and receptivity. They cooperate to magnetize your ability to attract (through desire), while they also integrate to reduce (through surrender) any compulsion to willfully make things happen, and to reduce any resistance to receptivity born of fear, doubt, or negativity. It is important to be aware of this dynamic of desire and surrender on all levels of interaction as it behaves differently given the context.

On a psychological level, we commonly think of the two processes of desire and surrender as being mutually exclusive. You either desire and pursue, or surrender and let go. One action is not compatible with the other. But on the spiritual level, desire and surrender are an alchemical team which both desires to experience God fully while also surrendering to that Higher Power. On a spiritual level, desire and surrender actually augment each other's power.

At the level of manifestation through attraction, your personal desire to manifest echoes God's desire to create. You are made in the image and likeness of God, a piece of spirit made flesh. Your desire to co-create with God can thereby attract unlimited resources enabling the process of manifestation.

At the level of manifestation through receptivity, your surrender provides the ideal environment in which manifestation can occur. Surrendering your desire frees you of the fear that it will not happen and moves you to acceptance and openness to come what may, "Not my will, but Thy Will." Surrender fuels receptivity is the same way that desire fuels attraction. It allows you to trust and stay open even when progress is slow, stalled, or stopped altogether. This openness through all types of "manifestation weather" enhances receptivity and the magnetic power of attraction, allowing momentum to build over time. Desire that is rightly sustained within the co-creative partnership increases attractive ability. Surrender that is rightly sustained within the co-creative partnership increases receptivity. The dualities work hand in hand, desire with surrender, attraction with receptivity.

As part of your Heart Journey spiritual path you need to temper an aggressive approach to making things happen, and instead increase your ability to receive by strengthening your attractive and receptive muscles. You do this by increasing both your desire and your surrender while always maintaining a balance between the two. Patience is a virtue in this process. These are subtle muscles and the balance must be finely tuned. You must open when you would close, receive when you would refuse, give when you would deny, and desire through it all while surrendering the results.

In some situations, receptivity is not only more effective than action, it is the only possible technique for the task at hand. For instance, you cannot make a butterfly land on your hand. You can only sit quietly among the butterflies hoping and waiting for one to light. You might hold flowers in your hand or sugar water in your palm, but it is the butterfly who is drawn to you through attraction and receptivity. It is your job to set the ideal stage for what you wish to happen and then wait patiently. Getting a butterfly net and capturing a butterfly is not the same. This is a "will-based" action that might injure or destroy the very prize you seek.

In the same way, you cannot "go get" or force love. The moment you use force, you lose completely. You can never capture love. You can only open to love and flow from it and with it through an open heart. In this way, you attract what you want by becoming what you desire, i.e., love, then surrendering to it, and remaining open to receiving it.

Breaking this down, step-by-step, the initial desire is to be loved. You start by being loving, then continue to love in all situations until finally you become the personification of love. At this point you are love. By being love and loving well, you become loved, the manifestation of your original desire. By surrendering to that which you desire (in this case love), without fear (of not being loved), without conditions (under which you will love), or control (expectations regarding the responses of others), you become the pure, surrendered manifestation of that which you sought, fulfilling your desire. This progression is innate to the laws of manifestation through attraction and receptivity and it requires the balance of desire with surrender.

A Focused and Sustained Potent Thought

Energy follows thought. Though desire fuels the manifestation process, thought directs the co-creative energy into a particular form or result. It is the pattern or template for manifestation. After you desire it, you must think it, and think it consistently over time. If desire were the water in a hose, the hose itself would be the mechanism giving you the ability to aim and direct the water to quench and maintain your garden. In this analogy, the hose is to water as the focused thought is to desire. If you remember to water your garden every day, regardless of the heat and your busy schedule, you sustain your garden over time and will be rewarded with beautiful flowers, fruits, and vegetables. Likewise, when your focused thought is sustained daily and over time, your desire is more likely to manifest or bear fruit. Now, you cannot actively force your garden to grow, only nurture and support its growth, supplying what is needed. You also cannot force manifestation through attraction and receptivity.

Your Heart Journey contract is your focused thought that you need to sustain for manifestation to occur. This is why a simple contract is best since you can carry it with you in your head and heart. In Part One: The Initiation, you were instructed to make your contract concrete and specific. The reason for this is that the more focused your thought, the more likely it is to manifest in the physical world in a measurable way. Your desire or vision has definition when your thought is focused. A vague or confused contract does not have the same formative ability and will not channel co-creative energy as effectively. It is still possible, but less likely. Returning to the image of the garden hose, if you set the spray on wide and fine you might also be watering weeds and your sidewalk. Your water usage is less efficient and less focused. Your diluted efforts will not get you the exact results you desire as weeds will outpace your flowers and take over your garden. More work will be required to grow and maintain your garden. In the same way, competing desires have built-in distractions. With complex Heart Journey contracts you might wish to organize or prioritize desires.

Translating your desire into meaningful symbols, applications, or wording was an important step in writing your contract and not necessarily an easy thing to do as translation can be an acquired skill. Words and symbols are sometimes too small for a vision, but they do enhance the movement into matter. The process of translation is not over and continues throughout your Heart Journey. As you progress and establish a co-creative partnership with God, modifications will be needed to guide your desire smoothly into manifestation. You will be called on to revisit your translation repeatedly as new options or situations arise. Make appropriate fine-tuned adjustments in your focused, sustained thought, or major course corrections regarding methods or results.

On the other hand, you might need to revisit your translation and make adjustments because expectations are not being met and events are not progressing according to plan. Translation of your desire into a focused thought is an ongoing practice meant to keep you on track. Revisiting your contract and translation keeps your focused thought current and responsive to feedback from your co-creative Partner and conditions impacting your journey.

Although adjustments are made, you still need to sustain the central theme of your focused thought. You must consistently want what you desire day after day (within reason). Minor corrections are fine, but you do not want to desire one thing one day and then a different, mutually exclusive option the next day. Do not impede your Heart Journey contract with competing desires. Scattering your thoughts and energy dilutes your ability to attract. So stay focused! Your desire and translation should stay basically the same throughout the manifestation process.

In addition, you do not want to weaken your desire and focused thought through chaos, doubt, or fear. Mixed emotions and internal or external conflict can distract you from your vision and deplete the potency of your thought and desire, thereby derailing the manifestation process. Negativity also leads to contraction, diminishing receptivity. Manifestation cannot occur under these circumstances because magnetism (attraction) and openness (receptivity) are lost. Quality and consistency over time are needed. You must sustain a focused thought consistent with God's guidance that is filled with desire while surrendering the results throughout the manifestation process. All this needs to take place within an emotional climate of faith, hope, inner peace, and heart openness if attraction and receptivity are to be maintained.

Flow

No one would attempt to fly a kite or sail a boat on a windless day. No one would try to grow a garden when the weather is freezing cold and there is snow on the ground. A baby cannot be expected to walk much before a year old no matter how strong his or her legs appear to be at five months. What we might think of as common sense is actually an awareness of "flow" in its most physical and observable form. Flow is associated with the natural order of things that states there is a time for everything.

> *"To every thing there is a season, and a time to every purpose under heaven.* (Ecclesiastes 3:1, KJV of The Holy Bible).

Everyone has experienced the wisdom of paying attention to environmental conditions when attempting to accomplish a task. But when dealing with your co-creative Partner in the process of manifestation through attraction and receptivity, you must also pay attention to spiritual or energetic flow. On an esoteric level, flow is timing according to ease and difficulty. Though this might seem like a subtle dynamic, it can actually be quite obvious. Each step is accomplished easily as everything falls into place. Your actions seem effortless, yet still successful. Whatever you need is available when you need it. You know when to move ahead and when to wait for the next go-round. You are never rushed, late, or ahead of your time. You are able to pace yourself and keep a balanced schedule that includes family, friends, exercise, and rest. Progress comes easily, either bit-by-bit or in a single act. When there is ease, you have the sense that God is with you.

On the other hand, when everything is difficult and efforts fail no matter what you do or how hard you try, there is no flow. You are not being assisted in any way, shape, or form, and instead you feel thwarted. Everything seems to be going wrong and you cannot get a break. You struggle for each step and still progress is denied. Freaky things happen. Problems come out of the blue. People get sick, your car dies and you miss the plane, or are called away at the worst possible moment. Paperwork is incorrect. Money dries up. The dependability factor falls to zero as you cannot count on anything being what it is supposed to be, or doing what it is supposed to do. What is beyond your ability to control is out of control, but then nothing you do works either.

When there is no flow, you need to step back, reflect, and check in with your co-creative Partner. There can be a number of reasons for the difficulties, a lack of flow being one of them, but you will never know what is going on until you sit quietly with your co-creative Partner and check in. Your timing might be off. You might be attempting to do something in the wrong manner or through the wrong means. You could be totally off track or not in accordance with Divine Will or the highest good of all involved. These are just a few general possibilities, but the reasons can be numerous and highly specific on an individualized level.

The bottom line is that if there is no flow, you cannot manifest through attraction and receptivity, and you might not be able to manifest through force either. This is why communication with your co-creative Partner is so important. It can mean the difference between success or failure, effortless progress or spinning your wheels and expending great effort while going nowhere. Although flow might seem like a force too subtle for common awareness, consistently paying attention to "what is" and "what is not" working, how, and when, can sharpen your senses and bring this element clearly into the light of day.

Example of Manifestation within the Flow

I was invited on a tour to Sedona, Arizona. The tour itself would be free including lodging, however, I needed to cover my own airfare. I said to God, "If I am meant to go, make it happen." Within three hours a friend who was already scheduled for the tour called with a free companion ticket. I went to Sedona with all expenses paid.

In this example, all three elements discussed so far were present. My desire was to go to Sedona, and I clearly stated that I needed a plane ticket to get there. I asked God, my co-creative Partner to help me with a ticket, but then surrendered the results. I was willing to stay home if that was in my best interest or for the highest good of all involved. Obviously, flow was with me as a ticket appeared in a matter of hours. Ease like this that is swift, effortless, and complete is always highly significant.

On the other hand, my search for the guru or master, see Chapter 8: Example of Difficulties and Lack of Success, was not so successful. The desire was there and it was clearly stated in a focused and sustained thought that was held over a year's time. Still there was no flow and this was not to be.

Manifestation through attraction and receptivity can take time. Not all manifestations happen quickly. Many take months, some take years, especially when the vision is a big step or a complex process. As a rule, the farther you are from the goal when you begin your journey and the more involved the transition, the more time needed for manifestation to occur. Breaking your goal down into small stages will sustain and guide you along the way. In the interim, you need to stay in communication with your co-creative Partner and pay particular attention to the ease and difficulty associated with each step along the way.

Finally, to be at your best and in touch with the flow, you must be clear-headed, calm, loving, and open. Daily meditation will help you do this even in stressful times. It is difficult to sense the flow when your emotions are running wild. Anxiety increases indecisiveness, making signals appear mixed and inconclusive. Additionally, though the grace of God is readily available to all, it is difficult to connect to or experience it when you are angry, chaotic, doubtful, or unable to trust and follow guidance. In these cases, grace is like water rolling off a duck's back. There is no true meeting, recognition, and awareness of support. You need to maintain a calm, loving, and loved attitude that is in harmony with God's companionship. Emotional equanimity helps you remain focused and connected, alert to flow, timing, obstacles, and ease.

Avenue for Manifestation

For manifestation to occur, there has to be a means or "avenue" by which things can materialize. The avenue for manifestation is the fourth and final element you need to foster and develop as you attract and receive. Desire is energetic intent and not method. It is the fuel for the process. A focused and sustained thought is the translation that channels the energy of desire into form, but it is not method. It is the template or idea. Flow is Divine assistance, timing and the ease with which the whole process occurs, and also not method. The avenue for manifestation is the physical means by which the other three elements come together and the end result appears.

In the Sedona example given above, the avenue for manifestation was a promotional companion ticket issued by a credit card company to my friend. In the example involving the search for a teacher and a guru, the avenues for finding a master included a meditation course, a listing in a new-age newspaper, and a lecture at a local center. Any one of these steps could have led me to a teacher, but it was not to be, and obviously there was no flow.

The avenue for manifestation may or may not be within your control and might be totally unknown to you. You do not necessarily have to know in advance how things will come to pass though many times that is the case. I had no control over the plane ticket to Sedona and had never heard of a free companion ticket. It came out of the blue, with no foreknowledge on anyone's part, not even my friend's.

There are two different processes associated with the avenue for manifestation depending on the extent of your involvement. In the first venue, you do not and cannot know how fulfillment will occur. It is not your job because you are not a major contributor to your success. Everything is essentially beyond your control and the ball is in God's court. There is little you can do other than make your request and then remain open, attractive and receptive. The rest depends on grace and whatever is for the highest good of all involved. This is a risky play that may or may not work, but sometimes you have no choice. You can't do it on your own.

In the second venue for manifestation, you not only have some idea about how manifestation might occur, you also have a plan or the beginnings of a plan. This is the best approach to take when your desire involves a multistage process that you need to be intimately involved with over time, putting forth effort and developing the necessary skills. With this type of journey the ball is definitely in your court and you are a major contributor while God is on your support team.

For example, suppose you want to become a doctor in a third world country. You will not be gifted with an instantaneous medical degree! You have work to do. If you are fresh out of college, you need to go to medical school. If you are fresh out of medical school, you have to complete an internship. Even then there would be a foreign language to learn. The avenue for manifestation is clear from the beginning and you understand your role. You have to put in the effort and develop your skills over an extended period of time as your part of the deal. Though the ball is clearly in your court, God is not totally out of the picture. You can receive Divine support. Along the way doors can fly open for you. You might get scholarship money for school and incentives for opening a practice in an underprivileged or rural area. Through grace you can develop special healing talents and insights that go beyond your training. Easing your tasks and clearing the way are God's part of the deal. Commitment to a path, no matter how long it might take leads to support and resources becoming available when you practice manifestation through the process of attraction and receptivity.

Suppose you are not interested in developing skills. You are comfortable with the skills you have and wish to delegate tasks to skilled labor. This is still an avenue for manifestation. For example, you love to design clothing. You choose the fabrics, draw your designs, and fit the clothing to the model, but you do not want to sew the garment or create the patterns for different sizes. You are also not interested in marketing techniques. You know where your talents are and where they are not. You are not interested in developing new skills. You prefer to attract and hire the best people for the job. This is the format your avenue for manifestation will take.

Sometimes you know how things will work out and sometimes you are clueless. Sometimes you are doing nothing at all other than waiting for a sign. Sometimes the way becomes clearer as you progress or you simply put one foot in front of the other, moving along toward your vision blindly. A plan can emerge all at once or be revealed piece by piece.

Example of Following Blindly

I made a special pipe bag for a Native American pipe carrier. The bag was suede and I wanted to put a beaded hummingbird on the front of the bag. For two days I struggled with a needle and thread, trying to create a pattern that looked like the bird. I managed to create most of the body, but was having trouble with the wing. The suede was tough to work with and my fingers became sore. I became discouraged by my lack of success. I begged God for assistance as I ripped the wing out again for the umpteenth time.

> "I can't do this. You have to help me!"
> The thought voice relied, "Are you ready to listen?"
> I replied, "Yes."
> "Then put this bead here," said the voice in my head.
> I asked for a complete description. "What will it look like?"
> Again the single directive, "Put this bead here."
> I resisted. "But I want to know where we are going!"
> "Put this bead here."
> I pleaded, "I need to see the big picture!"
> "Put this bead here," was the only response.

I could tell I was not going to get anywhere with my objections. If I wanted to succeed I was going to have to go along with the blow-by-blow, bead-by-bead instructions. For thirty minutes, this was all I heard as I worked and followed instructions: "Put this bead here. Then I began to complain again.

> "This is wrong. The beads are going in the wrong way."
> "Put this bead here."
> "But these beads are sticking up out of the bird!"
> "Put this bead here."

"This is crazy," I thought. "This is not looking like a hummingbird and God should know what they look like." But the voice was insistent and would not stray from the one bead at a time directive. I finally decided to continue and ultimately prove God wrong! But then a miraculous thing happened. The hummingbird began to take flight. It was no longer a hummingbird sitting on a branch, it was now a hummingbird landing on a branch with its wings fully extended and up, something I had not thought of and had no intention of doing. In less than an hour, the hummingbird was done. It was perfect and beautiful, and I learned a valuable lesson about trusting God. Sometimes you just have to put one foot in front of the other without ever knowing exactly where you are going or how you are going to get there.

Knowing the step-by-step plan at the outset of your Heart Journey contract is nice, but not essential. You can develop a plan as you go along or watch one evolve over time. This can be a real lesson in letting go and letting God. As you journey, doors can open, options might arise, options you had not thought possible. You do not have to know how fulfillment will occur as long as your goal is believable and you trust that it can be done. The avenue may become clear to you over time, or it might not be your responsibility at all. The ball can be in God's court for the initial steps or even for fulfillment.

Keeping your options open is essential for maximum Divine assistance and benefit. You never know how things will play out so allow for expanding horizons. In fact, a policy of openness in all areas of your life is advantageous. Generalized openness increases opportunities for multiple benefits since abundance will not be limited to Heart Journey contract items only. As your ability to manifest through attraction and receptivity increases, abundance can affect a broad range on life situations.

Furthermore, you can assist the process by actively cultivating and enhancing ways to generate abundance. A client spoke to me about how she needed money for dental work and a new roof on her house. All told, she had to come up with $10,000. Several days after realizing this, she received a letter from her stock broker containing a check for around $10,000. He had been forced to liquidate some assets and sent her the proceeds. It occurred to me at the time that this was one avenue for the manifestation of abundance I did not have and needed to develop.

The danger associated with having a ready-made, well-defined avenue for manifestation is that you might narrow your thinking to one option or plan, presuming that this is the only way manifestation will occur. Do not limit yourself! A client with a business idea turned down several offers for assistance. He wanted an exact amount of money from an investor he did not know at a specific time. He thereby complicated and restricted his options for receiving with his preconceived expectations. In the end he missed out entirely.

Through Divine communication you will ascertain your role in the process. Make sure you fill that role to the best of your ability by putting in the effort and developing the necessary skills. Remember, God helps those who help themselves! In the meantime, do not let your desire become deflated because you do not know the method by which things will manifest. Maintain your desire. Sustain your focused thought, and do not fall into the trap of trying to make things happen. If you stay calm, focused, and connected to your co-creative Partner everything will become clearer in time.

If you have a vague sense of what needs to be done and your project is extensive, break it down into units and then choose your first steps. Trying to deal with a major project all at once can be overwhelming. As you make your way through each piece, keep in close contact with your co-creative Partner so insights will arise regarding the particular task you are working on. This helps you to narrow, yet maintain, your focus. The constant influx of detailed information will help you adjust your plan step-by-step, enabling you to hone in on immediate tasks while staying true to your long range vision. Ongoing support such as this is a major advantage in the successful manifestation of any long range vision.

For some people and situations, the avenue for manifestation is the most difficult step in the process of manifestation through attraction and receptivity. This is true whether the project is complex and long-term, or simple and quick with things appearing out of nowhere. For other people and situations, this step is a snap as doors seem to fly open immediately. No two journeys are the same, even for the same person. Every situation and process of manifestation through attraction and receptivity is different and will exhibit its own characteristic unfolding and internal timing. People are different in their ability to desire. Translations of desire into a focused thought might need adjustment and flow is constantly changing. It is impossible to tell anyone what to do, what not to do, or exactly how things will progress. Only the pertinent signs can and have been given to help you understand your own journey. It is up to you to combine these four elements:

1. Desire tempered by surrender
2. Defined by a focused and sustained thought
3. Moving with the flow
4. Through an avenue for manifestation

Picture a parachutist who wishes to land in a small ring on the ground. He must pull on the ropes, constantly making adjustments to navigate his way into the prescribed area. The process of manifestation through attraction and receptivity is not a static process. It does involve navigation as numerous adjustments, both minor and major, might be needed. You will be guided as you move closer and closer to your manifestation goal by the signs related to flow and Divine communications.

Gratitude

Never take your abundance or co-creative Partner for granted. Be thankful for each step towards manifestation as it is truly a gift. Remember to be thankful for each failed attempt also. There is learning, wisdom, and love in each interchange even when it is not readily apparent. First impressions are not what they always seem. Frustration and hardship can breed courage and insight, or they can be the means by which your course is redirected. Valuable lessons are innate to Heart Journey and you never know when you are dealing with a teaching situation. What might appear to be a struggle could really be an attempt to get you to "Put this bead here!" You won't know what the end result will be or where you will end up until you go with it completely while acknowledging and appreciating the journey. What seems like a denial might open a door to accelerated growth, achievement, and manifestation. No matter what is coming your way, be thankful. Know that God is always with you, guiding you, with purpose and your highest good in mind.

Chapter Twelve:
Troubleshooting Communication

Introduction to Troubleshooting

Manifesting through attraction and receptivity is not always an easy process and neither is it foolproof. It requires the delicate art of skillful navigation to bring your vision into form with the full participation of your co-creative Partner. Your role is to become a Heart Journey alchemist applying the right amount of desire tempered by surrender, with effort and/or skill, to your focused, sustained thought within the flow. To balance all the elements and come up with the best combination, stay in close communication with your co-creative Partner and enhance your receptivity with an open and loving heart. All this might sound like trying to pat your head while rubbing your tummy, but it can fall into place and come together in an instant or in a step-by-step process that takes years. If you just stay with the unfolding, you will begin to attract the resources and insights needed to know how, when and where to apply your skills and efforts.

This chapter and the four other troubleshooting chapters that follow deal with the common obstacles an individual on a Heart Journey might encounter; however, it is very unlikely for anyone to encounter all or even many of these obstacles. If a problem arises, it will be with one of the four elements needed for manifestation through attraction and receptivity, or the failure to establish clear and insightful communication with your co-creative Partner. To systematically troubleshoot the process, it is best to start by assessing communication with your co-creative Partner since strong communication is the remedy in many situations. Once you are confident that communication is established and helpful, move on to evaluate, one by one and in order, the four elements needed for manifestation until you locate the problem area.

Start Troubleshooting by Communicating with God

Assess the Strength of the Connection

When nothing is happening and you have not made any progress in months, the very first step in the troubleshooting process is to look at the level of connection and communication with your co-creative Partner. The connection is well-established when it involves daily contacts on your part. This means you spend quiet time in meditation, reflection, or in nature, listening every day. In all instances, troubleshooting the manifestation process, regardless of where you think the problem lies, starts with spending quality time with your co-creative Partner. This is the fastest and surest way to ascertain the nature of any problem and comprehend the appropriate corrective action you might need to take. Much can be gained from simply checking in.

The length of time you spend in reflection should be sufficient to support a growing and continuing relationship. Do not shortchange your time with God if you wish to receive Divine guidance and assistance. The co-creative partnership is crucial for manifestation through attraction and receptivity. Without the connection you are working alone in a vacuum on a do-it-yourself, self-willed project. The actual length of time you spend in reflection, whether twenty minutes or an hour, is highly individualistic. It depends on your ability to quiet your mind and enter into a reflective space. The surest signs that you are spending enough quality time are that you are at peace with the manifestation process and you trust your co-creative Partner. If you embody these two emotions, the co-creative partnership is strong and supportive. A lack of guidance or delayed communication, (according to your time frame), is not a sign of failure or deterioration of the co-creative partnership as long as peace and trust are present. A lack of progress in regard to manifestation is also not a sign of failure or deterioration of the co-creative partnership as long as peace and trust are present. The presence of these two calming emotions is highly significant of Divine interaction. Keep in mind that the manifestation process through attraction and receptivity works within God's timing. Be at peace and trust in God's plan.

If, on the other hand, you feel thwarted in your efforts to manifest, frustrated with the co-creative partnership, and disheartened by the lack of success, you are not spending enough quality time in reflection. These negative emotions and loss of comfort are important to note. They indicate that your connection to the Divine is weak and your belief in co-creation is fragile. Impatience is man-made and in keeping with self-will. It denotes a lack of surrender to Divine timing or guidance and a decreasing commitment to your Heart Journey contract. If you have no sense of peace and distrust your co-creative Partner, your connection has suffered and you may be seriously off track.

If your connection is strong and stable and of good quality, but you are not aware of receiving any responses to questions, support, or guidance, you may not be fully sensitized to all the different forms communication can take, i.e., symbols, signs, coincidence, ease,

God whispers, lucid dreams, and visions. Do not assume that God is not listening or responding. You can easily miss the signals if you are looking for the wrong medium, in the wrong place, or at the wrong time. You might be waiting for a thought voice message when there are symbols all around you. Or, you could be expecting insights during meditation when actually they are occurring while you are cooking dinner. Guidance can appear in lucid dreams instead of during the day. Beware of your expectations. They can filter out unexpected communications.

Remedy: If you feel frustrated or abandoned, without insight or support, you need to strengthen your connection by increasing your time spent in reflection or improving the quality of the time you spend with your co-creative Partner. Quality reflection is directly related to listening. Quiet your mind and remain open. Cut the dialogue. You can ask for help, you can seek guidance and insight regarding life's problems, but this is not the time to complain. Skip the details; God already knows. Your goal is to quiet the mind, not to replay life's events and dramas. Pray the solution, not the problem.

Regularity is as important as quality. Setting aside time each day breeds peace and reinforces trust through intimacy with the Divine. Sporadic reflection, rushed meditation, or a practice interrupted by noise, drama, or chaos will not foster a strong connection. Though your life might be filled with distractions, do not let them derail the communication process. Clearing your head will require concentration and training, especially in the beginning. Practice is essential. Turning down the chaos in your life helps. Find a quiet place. Learn to step back from unnecessary distractions so you can sit quietly. Regular, well-established, quality reflective time will lead to a stable connection, continuous guidance, and support along with feelings of peace and trust.

If communications seem few and far between review Chapter 8: Communicating with God to remind yourself of all the forms Divine communications might take. The "Rule of Three" in Chapter 10: Communication Guidelines might be particularly helpful in sorting out what is noteworthy when symbols are reoccurring in several different venues. Be open to whatever form communications may take and whenever they occur, regardless of how subtle, blatant, or weird they might be.

Evaluate the Nature of the Communications

If your connection is strong and stable, evaluate the nature of communications you are receiving or think you are receiving for their content. If you are receiving insights and you are being told to be patient, you do not have a problem. You need to wait. During this time it is important to maintain your desire and also sustain your focused thought. You are waiting for the timing to be right. For whatever reason, there is no flow at present. If appropriate, you might use this time to sharpen your skills. Continue with your quiet times of reflection and you will develop further spiritually. Even though there is no external progress toward manifestation, internal progress will be made and your co-creative partnership will continue to grow stronger by maintaining your practice. There is more to Heart Journey than just manifestation.

Communications can be subtle and easily misunderstood or distorted by the ego or the unconscious. This can be a real problem for the beginner. An important criterion for evaluating communications is whether or not they are consistent with your experience. Actions and events can speak louder than words. Contradictions between communications and experience are warning flags indicating self-contamination and human error on your part. God does not lie. In the best of circumstances, communications should go hand in hand with insights, progress, and ensuing events. This is not to say that communications are meant to be predictive. They generally are not, but there should be some correlation or confirmation.

The spiritual content or lack thereof in the communications you receive is another yardstick used to evaluate content. Communications which include flattery and praise are false. Though support is readily available and given in an insightful manner, ego strokes are just that, ego strokes. The flip side of flattery is condemnation and these false communications also originate from the unconscious. God is the personification of gentleness and does not stoop to guilt trips. If communications turn critical and blame you for the lack of success, you have definitely tapped into your own inner critic. God never berates. God is never angry at you or at your enemies, even when you wish it were so. This is a very negative distortion of communications by the unconscious which can also generate fear, competition, doubt, and control issues. None of these emotions is innate to Divine communications and should be either ignored or challenged as false. Negativity impedes manifestation and spiritual development. God is interested in the best that you can be starting with where you are now. Past mistakes or current deficiencies may be part of the learning process. You may be shown in a matter of fact manner the results of your decisions and actions. Natural consequences are also part of the learning process. View this information with gentle eyes as God would. It is meant to help you make better choices in the future. Learning to love yourself is part of Heart Journey and necessary for the heart opening.

Clarity is sometimes a problem in the communication process. Your connection is strong, the insights are uplifting, but the communications are confusing or unclear. You are not sure how the pieces fit together and they might appear to be contradictory. There can be various reasons for this confusion, but generally this is because accurate interpretation involves a learning process. Experience leads to mastery. Remember, you are not trained in interpretation. Also, the ability to interpret signs, symbols and other communications is linked to spiritual development. All this takes time; be patient.

Remedy: If communications are flattering or negative, review Chapter 9: The Nature of Communications in regard to what Divine input is like and what it is not like. Information in that chapter will help you avoid the pitfalls of negative emotions contaminating Divine communications and/or masquerading as the real thing. It will also help you avoid self-aggrandizement. Expect guidance to be uplifting and inspirational, never critical or flattering. Learning to discern mundane truth and also Divine truth from fiction is part of every Heart Journey. Criteria and application become clearer as you work with the communication process.

You are building a personal connection between the invisible spiritual world and the visible material world for the purposes of manifestation, insight, and spiritual development. These two worlds are already energetically linked, but they exist at different vibrational rates. The spiritual world vibrates at a much higher rate than the material world of gases, liquids and solids. The higher vibrational rate of the spiritual world supports the transcendence of time and space. The much slower vibrational rate leads to greater density and form.

You are learning how to navigate this energetic vibrational continuum through the assistance of your co-creative Partner. The path is highly individualized to reflect your own personal needs and skills. It differs from person to person. Your co-creative Partner is your mentor and guide for the journey. Consistency between communications and mundane experience is reflective of the link between the two worlds and is meant to keep you on track. Consistency is a crucial piece of information necessary for manifestation through attraction and receptivity. Information or guidance should be confirmed by events. For example, if you feel directed to apply for a business loan at a certain bank, the loan should be approved. If the bank does not approve your application, you should revisit the original communication. What went wrong? Did you misunderstand? Were you supposed to have a different interaction with this bank? Were you unprepared? Communications that are directive should be productive. Communications that are informative should be truthful.

Consistency is a noteworthy sign. God will never mislead you or give you false hope. God will always lead you to truth. Manifestation resulting through consistency between spiritual insight or Divine communication and the material world confirms progress: progress in regard to your understanding of manifestation through attraction and receptivity; progress in regard to spiritual development; progress in regard to your ability to comprehend Divine communications; and progress in the establishment and growth of the co-creative partnership. Depend on it.

When communications are confusing, the best course of action is to be patient. Wait for further information. Tell your co-creative Partner that you do not understand. Ask questions. Personal resistance, conscious or unconscious, can interfere with your ability to interpret or comprehend communications. Time spent in reflection will eventually burn off any resistance as intimacy with your co-creative Partner leads to trust and mental clarity. If confusion is related to a need for personal growth, time in reflection naturally leads to spiritual maturity. Stay with your practice and eventually things will become clearer. You will grow into the next step and then be able to take appropriate action with confidence. Interpreting a sign or symbol, and understanding a vision or whisper, are acquired skills in the communication process. It is expected that translation and application will be unclear at times and require practice, especially in the beginning. Translation is mastered through reflection and experience. Over time, as your co-creative partnership strengthens and your reflective mind becomes quieter, clarity will increase and confusion will cease to be a problem.

Falling into Prediction

As noted in Chapter 9: The Nature of Communications, there is a danger with prediction, especially for the Heart Journey beginner. Counterfeit communications often include unfulfilled promises predicting exactly what you want to hear including easy and immediate manifestation, or they portend problems and hardships that confirm your deepest fears. Neither piece of information is helpful. What you really want and need to know is what is the next step in the co-creative process and what role you need to play in bringing it about.

If you think you are receiving predictions involving people you know, love or hate, think again. Predictions concerning others are even more dangerous than predictions about yourself. This is a beginner's trap you should avoid completely! Ninety-nine percent of the time predictions involving others will be false. Skill in this area is outside the teachings of Heart Journey. Accuracy takes years to develop and even then you can be incorrect.

Your goal in Heart Journey is to grow in wisdom and lovingness, not predict the future. Heart Journey exists on a level of unlimited potential. You belie your potential when you take this detour. The underlying intent when making a prediction is to prove that something mystical or paranormal is happening to you. You have a newfound power. If you can predict an event and then have your prediction come true, obviously you know something others do not know. You are special and you have demonstrated this to others. You ego is happy and becomes even more ingrained.

You are on a mystical journey to learn the process of manifestation through attraction and receptivity. You are building a co-creative partnership with God. All this is at risk when you fall into predictions. In all honesty, with time you might experience some insight into the future, but except in terms of your own development and growth, it is unimportant. Your goal is heart openness leading to abundance through a strong co-creative partnership with God. This puts you squarely on a spiritual path. On the enlightenment scale, predictions are at the very bottom while wisdom is near the top.

Remedy: Don't expect predictions and don't ask for guarantees. Instead deal head on with your fears of both success and failure. It is your job to develop trust and do the work that needs to be done for manifestation to occur.

Don't ask about others. This is your Heart Journey. Be very clear that you want to be on "a need to know basis." If there is no reason for you to know it, you are not interested.

Should you become aware of prediction-like communications, reserve all judgment. Ask for clarification. Why are you being given this information? What are you to do with it?

Observation of your own unconscious is critical in dealing with prediction-like communications. They are frequently the product of your fears (negative predictions) or ego (positive predictions). Note the pattern or theme associated with the predictions. What do you stand to lose if the predictions are correct? Is this your greatest fear? What do you stand to gain if the predictions are correct? Do you feel special? Chosen? Your emotional response to prediction is an indication that the information is unconsciously generated. The best policy is to disregard predictions as tainted information until proven otherwise.

Faith in Your Co-creative Partner

Beyond the above mentioned problems with communication, you may be blocking reception if you are not totally convinced that God is on your side. Reassess your beliefs about a loving God and the possibility of making a direct connection with an all powerful, all knowing, omnipresent Being. Do you believe that you are unworthy of a co-creative partnership with the Divine? (Worth has nothing to do with it! The option was God-given at birth.) Do you believe that you are incapable? (God has a training program! You can get in on the ground level.) Are you fearful of an illogical response? (Generally, responses start out in the rational arena. You do not enter the irrational or miraculous level until you develop spiritually.) Are you waiting for proof? (Scientific proof isn't going to happen. Get over it!) Are you holding out for a mind-blowing experience and refusing to consider subtleties? (Mind-blowing experiences are very unnerving and take some getting used to. Better to start small.) If you have gotten this far in the communication process with no results, clarity, or responses at all, ask yourself these and other pertinent questions concerning your beliefs about God. This might be where you are stuck.

Remedy: Lack of faith in your co-creative Partner probably originated long before your Heart Journey contract. Impeding beliefs can be ingrained from childhood training and may take some time to dismantle. You are locked in an ideological conflict that challenges your very beliefs about God and the co-creative partnership. Awakening to this philosophical conflict now just means that you missed this step during contract formation. You have to take a step back until you believe that all things are possible with a loving God. Look at your religious or spiritual training. What do you believe versus what is merely ingrained? What precepts do you follow and actually practice? If you suspect that your thinking might be distorted, focus on your actions. Why do you do what you do? Is it out of fear or is it out of love? What would make you a better person? Do you respond best to gentleness and kindness? Is this what you would wish for from God? Reexamining your beliefs to determine what is truly your own and what works best for you can enable you to personalize your spirituality and redefine your relationship with God. Taking corrective action now will start to free you up and move you forward.

If you are comfortable with your co-creative partnership with God and you feel that communication is strong and understandable, you do not have a problem in this area. Proceed to the next chapter, Troubleshooting Desire to determine if your desire is strong enough and stable enough to fuel the manifestation process.

Chapter Thirteen:
Troubleshooting Desire & Surrender

Troubleshooting the Four Elements Needed for Manifestation

If your connection to your Partner is strong and stable, communications are clear and of good quality, your co-creative partnership in thriving, and you are getting insights into the process of manifestation through attraction and receptivity, and attempting to follow up on suggestions, any problem you are experiencing is not the result of communication or your co-creative relationship with God. You need to investigate further, in particular, look for problems with the four elements necessary for manifestation through attraction and receptivity. Any one of the following might be the source of stagnation.

1. Desire tempered by surrender
2. Focused and sustained thought
3. Flow
4. Avenue for manifestation

When things are not working, most people tend to think that the problem is in the flow or that their desire is not appropriate for the highest good of all involved. While this may or may not be true, most of the time it is not. Others might blame God when things are not manifesting according to plan, thinking God is not listening or responding. This is never true! There are many possible problems associated with manifestation through attraction and receptivity, or the lack thereof, and most of them have a human source and are subject to correction. Some can be remedied quickly and easily with insight and a change in attitude. Since numerous factors are within your control, it is important to troubleshoot all possibilities before laying blame, drawing conclusions, or becoming so discouraged you throw in the towel. In fact, you should never throw in the towel, no matter what the setback. There is something to be learned or gained from each and every co-creative endeavor, even those that are not progressing or those that have failed completely. Guidance on when to give up or make a major change in your Heart Journey contract comes from continued communication with your co-creative Partner. Guidance on what needs correcting also comes from continued communication with your co-creative Partner. Keeping the lines of communication open is essential.

To make troubleshooting your progress or lack thereof easier, manifestation problems have been broken down into separate chapters associated with each of the four elements already discussed; desire tempered by surrender, a focused and sustained thought, the flow, and avenue for manifestation. Distinctions are partly artificial because there is so much crossover between the elements, but the structure does provide a coherent troubleshooting guide that will help you think through your experience logically. It is important to first assess your desire and also surrender before proceeding to the next chapter. Be systematic and thorough as you work through the next chapters to determine where difficulty might lie.

Problems Related to Desire

When it comes to manifestation through attraction and receptivity, problems with desire include too much, too little, overall inconsistency, or issues associated with surrender. Your desire can be so strong it blocks awareness of options, alternatives, and guidance. Or, your desire might be too weak, erratic, or disrupted by distractions and contradictory emotions to fuel the process of manifestation. In order to manifest through attraction and receptivity, your desire must be strong and steady, but always tempered by surrender.

Too Strong Desire and Clinging to Expectations

Some individuals make the mistake of wanting what they want when they want it and how they want it, meaning they place limitations on their desire by being so regimented. Their level of expectation is rigid and far reaching, down to the smallest details. Some even set a time limit, as if God works on their schedule! God doesn't. In their desire to have it "their way," their vision becomes a model in concrete rather than a fluid response to evolving and unfolding patterns of growth. They develop tunnel vision which prevents them from connecting to options, secondary processes for manifestation, or alternative outcomes and upgrades.

For others, desire is born of desperation and urgency, rather than spirituality. They are in a crisis management situation looking for an effortless, quick fix to life problems they may or may not have created. They are shortsighted, never grasping the big picture or the potential innate to Heart Journey and the co-creative process. For them, there is only one option, one goal, one scenario for manifestation, and it needs to happen now! They are looking to be saved. Manifestation through attraction and receptivity is not a free ride, make-it-happen, power trip and rarely occurs in a panic-stricken environment.

Remember, communication with your co-creative Partner occurs in the silence, and attraction and receptivity occur within an open heart. These conditions do not exist in a panic state. Applying extra effort and control is not the answer to your prayers. You cannot get a flower to bloom by pulling on the petals!

When desire is too strong, it narrows or negates the person's ability to co-create and manifest. Untempered desire overshadows what really needs to take place and drives a wedge between the aspirant and God. Frustration builds. "Come on, come on!" The individual is so attached to expectations and dependent on specific outcomes or processes that he or she cannot see or flow with what is immediately available or arising in the future. Experiences become limiting rather than expansive as muscles tighten with increased tension. There is just too much riding on the outcome. Disappointment leads to further stress, then communication with God peters out and eventually stops because it is of no value or falls on deaf ears. The downward spiral can lead to heart closure thereby ending receptivity completely. Once this happens, there is no chance of attraction.

Remedy: Stay open and aware of divergent opportunities while you balance your desire with surrender. Begin to solve your own problems to alleviate stress in your life and undue pressure on the manifestation process. Turn down the volume so you can become aware of subtleties. Learn to be patient and concentrate on yielding to guidance. Surrender allows you to remain open and receptive to the co-creative potential for as long as needed. Set the stage, move with the flow, and do your part. When you truly balance desire with surrender, you will experience what a loving God can create for and with you if it is for your highest good and the good of all involved.

Close communication with your co-creative Partner also helps to dispel rigid expectations. Trusting that God sees down the road and knows the path better than you should convince you to let go and let God. Expect a periodic curve ball to come your way. It shakes up your expectations and keeps you on your toes, open to new options or upgrades. Although Heart Journey starts out with a formal contract, the path is actually a continuous string of modifications that keep you moving from one stepping stone to the next. Situations evolve and change. You must stay on top of the process, moving with the flow, and patiently awaiting instructions regarding the next step. For this reason, hold your vision loosely and temper your strong desire with equally strong surrender.

Heart Journey is a mystical path filled with mystery and hidden influences. If you travel with preconceived notions and control in mind, you will miss the whole point of the journey and co-creative process. You are meant to follow, not lead. You are supposed to learn, not know. You should grow, not look for a quick fix. Mysticism is about Divine mysteries that lay beyond your control. Mysticism is about surrender into what you do not know, cannot be told, would not have imagined, and can only discover through direct and quiet awareness. This is how wisdom and your co-creative partnership with God should and does develop. Unchecked desire and clinging to expectations blinds you to the co-creative potential, the wisdom that would arise, and ultimately, the process of manifestation. It is foolish to try to direct or manipulate when you are not in control. Accept that you do not know how your Heart Journey will play out and when.

Weak Desire

Weak desire does not elicit a co-creative response, nor does it foster the magnetism necessary for manifestation through attraction and receptivity. Without desire, there is no fuel for your Heart Journey. You are like a sailboat without a breeze, becalmed and going nowhere. You cannot be ho-hum about your Heart Journey contract. You have to really want it and want it consistently. What might look like a lack of flow when you are going nowhere fast can really be a lack of true heart's desire. When diagnosing problems, weak desire is always suspect before weak flow.

Your vision must reflect your own heart's desire. If your desire was not truly your own and from the heart when you formulated your contract, it will have less and less strength as time goes on. Others cannot sustain their desire through you and you cannot sustain the desire of or for another if you cannot find a reason to make it your own. Limp, half-hearted desires that are not representative of your wants and wishes either fizzle out completely or become more of an impediment than an asset as resistance rises.

Remedy: If you are bogged down going nowhere, reassess your commitment to your contract and vision. Desire wanes for a reason and it is your job to discover what that reason is, and then counteract it through corrective action. Go back to the process of formulating your contract. Was desire truly your own to begin with? What was your commitment then? What is your commitment now? Is your original intention still as strong and valid at this time? Does your contract feel right to you? Your desire must be totally yours and still valid.

If your vision is not exactly correct, but definitely in the ballpark, make adjustments to your contract that increase its accuracy and desirability. You grow with and into your Heart Journey contract and changes may be necessary along the way. If your contract is written, write an addendum or rewrite the statements that no longer apply. If your contract is visual, add, subtract, or refine the images or symbols as needed.

On the other hand, if your contract is really far afield from what you truly desire now, start over completely with a new Heart Journey contract. Sometimes external conditions change dramatically making your contract moot. This will have a serious impact on your desire and lead to a major change of plans even though your desire was strong and true at the signing. Ensuing events, changing circumstances, along with new revelations, deeper understanding, and spiritual growth can all impact and alter your vision. If desire wanes for these reasons, it is best to start fresh with a new contract rather than limp along with an amended or obsolete one. There are no repercussions for doing so. God understands that asking is a learning process, and in this case, one step back can be a giant leap forward.

A Comment About Passion

When passion is present, desire is rarely weak. Passion is an added bonus to your heart's desire since it is many times associated with a life-long dream or soul level pursuit. Passion gets in your blood, goes to the center of your being, remains foremost in your mind and heart, and never wanes. Those who are passionate about their Heart Journey contract tend to stay focused and energized until manifestation occurs no matter how long it takes. If you are passionate about your contract, your heart's desire will be strong and steady.

Conflicting Desires and Overly Complex Contracts

Conflicting desires can be innate to your original contract or the result of subsequent competing contracts. It makes no sense to put two mutually exclusive items into the same contract. This is counterproductive and God will not know what you truly want because you have not made a definitive choice. You cannot desire two mutual exclusive manifestations and expect results. The attractive ability of one desire will kill the receptive ability of the second desire and vice versa. They are like two enemies living in the same house fighting over resources for different outcomes. You have to be clear of interference and conflict on all levels to manifest. It is possible, though rare, that items in your contract only become mutually exclusive with time. This situation will be obvious to you in the choices you are asked to make. You will have to choose.

It is also not a good idea to put prioritized competing desires into a contract saying "If desire number one is not possible, then I want desire number two!" You are building failure into the contract right from the start, half expecting to fail by establishing a backup plan.

Competing desires are entirely different from "stepping stone" desires. Stepping stone desires are sequential steps in the manifestation process. For example, you apply to a college, secure a scholarship, get an education, and then find work in your chosen field. This is not an either-or situation, but a natural progression. Step-by-step components in your contract are appropriate and advantageous.

It is more likely that conflicting desires will come from layered contracts. Some individuals feel that if one Heart Journey contract is good, adding one or more subsequent contracts must be better. After composing and initiating their first contract, they initiate another, rather than working exclusively on one contract through to completion. Maybe they lose interest in the first contract or maybe they grow impatient. Regardless, as new contracts and desires build up, contradictions are likely to arise, creating conflict and weakening their original intent even if the contracts are focused on different areas of life. Even if there is no contradiction, the pile-on technique leads to an overall weakening of desire by scattering your focus, attention, skills and efforts. Contract additions generate impediments through competition. To develop spiritually and to get the maximum benefit from your Heart Journey, only work on one contract at a time.

The same tendency to weaken desire is also true with large, complex and multifaceted contracts. Although desires might not directly conflict, they can still scatter and dilute your attention and focus. Simple is best, particularly as manifestation generally involves a major commitment in time, energy, and resources on your part.

Remedy: If your contract has a problem with competing desires, whether prioritized or either-or, make a decision and start editing. Clarity is the best course of action and brings results faster than split decisions. In regard to layered contracts stick with your original heart's desire or the truest contract until manifestation has occurred. Discard any other contracts. Putting them away for a later date is not a good idea. A contract waiting in the wings implies that your present contract is a temporary situation that will be accomplished in the immediate future. This may or may not be true, but it puts pressure on you to get the job done and thereby weakens your surrender. The best and most productive policy is to clear the decks and focus on one contract at a time.

If you are getting bogged down with a complex, multifaceted contract, you have two choices. You can either envision a common theme to unify the individual items, or scale back and edit out the less important desires. When you unify items and see the separate desires working together towards a common goal, your energy and focus merge. The time span for the process of manifestation might lengthen, but sequential steps are more likely to be revealed. Then you will naturally narrow your focus and take things as they come.

If there is no unifying principle to be found in your complex contract, edit items out to lighten the load. Focus on one or two important tasks only. But before you do this, you have to be clear that the weight of the contract is too heavy and that it is the reason you are bogged down as opposed to an absence of flow. The difference between being overwhelmed by multiple desires and being stalled because of an absence of flow is seen in your efforts, skills and resources. God might be unlimited, but you are not. If there are not enough hours in the day, if you need to be in two places at once, if you are running on empty, and you bit off more than you can chew, you need to pare down your contract. If you are stalled with nothing to do, the problem is more likely to be an absence of flow, especially if you get negative responses to your efforts.

Sabotaging Fears and Other Negative Emotions

Fears are major impediments to desire. They constantly undermine the manifestation process through emotional vacillation when consistency is what is needed. The range of fears is unlimited and can even be contradictory. You can be afraid of success and at the same time afraid of failure, a true no-win situation. Fears do not have to be relevant to the current situation. They can be painful memories held over from your childhood or hurtful comments from a lost love relationship replayed at the worst possible time. Fears do not have to be rational. Their influence does not have to cause emotional instability to effect the strength of your desire and commitment. Fears, even weak fears, need only plant a seed and raise doubts to effectively impede manifestation. Even a low grade, generalized climate of unconscious fear can thwart attraction and receptivity.

Fears are not the only negative emotions you have to counteract. Depression, discouragement, impatience, lack of confidence, pessimism, apathy, guilt, regret, doubt, and anger are just a few other undermining emotions. Search your unconscious and emotional system for any negativity. Do you feel unworthy? (You do not have to earn the right to be co-creative.) Do you doubt the co-creative process and your ability to manifest? (Believing is seeing, not the other way around.) Do you distrust your co-creative Partner? (God is on your side.) A negative answer to any of these questions indicates a serious threat to desire.

Negativity of any kind can contribute to the instability of your desire, interrupting the fuel needed for manifestation. Two diametrically opposed emotions, (one positive, one negative), cannot exist in the same space at the same time, and unfortunately, negativity tends to win out repeatedly. Your desire can lose forward momentum to negative emotions at any time. A desire that is strong one day and weak the next is like a car with dirty gas. It sputters down the road with fits and starts, and eventually stalls. Inconsistency will have the same effect on your ability to manifest. Erratic progress or lack thereof will only serve to compound negativity, creating an escalating downward spiral.

Remedy: Guard against negative emotions and counteract their influence as soon as they come into awareness, and they will come into awareness. Replace disapproving thoughts with positive statements of support and hope. For example, replace a fear of failure with the statement, "I can succeed with God's help." Consult with your co-creative Partner regarding negativity and pray the solution. Expect to pass through a cleansing process innate to Heart Journey. Everyone who signs a contract and seeks to manifest a desire must face his or her inner demons, fears, and doubts. The very act of opening the heart is bound to stir up painful memories, old wounds, feelings of inadequacy, vulnerability, and negative emotions which must be resolved, healed, and released. Do not let the arising of these feelings and issues derail your progress. What at first seems to be troublesome, is actually expected and a good sign. It shows progress in regard to heart openness. Working directly to undo these emotional complexes will speed you on your way and stabilize a feeling of openness.

You have to maintain a positive emotional climate to protect your desire from self-sabotaging fears and negativity. Reflection and communication with your co-creative Partner can help you protect against negative emotions. Emotional healing can ultimately be a joyful passage of letting go and can accelerate the manifestation process. When there are no emotional impediments and desire is strong, manifestation can proceed, but when there are no impediments, desire is strong, and the heart is fully open, conductivity is enhanced and manifestation quickens.

Problems Related to Surrender

Inability to Surrender Control

Akin to clinging to highly specific expectations is the need to control the manifestation process and an inability to surrender. You are not in control, but your ego believes it can and should be. The ego lives for control. Its very survival depends on it because surrender heralds the death of the ego. The ego is the perpetuator of and the sustaining force behind self-will. The ego imagines itself as a separate and independent entity. It prefers not to share power with anyone, even God. Nor is it in the ego's nature to trust. It thinks it knows how and when things should proceed, and will attempt to out-perform your co-creative Partner by encouraging you to rush ahead and work overtime to complete the task without Divine assistance or guidance. This attempt at an end-run will arise whenever things slow down, seem stalled, out of control, or don't proceed according to plan, the ego's plan.

> "What are you doing? Nothing is happening! You need to act now or this will never get done! Listen to me! Here is what you need to do. I have a plan!"

Patience is a virtue the ego does not aspire to. Besides, the ego truly wants to lay claim to all the glory. It needs kudos to survive. Foolish pride!

The ego is not heart-based while surrender is. It is within the heart that we relinquish control, pass through the veil of vulnerability, learn to trust, and open fully to giving and receiving love and shared abundance. Surrender is the key catalyst to this process of heart openness. The ego resides outside the domain of the heart and assumes a position of power and control, vowing never to surrender power, never to be become vulnerable, and never to let you be hurt again. This is the ego's hook! The ego wants you to believe that you need its protection and control to prevent further emotional pain from abandonment, rejection, humiliation, and a myriad of other real or imagined offenses. Everyone has been hurt at one time or another and those not consciously aware of the ego's scam will readily accept the need for protection even when it makes no sense and actually thwarts the potential for future happiness. But the ego is fulfilled; it has a job!

True love is synonymous with surrender and heart openness. The ego is incapable of true love. It can only participate in mutually beneficial and comforting exchanges that directly serve its present purpose, wants, needs, or goals. The ego needs to get something from the relationship, and the relationship must be safe and come with guarantees. This is accomplished through control and conditional love. "I will love you as long as you do this for me or behave in this manner." This is not real love, but a false pretender. True love is unconditional.

The ego does not share toys and resources well either, unless there is some secondary gain to be had. Sharing abundance diminishes the stockpile and competitive edge of having more than anyone else. Even generosity can be self-serving when it comes with strings attached and a desire for recognition. The ego wants to be better than, numero uno in all things, and it is, the number one impediment to surrender, heart openness, attraction, receptivity, and the co-creative partnership.

All true spiritual paths eventually lead to surrender and Heart Journey is no exception. Surrender has been a major component of your contract from the very beginning. True love and shared abundance are part of the process related to heart openness and manifestation through attraction and receptivity. These developments are far more beneficial than anything the ego might concoct.

Remedy: The greatest boost to the process of surrender and the greatest deterrent to the control of the ego is the Divine upgrade. A picture is worth a thousand words. One Divine upgrade can diminish the power of the ego in an instant. You only need one "Ah-hah!" moment to see things differently. Once you witness the creative potential of God and the power of the co-creative partnership, you will immediately start to abandon the ego's need for control. Even if you are not the recipient of a Divine upgrade, but a bystander, it is awesome to see and will immediately get you to think differently about the ego versus surrender. Why would you settle for less when you can have more than you could create or imagine on your own? Why would you stay with a partner who pulls you down when you can have One who lifts you up? The ego will grow smaller with each upgrade.

If upgrades lead to the deflation of the ego's power and surrender leads to Divine upgrades, it is easy to see why the ego would fight for control, credit, and position. Now the question becomes, how do you get to experience an upgrade? There are no guarantees, but an important precursor to an upgrade is patience. Begin to delay your responses while observing events. Allow God more time to step in. You are not surrendering control completely, only deferring action. This will feel less threatening while still fostering conditions conducive to upgrades. Yielding a little will diminish control over time and begin the process of surrender.

The inability to surrender shows a lack of trust in God. Perhaps you are still inexperienced in regard to the co-creative partnership. Reflection and meditation support both your surrender and your co-creative partnership with God while undermining the ego's attempts at masterminding the process of attraction and receptivity. Establish a daily practice dedicated to communication with God and strengthen the co-creative partnership.

Weak Surrender to God's Desire

If your contract was built around surrender to God's desire instead of a personal desire, then your love for and devotion to God has to be passionate. Only the spiritually strong and ready individual should be on this path. Because surrender needs to be counterbalanced and reinforced by devotion to God, you must have already established a strong relationship with your co-creative Partner prior to signing the contract. In this type of Heart Journey, devotion to God mimics and replaces desire for something worldly. It is your close connection to God that keeps you on the right path while in total surrender and sees you through any difficult transitions no matter what is happening. This type of contract entails a more complete surrender than the personal desire contract because it encompasses all areas of your life. Its scope is unlimited. You did not just agree to God's desire, basically you agreed to whatever God desires. You gave your co-creative Partner carte blanche in determining your path. Total submission necessitates complete trust at the outset. You are starting your Heart Journey at a higher level of commitment and surrender than most and you need to be spiritually mature.

Your emotional state is key to understanding whether or not you are in a good place regarding your commitment and surrender to a God's desire contract. If you are calm and peaceful, your surrender is strong. It does not matter if nothing is happening or even if everything seems to be going wrong or falling apart. Periods of stagnation are to be expected with this contract and do not indicate weakness. Periods of external turmoil suggest cleansing and do not indicate that you are off course. Those people, places, things, and situations which seek to impede your progress and disrupt your serenity will fall away. Sometimes the drop off can be abrupt and shocking. But if you can continue to chop wood and carry water through it all with a calm presence and trust in your heart, you are in a good space doing God's work. Your surrender is strong regardless of what is or is not happening externally.

Spiritual development is the goal of this contract and more prized than any external manifestation. For this reason, God's desire contracts might involve little or no apparent external change while internally one moves to higher and higher levels of spiritual attainment. The real action comes with application. You will be called on to demonstrate your increased understanding and wisdom. Each wave of insight should be followed by the opportunity to practice. You must walk the talk, applying what you know to both personal issues and mundane situations to truly inculcate the knowledge. Application is essential for lasting spiritual progress with every contract, but especially with a God's desire contract. In this way, manifestation comes through application and demonstration as well as attraction and receptivity.

If you are anxious, confused, uncertain, and doubtful, your surrender is weak. Over time, your resistance will rise, your trust will waver, and sooner or later, your devotion will wane. Perhaps a surrender to God's desire contract should not have been your choice. Were you originally indecisive or unclear as to what you wanted? Starting from this position will only breed further confusion and anxiety while on your Heart Journey. Though you might be in close communication with God, increasing anxiety and negative emotions can indicate that you overestimated your spiritual maturity and are presently in the wrong type of contract. You have to totally trust whatever God is creating for you to continue on this path. If not, one or both of two changes are likely to occur. Either you discover what you do not want, (this is valuable information, but just a good starting point), or personal desire will start to build and reveal itself. In the end, all is not lost. Your just took a detour and can take corrective action.

Remedy: If you are in the right contract, and surrender is truly your path, meditation, reflection, and communication with your co-creative Partner should alleviate any anxiety and stress. You need to deepen your trust in God.

If on the other hand, you are basically at peace, but plagued by uncertainty, know that this is normal. God's desire contracts tend to generate great uncertainty and this is not necessarily a sign that your surrender is weak. Surrender is an emotion-filled, conscious act leading to subtle insights in the midst of great uncertainty. Communications are more elusive with a God's desire contract. You signed a contract surrendering to an unknown choice or series of choices. Uncertainty is built in. Use it to deepen your trust in your co-creative Partner. It may be your path to put one foot in front of the other without a clear picture of your destination. That's okay. One day you will look back and see how far you have come and what was accomplished. For the present, apply what you have been taught. Hone your awareness by recognizing the subtle ways God is directing your life and moving through you to manifest Divinity on earth. If you are not desiring, if you are not controlling or initiating things, then God must be doing everything. Sit back and marvel. Seeing your life evolve in God's own time and in God's own manner can be a major revelation.

In the same way you would protect your desire from fear and negative emotions, you should also protect your surrender. Surrender equals loss of control and can be a breeding ground for doubt and distrust if you are not vigilant. Be proactive. Guard your surrender by keeping your co-creative partnership strong. Periods of reflection are especially important when you are not sure of the path. You may need to increase your time in meditation to calm negative emotions and recommit to trust. Like the hummingbird on the pipe bag in Chapter 11: Example of Following Blindly, sometimes you must move ahead blindly, despite uncertainty, and "put this bead here."

If you are not able to maintain a high level of surrender and devotion, cannot trust completely, and/or feel that you are in over your head, rewrite your contract. There is a time and a place for everything. Now is not the time for a God's desire contract. Recognize where you are, your strengths and weaknesses, and begin again. Focus on personal desire even if your vision is not totally clear. Go with what you have and write a new contract. Things will become clearer with time.

The Swing of the Pendulum between Desire and Surrender

Fluctuations between strong desire and strong surrender are normal and do not present a problem. Though they should be well-matched overall, they are generally not equal all the time. The pendulum will swing back and forth with great regularity. Sometimes desire will be stronger and sometimes surrender. These swings should not be viewed as weakness or impediments. They are part of the natural adjustments made in response to differing situations as they occur in the manifestation process. When the ball is in your court, expect desire to increase to move you forward and into action. When the ball is in God's court or you must wait on the flow and correct timing, surrender will be the most prominent influence causing you to sit back, trust, and be patient. Over time you might feel the subtle shift from one influence to another. Swinging too far or staying too long in either desire or surrender will naturally trigger a return in the opposite direction.

After reviewing the material in this chapter and not finding an issue or having taken corrective action, you are ready to move on to troubleshooting your focused, sustain thought.

Chapter Fourteen:
Troubleshooting Thoughts

Introduction to Problems Related to a Focused, Sustained Thought

Troubleshooting starts with an assessment of communications with God and the strength of the co-creative partnership. It proceeds to a review of issues associated with desire and surrender. If you have worked through those troubleshooting chapters and found no issues, you are now ready to reevaluate your focused, sustained thought.

Your focused, sustained thought is the translation of your desire and the means by which this energy or fuel is directed into form. It is your impression of what the goal might look like when it is fully realized and how you might get there. Might is the operative word here. Your co-creative partnership with God necessitates flexibility. First and foremost, your translation should not be etched in stone. Rigidity and narrowness limits your options and awareness of alternatives and Divine upgrades. On the other hand, vagueness and a lack of specificity leave you hanging without a clear cut direction or goal. Definition is important as long as it is a flexible, workable definition that is sustained over time.

Problems Related to Focusing Your Thought

Once you moved beyond desire to a focused thought, you were no longer dealing with the space between you and God (meaning the heart), you were dealing with the space between your ears. At the time of the contract signing, it was your job to determine the translation of your desire into form through a focused thought. At this point in Heart Journey the job of translation has shifted. You must now use your mind to guide that desire and thought into manifestation by continually making the appropriate navigational course corrections after conferring with your co-creative Partner. Manifestation is subject to flow, or ease and difficulty.

Rigid and Narrow Focused Thoughts

Though you must keep your eye on the goal, this is no time for rigid and narrow interpretations. You created a blueprint for success at the contract signing, but that was then and this is now. Do not assume that you know how things will proceed. You don't! Your blueprint is no more than a vague outline of what needs to take place.

It is important to remember that you are more like an apprentice navigator with an outdated set of training maps than an experienced ship's captain who knows the seas well. God knows where the channel is deep, where the current is swift, and where you might get hung up on the rocks. God also has the weather (flow) report, great creative potential, and a big picture perspective. You, on the other hand, do not have complete information nor the creative potential of your Partner. You are better off conferring before acting, and taking your cues from above.

You have communicated your desire through your focused thought. You know where you want to go and what you want to do. But being convinced that you already know the way and the steps that need to be taken can limit your ability to perceive options and Divine upgrades along the way, or alternate avenues for manifestation. Your plans, regardless of how obvious they appear to be, or how essential you think they are, are still subject to modification or correction and may be totally useless. They were suitable as a starting point only, and may or may not be appropriate for the journey itself.

Another impediment associated with rigid and narrow thinking includes personal preference and prejudice. Heart Journey is not like a fast-food restaurant where you can have it your way. You have to go with the flow of what is arising easily. Manifestation comes in its own tailor made package and timing. Furthermore, heart openness is needed for manifestation through attraction and receptivity. An open heart does not discriminate on the basis of race, creed, religion, gender, age, sexual orientation, nationality, education, mental ability, or politics. You can be sure that God will reach into the darkest part of your heart and open it to the light. You will see where you are withholding and unloving. In all likelihood, the very puzzle piece you need will arrive in the form of your greatest resistance, even if you are resistant to loving yourself.

Remedy: Heart Journey is an on-the-job training experience without the written manual or even a job description. Your trainer is your co-creative Partner. You learn from direct experience with the manifestation process and through Divine communication and guidance. The only way to know whether or not the next step you have in mind is the most effective one is to remain in close contact with your co-creative Partner and follow God's lead. Be flexible. Your responses should be dependent on incoming correspondence. You must trust and follow God's lead openheartedly. Be mindful of your prejudices and resistances. Consciously work to remove them, regardless of their source or supposed justification. There is no reason or excuse for holding on to either. They will thwart your progress and come up again and again until you let go.

Example of Overcoming Resistance

June was not is a good position. Her marriage was falling apart, her business was declining, and so was her health. The longer she stayed in the marriage, the weaker she became. Finances were a determining factor in why she could not leave. She looked at her budget carefully and considered the ways in which she could grow her business and pay her bills. She could swing it if she did not have to make a car payment, but she still had 3 years left to pay on her compact car. In meditation, June received the message that she needed to ask for help. The message was loud and clear for three weeks, but June refused to make a request. Finally, the voice stated the obvious, "Then remain stuck!" The stark realization of this truth horrified June and convinced her to take action. She knew who to go to and immediately began to compose her request for assistance. When she did finally make her request, the response was, "I knew you needed help and wanted to offer, but did not want to offend you." The car payment was covered and June and her husband made plans to separate. Within six months of the separation, June's business grew increasingly successful and she returned to good health.

Inability to Focus and a Lack of Specificity

Some people get lost during their Heart Journey. They become becalmed with nothing happening in their lives or with their contracts. Assuming they are aware of the various subtleties innate to Divine communication, the next suspected reason for an inability to progress is an inability to focus or a lack of specificity.

Desire is the fuel for the manifestation process. Your focused thought channels desire into form and has to accurately represent your desire to initiate change. But once the contract is signed, it is your ability to refine your focused thought again and again to maintain or augment accuracy that keeps you moving forward. Think of a camera and the act of focusing the lens to make the image clear and sharp. Suppose you focus the camera and take a picture of an object twenty feet away. Now you move in for greater detail. As you move closer to the object you are capturing, you need to refocus. The static focused thought of your contract becomes an evolving process constantly in need of refinement. You have to be vigilant regarding focusing and refocusing your thought. Although it is true that some simple contracts manifest spontaneously without much attention, most contracts, especially complex ones, need continual refocusing to move forward and manifest.

Contract specificity provides a clear definition of your vision and generates indicators of progress. This is especially true if your contract is complex or a step-by-step process is innate to your vision. Being specific during the contract formation creates a measurement tool which helps you discern when you are on target or off track.

When I was gifted with the Tantric twin crystal, related in Chapter 1: An Example of Abundance through Attraction, it was clear that I had stumbled on my first important lesson in manifesting through attraction and receptivity. In my search for a guru or master, related in Chapter 8: Example of Difficulties and the Lack of Success, it was clear that I was off track. Feedback of this sort is commonly initiated by a specific request and is invaluable. It strengthens the co-creative partnership, and trains you in the process of manifestation through attraction and receptivity.

Like refocusing your thought, you must also continually define or redefine the next step as you move closer and closer to manifestation. Specificity relates to the process as well as the content associated with your sustained, focused thought. What action do you need to take and when do you need to take it? Or, is it time to sit back and wait? What are the present signposts for interim success that would let you know you are on track? What would indicate that you are off track? Even though you might have an overall picture of what needs to take place, you still have to accomplish tasks sequentially, in the right order and/or at the right time. Sometimes the ball will be in your court and you must take action to move things along. At other times, you should not be doing anything. You have done all you can do for the moment and the ball is now in God's court. You need to wait. Even at these times, if you are observant, you might still see things moving along. Specific items or situations you request or need can appear out of nowhere without any effort on your part. Movement occurs when you keep your focused thought current and applicable by being specific, concrete, and always contemplating your next step.

Remedy: Awareness is the key to maintaining clarity. A lack of attention to the manifestation process and a lack of communication with your co-creative Partner are both directly related to a lack of focus and specificity in the translation of your desire into thought. This results in the confusion and an inability to progress. How can you continually refocus your thought when you are not aware of changes and developments as they arise? How can you determine the next step when you are not cognizant of what is or is not working, which doors are opening and which ones remain closed. Ease and difficulty are major signals within the manifestation process. They provide clues to who is supposed to take the next step, you or your co-creative Partner, what needs to happen, and when. Signals regarding tasks needed for advancement can be subtle.

How can you receive detailed guidance when your co-creative partnership and communication are weak? Focus and specificity is dependent on continuing awareness and contact with your Partner. The best way to increase awareness is through daily meditation and reflection. By quieting your mind, you are training it to focus, prioritize, organize, and to listen. It may seem unlikely that entering the silence once a day would sharpens awareness for the rest of the day, but it is certainly true. When you turn down the volume, you attune your senses and become aware of communication subtleties and feedback.

If you started out with a focused thought in your Heart Journey contract, but lost definition along the way, this is due to a lack of attention to your contract and recent feedback, or to underdeveloped communication with your co-creative Partner. You need to recommit to your contract, or refocus your thought in light of recent events and Divine input. Take time out! Step back from doing and enter into the silence. Ask yourself these questions. Am I on target? Is my focused thought as true to my present desire and vision as it can be at this time? Is it still representative of my original desire? If things have shifted, is it with good reason? Have I lost sight of the goal?

If you can now see that your original contract lacked a true focused thought, you need to amend your contract or possibly start over. It is not a failure to start over. Remember, Heart Journey is a learning process. You are in training. There is no right or wrong, only education in the manifestation process and the co-creative partnership. It is better to start over than to limp along with an impotent thought. Your focused thought is the mechanism by which your desire moves to form. It has to have definition and validity or there can be no formation.

If your original contract was and still is focused or has been refocused, but there are no signposts innate to your Heart Journey, you lack reference points in regard to forward movement. Signposts are indicators of intermediate progress and they lend specificity to your thought while keeping you on track. Without them, only the dynamic of ease versus difficulty and communication with God can provide you with reference points. Awareness is crucial in this case because regardless of how specific your focused thought is, you do not have a measuring device between the beginning of the process of manifestation and the endpoint. If this is the case, continuing ease is a good indication you are growing in your ability to attract and following the lead of your co-creative Partner. Continuing difficulty is a clear indication you need feedback from your co-creative Partner. Listen inward, reassess, and then regroup. Your efforts are probably thwarted with good reason and you will be redirected.

To promote greater clarity, ask your co-creative Partner specific questions regarding your progress and actions you need to take. Specific queries related to your Heart Journey contract lead to specific guidance. Be patient; answers come in their own time. Keep the lines of communication open even if you have to wait weeks or months for an answer. When the time is right, the answer will come. Once you receive an applicable answer, follow guidance and stay on task. If you have correctly understood the information received and taken the appropriate step, you should advance or be successful. If not, revisit the guidance you received and ask for clarification. Paying attention to the response to your efforts will give you good information regarding what works, what does not work, and how to proceed. Repeating this process in cooperation with your co-creative Partner eventually leads to successful manifestation. Do your part in a timely manner as this creates momentum. There may be many communications and many course corrections needed as you refocus, define, and renegotiate the process of manifestation through attraction and receptivity.

If you are still unsure of the next step even after much reflection, communication, and soul searching, test the waters by attempting the best step possible. Perhaps you simply need to prime the pump. If your best next step works and it gets the ball rolling with ease, good, you are on your way. If this technique leads to obstacles on three attempts, there is definitely a problem and you need more time in reflection, meditation, and communication with your co-creative Partner. In this situation, the next step is not the problem. The issue is much deeper and you need to listen more closely.

Problems Related to Sustaining a Focused Thought

Even when your thought is correctly focused, the inability to sustain your thought over time leads to missed opportunities. Our lives are filled with distractions. We all have busy schedules, jobs, and families. We are rushed, spread thin, and on overload. Our attention is routinely scattered in our attempts at multitasking. When things breakdown or need repair, our lives can spiral out of control and into crisis management. In this climate it is tough to focus at all, let alone sustain our focus.

Your focused thought guides the energy of desire into form during the process of manifestation through attraction and receptivity. Because this process normally takes time, your focused thought must be sustained for however long it takes, even if that is weeks, months, years, or indefinitely. Problems arise when you lose sight of your contract and focused thought. It is not effective if you put your contract away in a drawer and forget about it for weeks on end. It is not productive if you become distracted by matters less important, but more immediate. Your focused thought will not be sustained if you cease to communicate with your co-creative Partner. You will definitely get off track. Waiting for God to make it all happen is sheer laziness and will not sustain your focused thought and move it to manifestation. Inattentiveness in any form weakens the ability to sustain your focused thought. The longer the inattentiveness, the weaker the thought, and the less momentum manifestation has. Only consistency, day in and day out, sustains, and sustaining your thought is every bit as important as focusing.

Remedy: Attention to the Heart Journey process and communication with your co-creative Partner are the keys to sustaining your focused thought despite worldly distractions. Quiet time will enable you to screen out interfering influences and life's chaos, at least temporarily. That may be all you can or need do. You cannot completely change your life or withdraw from responsibilities, nor should you. The goal is to balance inner spiritual growth with worldly interaction. You can empower yourself, your vision, and your life with daily mini retreat sessions. You only need to take as much time out as is effective, but consistency is important. This will give you a space for receiving co-creative guidance and sustaining your focused thought.

It is helpful to have a reminder of your contract in plain sight to reinforce and sustain your focused thought on a daily basis and to remind you of your vision when making decisions. This can be the contract itself or a symbolic representation. Some people place it wherever they will see it first thing every morning. Others place a symbol in their car or a copy of the contract with their schedule. The screen saver on your computer can also be an appropriate reminder.

Problems Related to Thinking

Excessive Thinking

In the co-creative manifestation process, your mind should assume a passive and receptive role more like that of an enhanced communication device capable of comprehension, interpretation, and organization before carrying out tasks. Co-creation requires an open channel to your Partner and an ability to perceive subtleties on many levels. In the ideal situation, all your senses become heightened. This is best accomplished when your active, technical, thinking left brain quiets down a bit, and not just in meditation.

Mental processes need to turn inward rather than outward. You need to be listening rather than talking in your head or planning things out in advance. Remember, you are a student; you are in school and should be listening to your Teacher and Mentor Who speaks very softly. If you continually gossip with others, daydream about the future, or critique the process, you will miss the lesson. In the same way that the heart needs to be open and receptive, your mind must also be open and receptive. If you remain in an active, highly intellectual, dominant role, you will miss the co-creative interchange and partnership.

We tend to live more in our heads than in the present moment. We want to plan things out in advance and understand exactly how things work. We constantly daydream about future scenarios that may be totally unrealistic. All our creative energy can get projected into the future, instead of focused on the here and now. This fantasy world does not exist and could never exist without a connection to the present and our co-creative Partner because we will miss cues as they arise and will fail to take the necessary steps to get to the future we are so desperately dreaming about. An overactive mind can leave one disconnected from the present moment and wandering in limbo.

Ingrained thought patterns, preferences, and even personal agendas can interrupt your ability to listen and respond appropriately. Despite what you might expect, despite what you might be addicted to or used to, you do not need to think you way to manifestation. You need to communicate your way to manifestation, and that involves listening.

Remedy: Whenever thinking competes with your ability to perceive, it should be temporarily suspended. To slow thinking down, modulate your breathing. Close your eyes and take prolonged deep breaths. Exhale slowly as you focus inward. Note your feelings and emotional state. Are you agitated or anxious? Can you instill calmness? Be aware of your body and any impressions that occur. Where are you tense? Relax your muscles. Continue the slow breathing until thinking slows and the body calms.

Now look inward. Allow sensations to arise. Become aware of subtleties, but do not rush to interpret. This is not the time to start analyzing. Simply note. You are stepping back, not only to gather insights, but also, and perhaps more importantly, to retrain your mind as a tool. You are consciousness; you are not your mind which is meant to be the vehicle by which your consciousness manifests. Your mind is not supposed to be in control of your life. Your mind is not supposed to derail your life by being out of control. The mind is meant to be under your control and it can be trained through meditation. This requires time and practice, for some more than others.

By closing your eyes and modulating your breathing, you can shift your mental abilities from output, such as commenting, analyzing and planning, to input, such as listening, reflecting, and observing. By simply following your breath, you can still your mind and quiet your thoughts. In time and with patience, subtle sensations will arise more readily and grow into perceptions. Once you have emerged from the quiet period of slow breathing, you can ponder these perceptions and insights.

Rationalism and the Need for Logical Explanations

Left brain rationalism, logic, and science can be valued more than imagination, artistry, mysticism, and right brain processes. Scientists are interested in proof. That which cannot be proven, can be discounted. Schools emphasize academics as both art and music classes are cut. Psychologists have labeled visions hallucinations, making no distinction between spiritual visions and abnormalities. Most religions do not prepare followers for mystical experiences. They are considered inappropriate for the layperson who is left to depend on intermediary such as a priest, rabbi, or guru for their connection to God.

What is the result? Your left brain may be overly developed leaving you dependent on rational analysis, logical thought, and scientific proof. What you have been taught by others and what they think can carry more weight than what you experience, feel, or know to be true. Your right brain can be less developed than your left brain unless you are an artist or musician. Your mystical training is probably nonexistent. Added to this lopsided development and lack of training is a fear of losing your mind. No one wants to have what psychologists define as abnormal episodes, whether they are hallucinations or irrational experiences.

For all these reasons, you may adhere to rationalism and seek logical explanations for your experiences, especially early in your Heart Journey. At some point all logic and reason will fly out the window. Time will warp or collapse. Distances will not matter. Any number of distortions will occur. Sooner or later you have to let go of the need for proof, or the need to understand how or why some events take place and even their meaning.

Remedy: You have to go into Heart Journey with all your senses awakened and your heart and mind open. What is impossible and illogical is as likely to occur as what is possible and logical. Miracles do happen! You want them to happen, so do not resist them, discount them, or explain them away. Your experiences are your experiences, whatever they may be. At some point, logical cause and effect reality falls away, (example: if this occurs, then it causes that to happen). Cause will no longer be a requirement for effect. Effect can occur without cause and vice versa. Sometimes events are coincidental, but not necessarily. Like your experiences, events just are.

Suspend judgment of irrational experiences as long as they help you to grow in love and wisdom. Embrace whatever is emerging and in keeping with spiritual growth. As disconcerting as initial experiences might be, they will become more familiar and matter of fact as time goes by. Understandable patterns may develop. There is no need to explain experiences to others or to justify them. They may discount what you say. If you do not understand, ask your co-creative Partner for clarification or wait on further insight. The most important task is to accept and honor irrational experiences as long as they meet the guidelines mentioned in Chapter 8: Communicating with God, and Chapter 9: The Nature of Communications. It is especially important that you do not overanalyze your experiences or seek rational explanations. Miracles, no matter how big, small, extraordinary, or even mundane do not lend themselves to logical, irrational explanations.

Example of Surrender to a Divine Upgrade that is Irrational

I was coming to the end of a spiritual transition in my life and I wanted to celebrate the passing. I decided to drive from my Maryland home to Washington, D.C. and take my first Kundalini Yoga class at the local center there. It was a beginner's class. We did a number of physical exercises with controlled breathing, which were not particularly difficult, demanding, or unusual. I had a good time and then left for the hour-long drive home.

I was well into the drive home, about forty-five minutes out, when I reached Silver Spring, MD, or so I thought. While sitting at the stoplight waiting for it to change, I glanced over at the department stores. Before my eyes, they collapsed and reformed into the Smithsonian Natural History Museum and the surrounding buildings on the mall in downtown Washington. I thought to myself, "How can this be? I just looked at the large green beltway sign that said Bethesda!" As I looked back at the sign, the letters moved around on the green background and regrouped to say, "Bridge to Virginia."

I really snapped to attention at that point and became extra alert. I was not sure where I had been over the last forty-five minutes, but I certainly was not headed in the right direction. I immediately got back on course, remained alert, and made it home safely in about an hour.

That night as my body slept, my consciousness woke up to a strange energy coursing through my system. My consciousness immediately recognized the energy and knew I had the option to travel out of my body. The thought voice in my head asked if I wanted to do this and I replied, "Yes!" With that the vibrational rate increased and I shot out of my body and into hyperspace. Stars flew by and the scene was similar to what you would see in a Star Wars movie. A presence came with me. I am not sure if it was the thought voice, my higher self, my soul, or a being, but there was a presence behind me. We slowed to a stop before a huge book. I was told it was "The Book of Knowledge." The book opened and I was able to read it, however, I could not retain what I read. The voice behind me said, "It is not time for you to know what you know, it is only important that you know that you know." The book closed and I was instantly dragged back through space and returned to my body. I knew the experience was over. I understood that physically I was still asleep, and so I let my consciousness slip back into sleep also.

My idea of a spiritual celebration was my first ever Kundalini class. It was a great class and experience. But God's idea of a spiritual celebration was my first ever out of body experience, astral projection, and hyper travel through the universe to read the Book of Knowledge. What a Divine upgrade! God had a better idea that was far more creative, but in many ways, irrational. Though my body was asleep, my consciousness was not. This was not a dream or even a conscious dream. There is a world of difference between dreaming and being consciously awake while the body is asleep. Your consciousness is literally awakened suddenly in response to a stimulus in the same way that your body would awaken to the sound of an alarm clock, but in the former case, only consciousness is aroused while the physical body still sleeps.

Chapter Fifteen: Troubleshooting Flow

Introduction to Problems with the Flow

You have gone through all the troubleshooting material presented in the previous chapters and you know you are doing your part in regard to manifestation through attraction and receptivity. Still, nothing you do seems to work or come out right. You might feel that you are not getting any Divine assistance since there is no ease in the process, only difficulty. Maybe you feel your efforts are being thwarted or delayed. Perhaps the timing is off. Opportunities come too late, too soon, too slowly, or pass too quickly. Whatever the reason, you keep missing the boat or the boat never arrives. In situations such as these, most likely the problem lies with flow.

Flow is like wind, and in this case Divine wind. When there is a tailwind, you move ahead more easily and everything you need seems to fall into place. When there is a headwind, you are thwarted in your attempts to proceed. You do not have what you need when you need it and obstacles arise. When there is no wind, you are becalmed and not moving at all. Like the direction and speed of the wind, the direction and speed of the flow creates ease or difficulty in regard to progress. Ease or difficulty within the flow is always significant and meant to be a sign or subtle communication from your co-creative Partner to guide you toward manifestation through attraction and receptivity. It is your job to learn to read the flow, eventually harnessing your desire and focused sustained thought to ease and the flow's tailwind. In the same manner, you are to avoid difficulty or the flow's headwind. In order to master the process of manifestation through attraction and receptivity, and be guided by ease and difficulty, you have to be able to interpret flow. Which way does the wind blow or what is the direction of the flow? Will it move you closer to your desire or push you away? When is it time to move forward? When is it time to wait? Does the flow require an immediate response? Is the flow likely to be sustained over time? Should you change course or has the flow shifted direction? The answers to these questions are found in the flow and your experience of ease and difficulty.

Most problems with the flow require you to make adjustments. You must modify your efforts to align and pace yourself with the flow, heading in the direction of ease at the same speed and avoiding areas of difficulty. Be patient when the flow is slow; reassess when you are stopped in your tracks. Speed up when the flow is fast; strike while the iron is hot. You have to be the one to change; you cannot change the flow, though sometimes it will recycle and come around again at a later time. But for the most part, the flow simply is. It is as wild and uncontrollable as the wind. If you understand the speed and direction of the wind, you can fly a kite or sail a boat. If you understand the speed and direction of flow, you can manifest with ease and avoid setbacks or disruption.

Moving Against the Flow

Ease indicates that you are going in the right direction, moving at the right speed, completing the next step in a timely manner. Under these conditions progress can become almost effortless. When you are in the flow and correctly aligned, everything clicks.

On the other hand, difficulty indicates that you are going in the wrong direction, doing the wrong thing, at the wrong time. Tasks become much harder than they need to be, doors close unexpectedly, deals fall through. You feel like you are struggling, doing all the work but getting nowhere. Every attempt is thwarted. Difficulty, major setbacks, and disasters within Heart Journey are often God's way of telling you, "No!" Something is wrong. The simplest explanation is that your timing is off. You are rushing ahead when you really need to wait on the flow for assistance. It takes time for favorable conditions to develop. The more complex your contract, the longer the process will normally take. Another possibility is that the next step you are attempting to take is incorrect. The order of tasks might be incorrect or the task itself might be incorrect regardless of order or timing. In the worst case scenario, and perhaps the least likely, you have to consider the possibility that your request or contract is being denied or qualified. In other words, difficulty is not a matter of timing or correct action; problems run much deeper and your contract either includes a major flaw or is inappropriate in regard to future developments you may or may not be aware of.

Remedy: To determine whether or not you are working against the flow, use the Rule of Three mentioned in Chapter 10: Communication Guidelines. When you attempt the same task three times in three different ways and it fails each time, you need to reassess. You are fighting a headwind and being told "No!" You are probably moving in the wrong direction, doing the wrong thing, at the wrong time or speed. Adhering to the rule of three will save you a lot of time, effort, and resources. It is better to stop, listen, and make the appropriate adjustment than continue to try to force an unworkable option.

In the best of situations, failure or difficulty is a call for reflection and communication with your co-creative Partner. Perhaps all that is needed is Divine insight or guidance.

You might have gotten off track somewhere along the way. Communicating with your co-creative Partner should lead you to understand the exact nature of the problem. Then you can make the appropriate adjustment in timing, take corrective action, or identify a new course of action.

It is less likely that there would be a problem with the contract itself at this point if you originally spent enough time in reflection and communication with your co-creative Partner before the signing. But if you were off track from the beginning and just now realizing this, you need to abandon a dead-end situation. When you attempt to push things along despite consistent and continuing negative responses and obstacles you are working against the flow and Divine intent. Your efforts will fail, and fail again.

If you are uncertain as to the nature of the impediments even after much reflection and communication with your co-creative Partner, you should wait a little longer to see what develops. Conditions may change and obstacles may be removed with time, or a better option might arise. Be patient.

Unresponsive Flow

A lack of any response, either supportive or thwarting, is generally a clear indication that you need to wait or try something totally different. When the flow appears unresponsive, it is not that everything you try fails or that doors slam in your face; rather, you get little or no response at all to your efforts. Every initiative fades away for one reason or another. There is no feedback. It is like playing tennis alone without an opponent. You serve, the ball goes over the net, but it never returns and is lost. This lack of response can be directly related to elements outside of your control. You may be doing your part, priming the pump, putting in the effort, but through several attempts and initiatives, there has been no correlating response.

There is a distinction between the previous section, "Moving Against the Flow" and "Unresponsive Flow." In the former situation, while fishing you would cast your net only to snag it on the rocks. You run into obvious problems that prevent success. When the flow is unresponsive, you would cast your nets again and again, but never catch any fish. Most likely, you are fishing in the wrong spot, at the wrong time, or with the wrong bait.

Before you can identify the flow as truly unresponsive, certain criteria must be met.

1. You have to be a current and continuing active participant in the co-creative process.
2. You need to have initiated your part of the contract and completed all the necessary steps up to this point. (In other words, you are not sitting back expecting God to make something happen. You have done and continue to do your share, but at this point the ball is clearly in God's court.)

3. You make the effort to test the waters regularly with new and different initiatives.
4. You are in communication with your co-creative Partner and when you check in you are being told to wait.

If these criteria apply to your situation, conditions are just not right at the present moment. They need time to develop and become more favorable, or certain impeding circumstances need time to fade away.

Remedy: Under ideal conditions, the give and take exchange with the flow during the process of manifestation through attraction and receptivity is like a tennis match. It is a step-by-step process of volleys. You hit the ball over the net and then move with the returning ball. The ball comes back over the net left, you move left. The ball comes back over the net right, you move right. The ball goes long, you go long. The ball drops short, you move in. Your measured response must match the play to be successful and keep the ball in motion. As you return the ball back over the net, you have already developed a strategy and planned out where you expect and want the ball to land. If the ball never comes back over the net, you must wait for the serve. There is nothing else for you to do.

Similarly, when following your Heart Journey contract and desire, you initiate what you perceive as the next step needed for manifestation through attraction and receptivity. You need to move with the corresponding answer from the flow. The response to your initiative should give you clues on how to best position yourself for maximum benefit. Should you move left, right, back or up? If the response is an unexpected curve ball, major adjustments will be needed. Once positioned and aligned with the response, you should begin to formulate your next step. Take all this information to your co-creative Partner for discussion and reflection. Together you come up with a plan for the next step or set of tasks. Proceeding in this manner, step by step, in collaboration with your co-creative Partner will lead eventually to manifestation.

Obviously, if there is no response at all, this process is not possible; however, valuable information can still be gleaned. The lack of response should be reflected on and discussed with your co-creative Partner until you understand the reason for the lack of response and can make an appropriate adjustment. Either you need to try something new, (fish a different spot or use different bait), or wait patiently, (go fishing at a later date or time). Sooner or later, a different course of action will arise. In the meantime, there is always something to be learned from the flow's response, even when the response is no response at all.

Though external progress may be temporarily stopped, this does not affect internal advancement. It is still possible for you to grow spiritually and evolve under these conditions. Sometimes the most unresponsive circumstances are ideal for inner growth because they emphasize the need for trust. Continue to work internally on lovingness, gratitude, and communication while patiently awaiting the return of the flow.

Slow Moving and Stagnant Flow

In addition to a lack of response, the flow can be so slow moving as to become stagnant. This results from overwhelming complications that are self-made. "Unresponsive Flow" is an issue independent of your actions. It has to do with God's timing. "Slow Moving and Stagnant Flow" is a direct result of your decisions, actions, and life situation. The most serious cases associated with a lack of movement in the flow and resulting stagnation are commonly caused by:

1. A multifaceted contract: You start out with a contract that is so cumbersome your attention is scattered and therefore ineffective. You cannot concentrate your desire to focus with intention.
2. Overwhelming complications: Daily problems and difficult living conditions are distracting. You get caught up in crisis management, putting out fires instead of developing creative options and solutions. Overwhelmed by chaos, you cannot clear your head enough to get organized or productive.
3. Limited or no input on your part: Discouraged and exhausted or simply lazy, you start looking to be saved. You feel like you are incapable of solving these problems or carrying even a portion of the load. You cease all efforts and wait for a miracle.

If any of these factors weigh on your contract, then self-made complications can be impeding your interaction with the flow. Stagnation is almost guaranteed to occur when all three factors are present. For example, your contract or vision is very involved and addresses a complex problem while you are under difficult conditions that are highly dependent on God's miraculous input with little effort from you. A complicated situation like this is frequently more than you or the flow can handle because of dispersion of attention and mental concentration, dissipation of energy and resources, lack of creativity, and physical exhaustion. This is how the house of cards begins to fall apart and leads to stagnation.

For example, the Federal Emergency Management Agency's (FEMA's) response to Hurricane Katrina was totally bogged down both in regard to rescue and recovery efforts and disaster relief. Even years after the disaster, New Orleans residents were still living in trailers, the levies had not been completely rebuilt and secured, the police force was depleted, and whole neighborhoods lay in ruin. Problems were huge, complex and overwhelming. Many individuals lacked the resources and know-how to resolve and overcome impediments to rebuilding especially in the low lying areas. The government organizations meant to address problems were unresponsive or totally unprepared and overwhelmed by the nature and magnitude of the disaster. All of these factors contributed to a continuing blight and slow moving, stagnant conditions.

Complications are major distinctions between the previous section "Unresponsive Flow" and "Slow Moving and Stagnant Flow." In this situation, you might not fish at all because of a quagmire of your own making. Perhaps the bank has repossessed your boat because you are delinquent on your loan. Maybe you lent your nets to an acquaintance who left town with them. The end result is you are left standing on the dock hoping fish with jump out of the water into your arms. These are human made complications. Stagnation caused by complex contracts, overwhelming life problems, and human inefficiency is the signature cause of "Slow Moving and Stagnant Flow." You might think that the flow is unresponsive, when in fact you are creating and sustaining conditions that counteract flow.

The most dangerous situation arises when you do not realize what you have done. You assume that the flow is unresponsive, not weighed down by your self-made complications. You lose faith in the co-creative process and eventually cease all efforts. No input, no output! Economic and psychological depression can compound the difficulties you face. Your negativity is sometimes projected outward onto others. You expect to fail, and do not expect or ask for help from others. Your doom and gloom attitude becomes infectious and fosters a climate of apathy or hopelessness.

Remedy: In the best of circumstances, you align your desire and focused sustained thought to the movement of the flow, matching speed and direction so efforts can proceed as one with ease toward success. Your input and the feedback process keep things in motion. One factor feeds off another and momentum builds over time. It is like riding a bicycle. When you first get on, you have to pump to get the bike moving, but once you get going, pedaling on a flat terrain becomes easier. When confronted with slow moving and stagnate flow, an important factor to consider is when the slowdown began. Were you becalmed early on? If you were going nowhere shortly after signing your contract, you are more likely to suffer from a complex contract and overwhelming conditions. Stagnation is most likely human made and can be undone.

Hopefully, before conditions totally stagnate you check in with your co-creative Partner and take remedial action. If you are in communication, you will be aware of the slowdown as it is happening. Problems leading to stagnation are generally too big to miss and do not develop overnight. An ounce of prevention is worth a pound of cure! It is easier to prevent stagnation than to foster movement from a dead stop, so do not delay taking corrective action.

Assuming stagnation is directly related to complications you have created and your current situation, the best way to get things moving again is to simplify both your contract and your life. If you get organized and take it one step at a time, you can undo the gridlock associated with slow moving, stagnate flow. Start by breaking problems and goals down to single items, then prioritize tasks. Refocus your energies and resources by concentrating on one thing at a time. Slowly make you way through problem areas. Resist the temptation to start multitasking until you regain some momentum. If your goals are not all tightly linked together, consider dropping auxiliary goals or secondary requests. Simplify your contract as much as possible and stay with what is most important.

At the same time, reassess the complications in your life. Are they self-made or caused by others? Can you disengage and move on, or do you have responsibilities? Are the complications real or associated with sabotage and unnecessary drama? You sabotage yourself if you lend out your fishing nets when you need to go fishing. Others sabotage your efforts when they steal your nets or derail your plans with fabricated chaos. Protect your Heart Journey commitment from unnecessary intrusion. Weigh life circumstances honestly. An important step in spiritual growth is determining what is yours to address and what you need to release.

If you have done everything right, removed every obstacle, simplified your contract and life, and still feel stuck, you are probably "delayed." Delay is not associated with complications you create. It is an uncomplicated signal from God that the time is not yet right. Discussions with your co-creative Partner should help you make the distinction.

Delays, Interference, and Incorrect Timing

Delays and interference are usually indicative of incorrect timing, especially when you are waiting on someone to respond or something to happen so you can proceed. Delays are contingent on others, sometimes professionals, businesses, or government agencies. Delays are not related to complications you create, a distinction which separates them from stagnation.

By definition, delays in the flow are beyond your control. They have nothing to do with procrastination, apathy, or inattentiveness on your part and everything to do with predetermined and existing structures. Delays occur when the person you need to meet with has prior commitments, or services you need are not immediately available. You may be delayed by waiting periods for items such as licenses, permits, test results, or credit approval. Weather can be another delaying factor. What you need to proceed with ease is not available and still in formation. These limitations can be in place long before you signed your contract and began your Heart Journey.

Interference occurs when unexpected and disruptive events tie you up for days, weeks, months, or even years, monopolizing your time, energy, and resources. Interference arises from life's happenings that are beyond your control or related to situations that take precedence over your Heart Journey contract and desires. These include, but are not limited to, births, deaths, illnesses, calamities, unforeseen events, or crises. The sudden intrusion may be meant to derail you completely if you are headed in the wrong direction or simply delay your progress for the moment.

Remedy: There is a distinction that needs to be made between true delays or interference and distractions used as an excuse for an inability to stay on target. Your first step is to make absolutely certain that a delay is not caused by procrastination or inattentiveness on your part. Rather, the delay is beyond your control and the result of steps others need to take. You cannot look to the flow when the fault is your own.

In regard to interference, any change in your personal priorities can have a dramatic effect on your attention and progress. You cannot stay on target, doing what you need to do co-creatively for your Heart Journey contract when you suddenly decide a diversion such as cruise around the world is more important. Be clear about personal agendas and any inconsistency on your part. On the other hand, certain life situations and crises demand immediate attention and can preclude your Heart Journey contract. You must weigh the gravity of these situations and choose the most appropriate course of action after conferring with your co-creative Partner.

You are a spiritual being having a human experience, and perhaps human responsibilities are taking precedence over your contract for one reason or another. Be with whatever is arising. It is part of your training. This does not mean you cannot pick up the pace once matters are handled, but it can indicate the need to take a detour or wait patiently. Restrictions will be lifted eventually and at that time you will sense a change in the flow and be able to move ahead effortlessly and quickly, frequently making up for lost time. Why you were delayed might be a mystery that is explained later on, or perhaps, never explained. The important point to remember is that all is not lost or forgotten as long as your desire is steady and your faith in God is strong.

True delays and interference in the flow can be interpreted as a difficulty versus ease signal from your co-creative Partner. Your progress is interrupted for a reason and you are being told to wait. Though frustrating, developments can be purposeful and to your benefit in the long run. Learn to accept and work with, rather than against them. Maybe you are moving too quickly and your efforts are not in synch with the flow. More time is needed for conditions to develop fully or for you to evolve spiritually. At the very least, delays and interference allow for further consideration before decisions are final. Communicate with your co-creative Partner for further information on how and when to proceed, and what you need to do in the meantime. When faith is maintained, attractive and receptive abilities increase and the individual matures spiritually.

Sometimes delays, interference and interruptions are understandable. Your Heart Journey contract might require a lot of preparation or specific seasonal conditions. Technology might need to catch up with your creative ideas. Your business might need to develop products, build sales, and establish returning clientele before things run smoothly. Reflection and communication with your co-creative Partner can clarify the underlying causes. If you are being told that it is okay to wait and you will catch up later, impediments are not a permanent problem. For the moment, your timing is off and things will pick up in the future.

Example of Delay, Interference, and Incorrect Timing

Joann hated her job. She was ready to quit and had prepared her letter of resignation. She wanted to submit it to her boss as soon as possible, but something always seemed to get in the way. This went on for a week. First her boss was called out of town unexpectedly. Then Joann caught the flu and was at home sick for several days. When she returned to work there was a crisis that demanded everyone's attention. No matter how hard she tried, Joann could not arrange a time to meet with her boss. Before she knew it, it was late Friday night and everyone was off for the weekend. Though Joann was anxious to resign, intuition told her that something was amiss and it was okay to wait. There was probably a reason for the delay and interference.

When Joann arrived at work Monday morning, still carrying her resignation in her briefcase, it was announced that the company had been sold over the weekend. Every one of the employees would be offered a cash severance package with stock options based on how long he or she had been employed. Since Joann had been with the company almost since its inception, this was an appreciable amount of money, enough to retire. Only in hindsight did Joann truly understand that her timing was incorrect, but God's timing through delays and interference in the flow had worked to her benefit.

Quick Flow and the Need to be Prepared

Sometimes you have to strike when the iron is hot. When the flow is quick and the timing right, move without hesitation, especially when all the stepping stones line up and you can advance with great ease. This is your chance; this is a blessing, so take a risk! Manifestation through attraction and receptivity can occur spontaneously when the flow is quick. Sometimes this occurs after a period of stagnation or delay. While you wait through one postponement and/or interference after another, energy and anticipation builds. You may see necessary components falling into place one by one, but still there is no movement. Then the dam breaks. All the right elements are in place and everything moves swiftly forward as a unit. Delay and interference followed by sudden release can be God's way of setting an appropriate time schedule for manifestation. You need to be ready to go with the flow when this happens.

A shift in the flow is as recognizable as a break in the clouds after many days of rain. The sun comes out and warms your skin. Everything brightens. Delays and interfering life events fade temporarily or permanently. People come forward to take your place or lend a hand. Resources and contacts arise. Your schedule clears. You have the place, the time, the money, and assistance you need. When your ship comes in, get on board as quickly as possible. If you are used to interpreting the flow and are aware of the dramatic change, you can seize the moment with confidence!

When you are suddenly free from impediments and able to move ahead, you cannot know when or if limitations will return. The pressure is on to take advantage of the situation and leap from the cliff. You are less likely to waste time or procrastinate because of the past delays.

Remedy: When you are ready and prepared, quick moving flow or quick timing is not a problem, but what if you are not prepared or ready? What if you are taken by surprise? You have to assess the situation and make a fast decision. Do you go with it or not? Sometimes the flow moves too quickly for you to catch the ride and this is a problem. All of a sudden, life is moving ahead without you even though it is moving toward your vision. You have to either change your schedule to catch up or renegotiate the timing.

If you are caught totally by surprise and truly unable to catch the express train, negotiate for another chance; however, there is a big difference between fear or procrastination and the need for more time. If you hesitate out of fear or procrastinate and do not attempt to do your part when it is your turn to act, you may or may not be given a second or third chance. Reluctance or vacillation just when your moment arrives and the conditions are right is a serious trust issue that can only be addressed in communication with your co-creative Partner.

But if the situation is totally unworkable as it stands and another time would be better, confer with your co-creative Partner. Opportunities can come around again, even with a fast moving flow. Make the necessary adjustments and preparations should a second opportunity arise.

Example of Quick Moving Flow

My good friend was being sent to Hawaii by her company. She asked me if I would like to go along. We would be gone for two weeks. This was a dream come true, but the timing was all wrong. I had only 10 days to prepare. The school year had not yet started and my children would not be back to school making it necessary to find baby-sitters. But most importantly, I had a publishing deadline that could not wait. With great regret, I told my friend "No, perhaps another time." She doubted there would be second trip.

I thanked God for the opportunity. Gratitude is essential, even for missed opportunities, but I mentioned to God that the end of October would be better for me and I would have more time to prepare. When my friend returned from the Hawaiian business trip in early September, she called to say that a second trip to Hawaii was necessary and was scheduled for the end of October. This was a perfect opportunity to tag along. She invited me again and this time I accepted. My publishing deadline would have passed, my kids would be back in school, and as an added bonus I had just earned a free promotional plane ticket. Everything was falling into place. When you see ease and momentum like this, it is important to move with it and not miss the opportunity.

Chapter Sixteen:
Troubleshooting the Avenue for Manifestation

Introduction to Problems with the Avenue for Manifestation

Problems with the avenue for manifestation usually fall in your court. It can be your job to put forth the effort and develop the skills necessary for manifestation through attraction and receptivity to occur. In addition to the tasks before you now, you must maintain a conducive environment balancing all the elements mentioned previously and below in their most positive, heightened forms while maintaining clear communication with God and developing the co-creative partnership. Desire, surrender, your focus sustained thought, and flow are still necessary ingredients for manifestation and not just temporary guideposts to get you to this point. If you have not read through the previous troubleshooting chapters, you need to review them now before troubleshooting the avenue for manifestation.

If everything is in place, you need to close the deal. This usually means quality efforts and skills on your part are needed, but not always. Some individuals in some situations experience instant gratification, though this is not common. Some individuals in some situations experience long delays, even lasting years. This is also not common. Everyone else falls in between. Timing is somewhat dependent on the nature and complexity of your vision, the amount of effort and skill you bring to the table, your life situation, and how far afield you are at the beginning. Though your Heart Journey might seem lengthy to you as you worked though previously discussed issues, you are not done yet. Everything above simply sets the stage for what is to come. Now that you have laid the groundwork and establish a co-creative partnership with God, it is time to apply the right amount of effort and skills within the flow for the best outcome. As you begin to master this final element in the process of manifestation through attraction and receptivity, problems can still arise and corrective action will be needed.

Problems with Instant Gratification

It might seem to you that there cannot possibly be problems when you are able to manifest quickly, however, there are. Though some people might be capable of instant gratification, in the long run, a pattern of manifesting quickly can impede spiritual growth and the ability to focus and to attract over a longer period of time.

Instant gratification occurs when flow and desire are quickly matched through a potent thought and manifestation occurs without effort, skills, or sustained focus. Desires appropriate for instant gratification are generally uncomplicated, one-stage requests requiring only one or two elements to fall into place. The response is fairly immediate. One simply desires, and "it" simply appears, whatever it is. This is the express train to manifestation and some people are masters of instant gratification. They manifest quickly because they already are what they want and there is no need to become anything. They are there in their hearts and minds. Instant gratification has its positive rewards, but there can also be problems. It is not a panacea and it is not likely to occur all the time. It is those other times, those times of delayed gratification that can become more difficult and unmanageable for the masters of instant gratification for the following reasons:

1. The inability to cope with delayed gratification

Those who manifest quickly and effortlessly may not be able to cope with delayed gratification. They can lack staying power. Sooner or later gratification is delayed. This is incomprehensible to the masters of instant gratification. They cannot understand why delays occur when everything materializes readily and without their input. To them, delay is interpreted as a "No" from God and "wasn't meant to be." They assume incorrectly that their desire is inconsistent with the flow and Divine intent. They readily abandon their visions thinking since it isn't happening now, it will not happen ever. For them, delay equals denial.

2. A tendency to choose only simple, effortless desires

Because only simple desires move to manifestation quickly, the masters of instant gratification are less likely to elect complex or multi-staged visions that require effort, skill, or input on their part. Over time, they become short-sighted and lazy. Although manifesting simple desires quickly may be a product of attraction and receptivity, the process is less likely to be co-creative as human contributions shrink.

3. Limited communication with the co-creative Partner

When manifestation occurs quickly and repeatedly, there is the chance that time spent communicating with the co-creative Partner is shortened or even neglected. The ability to make adjustments, work through problems, renegotiate requests, and make major contributions to a long term process never develops. When gratification is delayed somewhat, a regular pattern of communication should be established in order to discuss options, changes, problems, and course of action. Navigational corrections are needed, perhaps daily. The co-creative partnership grows as you and God collaborate on your vision and this is the intent of Heart Journey. Attention to subtleties develops over time and an intimate relationship with the Divine results. When manifestation frequently occurs quickly and easily before the co-creative partnership has been established, spiritual development is curtailed.

4. Lack of spiritual growth and maturity

If the co-creative partnership fails to fully develop because of quick and easy manifestation, then spiritual growth will also suffer. Heart Journey is a spiritual practice build on desire and surrender through an intimate co-creative relationship with God. Spiritual maturity and character development occur through your communication with God, not through manifestation, no matter how quickly or slowly it occurs. When you do not participate fully in the manifestation process and co-creative partnership, you are left unchanged and reduced to a bystander.

5. Ego inflation

The previous four issues, when allowed to develop into full blown problems, lead to ego inflation. The ego will assume responsibility and credit for manifestation in one of two ways. The ego might take over control as soon as there is a delay, forcing things to happen, ("my will, not Thy Will"). Needless to say, you are no longer on a Heart Journey when the ego starts bypassing God and drawing up a to-do list.

On the other hand, when everything manifests suddenly, the ego can assume, either consciously or unconsciously, that God is at his or her command. One need only ask and God will provide. Isn't that how it works? An attitude like this sets the stage for a fall. I have seen this again and again in those who profess to manifest unconditionally. Sooner or later, the totally material, ego driven, Gimme God philosophy proves false because, no, it does not work that way. God is a beneficent parent Who wants what is best for the children (spiritually) and sometimes what is best is to say, "No!" The true purpose of manifestation through attraction and receptivity is not manifestation. It is a pathway to spiritual growth and heart openness through a co-creative partnership with God.

Remedy: Don't be fooled into thinking instant gratification is the only form of manifestation through attraction and receptivity. Delays are sometimes advantageous and necessary for long term plans. If you dream big, the process will take longer and you must grow and mature with your dream, learning to sustain your focused thought and efforts over time. Each situation has its own individual needs and potential. There is nothing wrong with instant gratification per se and there is also nothing wrong with delayed gratification per se.

Instant gratification is a blessing from God and should be viewed as such with gratitude and humility. It is not a given and should not be expected. You may have a good run of success, but sooner or later delays will occur. It might be a single delay that lasts for a relatively short period of time or a long delay that lasts years for one reason or another. In either case, you must stay committed to your co-creative partnership in all types of weather.

The important point to remember when instant gratification occurs is that you must maintain close communication with your co-creative Partner even though there are no problems to discuss. God is more than manifestation tech support! You do not need a problem to communicate. You can express your gratitude or just sit in the silence listening. Maintaining your connection will keep you from falling into the five pitfalls associated with instant gratification mentioned above. The surest way to avoid losing your way while on Heart Journey is to fully develop your relationship with God and trust in the guidance you receive.

Problems with Delayed Gratification

Delayed gratification is common and occurs for many reasons. To begin with, your contract might involve a lengthy process. It normally takes time for visions and thoughts to move from the spiritual plane into material form as energy must be condensed into matter. Manifestation through attraction and receptivity is especially slow the first time you attempt it because there are subtle understandings that cannot be taught and only come into awareness through experience. Do not become discouraged when the process takes longer than you expect.

When gratification is delayed within the avenue for manifestation, the ball is usually in your court. You have brought together the other elements necessary for attraction and receptivity. At this stage, developments can be totally dependent on your skills and efforts, and you are probably responsible for any delay.

Problems with delayed gratification within the avenue for manifestation generally result from what you do or don't do physically in addition to any of the previously mentioned elements. Your job is to balance desire with surrender, sustain your focused thought, and communicate with your co-creative Partner while staying in the flow. If all these preconditions are met, you will know when to act and what actions are appropriate. The actions that you take, in most situations, become the means or avenue for manifestation. Although it is possible that the means will simply materialize, it is more likely that your efforts and skills will be needed. When everything else is in place and delays arise at this point in the process, assess your own behavior. Assume that the ball is in your court. Confer with your co-creative Partner. What are you doing? What are you not doing? Listed below are the possible causes for delay. Within the discussion of each of these behaviors are suggested corrective actions you can take.

1. Procrastination and an inability to follow through
2. Counterproductive character traits and self-sabotage
3. Lack of sincere effort
4. Impatience and overcompensation
5. Lack of essential skills
6. Preconditions
7. Chaos, disorganization, and other distractions
8. Complexity
9. Renegotiation
10. Never getting started
11. Lack of financial support
12. Lack of moral or ethical integrity

1. Procrastination and an Inability to Follow Through

You cannot procrastinate or leave your part undone and still expect to manifest. Because this is a mystical process that involves the combination of attraction and receptivity within the flow, procrastination leads to incorrect timing. The flow waits for no one. You literally miss the boat, that special moment custom made for you when all the preconditions were met, everything is in balance, and the time is right to move forward. Your chance may or may not come around again. It should have been a major balancing act up to this point. It is best not to drag your feet and miss your opportunity. Strike while the iron is hot. Be on time when you apply your efforts and skills.

There is another reason to not procrastinate. Your desires and visions are never solely your own. They eventually merge into the collective unconscious and the minds of others. The hundredth monkey theory states that learned behavior can spread spontaneously from one group of monkeys to other monkeys when a critical number (in this case one hundred) is reached. The learned behavior does not have to be witnessed to spread, nor does there have to be any contact between the teacher of this behavior and the student. As soon as consciousness reaches critical mass, concepts are passed on by an unseen mechanism. Others will be seeded with the same vision you are having. Though you may delay, they may not. You might be left behind even though your contract started out as a one of a kind brainstorm.

You will never get off the ground if you do not follow through on the insights provided to you in your conversations with your co-creative Partner. Guidance is a gift and needs to be honored with action. Communications that fall on deaf ears eventually cease. Going back to the tennis game analogy, when the tennis ball is over the net and coming your way, you need to act and make an appropriate response. If you miss the ball consistently, the volley will die out and be difficult to restart.

When you honestly cannot get to the task at hand for one reason or another, there will be another chance. There are times when life situations interfere beyond your control. This is not procrastination. This is interruption of the flow. Maintain your balance and stay prepared for your future opportunity.

Remedy: Pay particular attention to deadlines whether they are man-made, Divinely inspired, or the result of natural consequences. You can set your own man-made deadlines to move your contract along so you are prepared and ahead of the game. These should be step-by-step deadlines that inch you towards success while communicating with your co-creative Partner. You do not want to get too far ahead. That generally entails extra and wasted effort. Divinely inspired deadlines are usually perceived intuitively. Those deadlines that are linked to natural consequences might be set by seasonal changes, age related limitations, health considerations, or responsibilities to children or elderly parents. In all situations, it is best to act and complete tasks when the conditions are right. They will not stay that way forever.

2. Counterproductive Character Traits and Self-Sabotage

Sometimes the vision is strong and true, but your ability to act is muted by a negative self-image and counterproductive character traits. If you are a passive person who normally lets life happen out of weakness or neglect, your ability to effect change is underdeveloped. You cannot be wishy-washy about your contract and Heart Journey. You must be strong enough to follow your co-creative Partner's lead. The goal is in sight. Don't give up now.

You are God's ambassador and right hand representative on the earth plane. Whether you believe it or not, you are a powerful person who matters in the grand scheme of things. Everyone plays a role in universal consciousness regardless of any contract or spiritual awareness. We are all participants, willing or not, conscious or not, effective, ineffective, or even detrimental.

Your ability to desire and then respond in a proactive manner to life situations and your co-creative Partner's communications is essential to your ability to attract, receive and move ahead with your Heart Journey contract. It is also essential to character development and spiritual maturity. Heart Journey is programmed to change you for the better. Of course you will be challenged! God wants you to grow, manifest, and succeed. Any character weakness, inhibition, and resistance at this point undermine all that you have learned and how far you have come.

Remedy: You need to be all that you can be. Nothing will move forward externally until you begin to strengthen internally. Start by believing in yourself. Your history is the past and does not define who you are at this moment. Success and change can always occur from this point forward. Any trait or negative pattern of behavior can be changed when you pray the solution and not the problem. Confer with your co-creative Partner. Ask God to show you how to modify your behavior, and then make a firm commitment to do so. Take it one step at a time. Do not bite off more than you can comfortably chew. If you have to, start by role playing. Act as if you are the person you want to be. If you pretend long enough this will result in becoming the person you want to be when it is no longer an act but the real thing. Step by step you can build the strength of character needed to carry out Divine Will and your Heart Journey vision.

3. Lack of Sincere Effort

Half-hearted efforts will get you nowhere. Nothing less than your best will do. This is not the lazy person's journey to manifestation and enlightenment. You cannot be a minimalist in regard to your efforts and expect to be rewarded with manifestation and spiritual growth. In your communications with your co-creative Partner, it will become very clear what you need to do. Maybe it is a little, maybe it is a lot, but nothing less than what is asked of you or required will suffice.

The process of manifestation through attraction and receptivity is a mystery to begin with. Do you really want to change the formula set forth by your co-creative Partner by doing less or other than asked? Do you think you know better? Do you think your co-creative Partner won't notice your half-hearted attempts? What if God's responses were half-hearted? Do you want a co-creative Partner who phones it in? When you know what you need to do, make sure that you do it, totally and completely, to the best of your ability.

Remedy: Heart Journey is about opening your heart to loving God, others, and yourself more fully. If your heart is truly open and loving, you will be joyful in all that you do. It is an act of self-love to be the best that you can be and successful, not just because of the success or reward, but because of the pride you have in the good work that you do. It is an act of devotion to God and the co-creative partnership to succeed. It is also possible that succeeding will show your love for others who might benefit in some way from your efforts and vision. You deserve to be accomplished. At this point, you have come a long way. You formulated your vision and translated it into a focused and sustained thought. Then you learned to interpret the flow and established an intimate, co-creative partnership with God. Now you need to close the deal and manifest your vision with a total commitment to the final steps. Trust in the help of your co-creative Partner. Don't sell yourself, your vision, or your Partner short. You can do more. You can be more. Give it all that you have.

4. Impatience and Overcompensation

Don't attempt to outdo God. The co-creative directive in manifestation through attraction and receptivity is to do your part, no more and no less, in a timely manner. Rushing ahead out of impatience or putting too much effort into the process to get it done as quickly as possible is as counterproductive as too little effort. It weakens the co-creative partnership, negates receptivity and your ability to attract. Pushing matters through when progress is slow because you are anxious and impatient is an example of the small self-will overriding Divine Will. When progress is slow, it might be because it needs to be slow.

One of the mysteries of manifestation is how you can be in the right place at the right time to attract and receive. If you are pushing the envelope, rushing ahead when you need to wait, and ignoring your co-creative Partner's input, you will miss your window. Opportunities for attraction and receptivity are not straight line trajectories. They are windows in time and space. You need to be positioned correctly to take advantage of them. This is not something you can figure out on your own. Only God will know when the right window will open.

Remember the story of Joann who wanted to submit her resignation but was thwarted a number of times, (see Chapter 15: Example of Delay, Interference and Incorrect Timing). Then without warning the company was sold and she was given a severance package. This was clearly a window in time that she could not see or know of in advance. But God and the flow determined the correct timing and it was to her benefit to wait one week.

Remedy: Close communication with your co-creative Partner helps you determine exactly what to do and what not to do when and where in a step-by-step manner. Communication is essential because your level of contribution will differ from project to project, person to person, and situation to situation. Tasks will change over time. There is no set pattern when it comes to manifestation. What you need to do when is individualized for your vision, specific for your talents, abilities, and where you are in the manifestation process. This is not a one size fits all program and there is no preconceived game plan to follow. Manifestation through attraction and receptivity is a mystery and the only way to enter the mystery and stay with it to the conclusion is through continuing and intense communication and cooperation with your co-creative Partner. Do not rush ahead thinking you know better.

5. Lack of Essential Skills

If you do not have the skills needed for manifestation then you must acquire them or get help from someone who does have the necessary skills. Either of these paths will work as long as the quality and expertise are there. Without them, results will be less than desirable or may not manifest at all. If skills are required, your first task will be to determine which path will best serve your vision. Should you develop the skills yourself or should you seek assistance in this matter?

The key question to ask yourself is whether or not you truly wish to acquire the necessary skills. Is it simply a means to an end for the sake of manifestation or are the skills innate to your vision and who you wish to become? If you are determined to develop your own skills as part of your Heart Journey, then be prepared to master the task at hand, whatever it is, and regardless of what it takes or how much time is required. Know that a temporary delay in manifestation is mandated in this situation as it cannot occur until you reach a certain level of proficiency.

For example, if you wish to film a documentary but do not have any previous experience or expertise as a director or film maker, discuss this with your co-creative Partner. What is the real goal here? Do you want to become a film maker or do you simply want to get your message across? If you want to become a film maker, then it is appropriate to develop the necessary camera and directing skills. You can take a course, go to school, or apprentice with a film director. There will be a serious learning curve and educating yourself will take time, but this will probably be your future profession and life-long pursuit. Your focused sustained thought should reflect this ultimate career goal. "I have become a highly skilled director and film maker." Generally, the farther your vision is from your starting point, the longer the process will take. The further along you are regarding skills and experience when you sign your contract, the shorter the time span before manifestation.

On the other hand, maybe you never intend to become a film maker per se. Instead, you simply want to get your message out and have impact. You and your co-creative Partner might decide that the best course of action would be to write a script and then attract a camera crew and director. If so, your focused sustained thought should reflect this ultimate goal. "I attract the best people for producing a film from my script that conveys this all important message." In this case, there is little or no learning curve. You are already a writer. You have the idea for the script already worked out in your head. Delays will tend to be shorter.

Remedy: When the question of skills applies to your contract, a preliminary step to the avenue for manifestation will always be the determination of who will be the skillful one. There is a fork in the road and you will not move forward until you choose the path that is right for you and your vision. Do you want to acquire the necessary skills or do you want to delegate the responsibility to someone who is already an expert? In most situations, your co-creative Partner will be amenable to whatever you want to do. The choice is yours, but you must be definitive. You will progress until you choose. Once the decision is made, the sustained, focused thought and the avenue for manifestation attain greater clarity. At that point you should begin to move forward.

6. Preconditions

You might be tempted to make the process of manifestation more difficult than it needs to be with preconditions to your contract. This problem is akin to the previous section wherein a skill might be required, however in this situation the motivation is not to acquire needed skills, but to obtain unnecessary credentials or experience. For example, you might decide that before you become an artist and sell your paintings, you need to study art history or get a degree in fine arts. The root of the problem is that you lack confidence in your abilities and feel that only a certificate or degree will give you credibility. God does not require a piece of paper for you to succeed and neither should you. Do not fall into the credentials trap. Occasionally, legitimate prerequisites will come up. Certification is necessary for certain professions such as in the medical or healthcare field, but if certification is not specifically required of you, be hesitant to place preconditions on yourself and your vision. There are innumerable "American dream" stories of individuals who dropped out of college or never completed their education but succeeded because they had an idea that would not wait. They made it big on passion and creativity and so can you.

Remedy: It is okay to acquire necessary skills. It is not okay to fabricate hollow preconditions to your vision and needlessly delay the manifestation process. Pieces of paper that do little more than add credibility to your efforts are a waste of time. Carefully assess your reasons for any precondition that you set. What will you gain? How much time will you lose? Does the precondition that you are setting involve a necessary skill? Is there a professional requirement that you need to adhere to? If the precondition you are setting does not involve a required skill or certification, why are you derailing your ability to move ahead? Do not delay the manifestation process over prerequisites you do not need.

7. Chaos, Disorganization and Other Distractions

When your life is chaotic and you function in a constant state of crisis management, you seriously limit your ability to move forward. Your vision will either be delayed or completely derailed. The process of manifestation through attraction and receptivity requires focus, and a focused, sustained thought. When your attention is scattered by daily disruptions, focus is lost repeatedly and the effectiveness of your thought becomes limited. Chaos makes it difficult to carve out enough quiet time to communicate clearly with your co-creative Partner. This impacts your creative potential. In addition, chaotic conditions keep you from perceiving opportunities as they arise and taking full advantage of them in a timely manner. As you know from the discussion of the flow, timing is very important. Chaos and the distractions it brings rob you of your true potential by reducing your ability to focus, communicate, create, and respond. The greater the chaos, the more negative the effect.

In regard to generalized disorganization, you cannot pursue a spiritual goal or vision while ignoring mundane physical needs such as health, finances, and personal relationships. You need to take care of your body; it is a temple for divinity and an important tool in the process of manifestation. When you are sick or disabled, your options can be limited. Pay your bills on time; you cannot expect to receive abundantly when you withhold from others. Relationships and families come with responsibilities especially when children or the elderly are involved. Fulfill your obligations with on open heart. Be kind and helpful to others. Heart Journey involves the integration of higher with lower, body with spirit, and the spiritual with the physical through an open and receptive heart. You cannot integrate what you disrespect and you cannot manifest without integration, balance, and heart openness.

Remedy: Before you can truly troubleshoot the cause of the chaos affecting your progress, a distinction needs to be made between the chaos you create and the chaos created by others. First, determine the source of the disruption. Second, determine what is a real, unavoidable crisis, (reflective of the flow), and what is artificially made and perpetuated disruption, (an indication of sabotage). Third, consider the appropriateness of your response to the disruption.

If you are the one generating the chaotic or disorganized conditions under which you live, then you are probably using the distractions as an excuse for not manifesting or doing your part in regard to your vision. You are avoiding the tasks before you, perhaps out of a fear of success. You need to reread Chapter 13: Sabotaging Fears and Other Negative Emotions.

If that information does not apply, it is possible that you have developed a life pattern of only succeeding when under pressure or faced with a deadline. Some individuals can't manifest until their backs are against the wall and they are running out of money, or faced with a similar crisis. This process is not manifestation through attraction and receptivity. This is manifestation born of desperation. Although it is true that the energy and activity associated with manifestation through attraction and receptivity generally rises shortly before materialization, desperation is not part of the equation. If you have a pattern of being a clutch player and can only manifest in an agitated frenzy, you can do better. Not only will you be less stressed, you will also be more productive.

If others are responsible for the chaos in your life, this can be an indication that the flow is not with you and your timing is off. Are the problems and crises involving others essentially unavoidable? Are they long standing and/or related to physical or mental illness, disability, accidents, young children, or elderly parents? Certain life problems mandate your attention and must be addressed. You should delay your vision if the flow is truly not with you anyway. (See Chapter 15: Delays, Interference and Incorrect Timing.) If the flow is with you, you must double your efforts, addressing unavoidable problems while also attending to your vision.

If the chaos and disorganization is unnecessary and perpetuated either consciously or unconsciously by others, you are being sabotaged and derailed by someone close to you. There may or may not be anything you can do about the behavior of others. You can try to address the issues with them or shield yourself, but in this situation self-empowerment will only occur when you assess the appropriateness of your responses to the interference. Do you enable this other person in some way? Do you cover or make things right for your saboteur? Let responsibility fall where it may. You do not have to do everything for everyone else before doing something for yourself. Your contract is not meant to make your responsible for everything and everyone in your life. It may be time to disengage. Move along so you can become a stronger person and inspiration for others, rather than a derailed, and probably ineffective savior.

8. Complexity

Complex visions and multi-staged endeavors are commonly associated with delayed gratification and necessitate major contributions on your part. The benefit of this slower pace is that it lends itself to major long-term projects and even life-long pursuits. This is where you get to dream big, but you will need to sustain your focused thought over the required length of time and make the appropriate adjustments in your vision for each stage of the process. Occasionally, all your skills and efforts will only produce minor progress while there are still many steps to take. Do not get discouraged. Keep in mind that because of the complexity of your vision, numerous factors have to come together for manifestation to occur. If instant gratification is the express train to manifestation, then choosing a complex vision gets you on the local. It is the nature of the vision. If you focus inward and communicate with your co-creative Partner, you will have a sense of the schedule, understand why this is so, and know what role you play in the step-by-step process.

On the other hand, you may be weary of the whole process. It is important to keep your vision simple. If matters are cumbersome or seem to be dragging on, you are probably aware of the wisdom in those words. A simple contract is best especially for your first attempt at manifestation through attraction and receptivity. An early success is advantageous in understanding how the process can work, but then a life-long passion can do a lot for a complex contract.

Remedy: There is truly no right or wrong in regard to simple or complex contracts, there is only what you choose to work with at any given time. If you are getting discouraged, you might wish to pare down, prioritize, reorganize, or break your contract down into steps or something more manageable. Revisit what you think you can handle and how to proceed.

9. Renegotiation

Renegotiation is the technique used when the manifestation that arises is not exactly what is wanted, but close. It is the best way to deal with unknown territory that reveals itself in increments. In this situation, manifestation itself frequently leads to a realization that new criteria need to come into play if you are to move closer to what you really want. Renegotiation is a back and forth, repeated specific request and co-creative response process that helps you refocus your thought again and again, and refine your desire. It can be a short term process or involve numerous steps.

Remedy: Everything is negotiable and if the first materialization is not a total success, you can adjust your desire, refocus your thought, (making it more to your liking), and request again. You can keep renegotiating and manifesting until you get exactly what you want. Just politely turn down inferior manifestations, thank God for the offering, but then restate your wish with the needed adjustments or upgrades. The goal is to keep improving and moving forward. When subsequent manifestations cease to improve or stop altogether, you know you have reached the endpoint.

Renegotiating your contract or vision is not for everyone and every situation. It certainly does delay manifestation through attraction and receptivity, but sometimes it is the best way to zero in on what you truly want when there are many unknowns. Renegotiation is best used for single or continuing adjustments to your already existing contract. The example below will give you good insight into this step-by-step process and how it will refine your vision.

Example of Renegotiation

John was a sedentary middle aged man. He realized he needed to join a health club and get some exercise. He was offered an unsolicited free visit to a local health club. John knew this was a sign that confirmed what his body was already telling him, so he made an appointment to visit the club.

The club was very nice. The people were friendly, but it was too expensive for his budget. The club wanted one hundred fifty dollars to join and forty dollars per month. John was a little disappointed, thanked God for the offer, but made a request for a cheaper club.

Much to his surprise, within days a coupon came in the mail for fifty percent off the membership fee at another club. So John called and made an appointment. The club was large and spacious with lots of equipment and a sauna. The membership fee was only fifty dollars to join with a thirty-five dollars monthly fee for a limited visit membership. The price was greatly improved, but John wanted unlimited visits. He also decided yoga, a Jacuzzi and steam bath would be nice. John chose to keep on looking. He thanked God for the offer, but requested a cheaper place that would have the extra amenities he liked.

This time John decided to help things along and take the initiative. He made a few calls when he got home. He immediately found a place with a steam bath, Jacuzzi and yoga. It was everything he wanted and the price was right, fifty dollars membership fee and thirty-three dollars per month with unlimited visitation. But it was farther from home than he wanted and it was not a clean establishment. John once again thanked God and said that everything was fine, but closer and cleaner would be better.

At this point the manager of the club he was visiting informed John that a new club had just opened closer to his home and he might wish to go see it. As it turned out, the new club was sunny and bright with a sauna, steam bath, and Jacuzzi. The cost was the same, fifty dollars membership fee with thirty-three dollars per month for unlimited visitation. They did not have yoga yet, but were in the process of negotiating with the teacher from the sister club. And the place was much cleaner.

John immediately signed on the dotted line. He knew this was the place for him. Though there had been delays in the process, he had stayed with it until completely satisfied. He negotiated and renegotiated his vision as he got closer and closer to what he wanted. Each step required gratitude for the previous manifestation and a refocused thought reflecting new insight and information. At each stage, John applied the right amount of effort to continue moving forward, but he also surrendered his desire and held it loosely until he got more of what he wanted. He did not jump at the first offer. Eventually he reached a point when he realized that the price was as low as it was going to go and only the majority of his expectations could be met. He got the fee that he wanted, but had to settle for the promise of yoga. This is as far as the manifestation process through attraction and receptivity would take him. Along the way he learned how to speed up the process by taking the initiative and placing a few telephone calls. John remained calm and unemotional throughout the process, and he stayed in the flow and in communication with his co-creative Partner.

If this had not worked out the way it did, if things had not been moving forward, John would have gone off in another direction. But as long as the path was somewhat fruitful and producing a better and better response, he continued. He ultimately got most of what he wanted through renegotiation, being grateful for what was offered, but then refocusing and refining his vision step-by-step.

10. Never Getting Started

It is so discouraging to come this far with your desire and focused, sustained thought, and not progress at all. You are stuck with only the first two elements needed for manifestation. The final two are missing. You have no sense of flow and you do not know what action you need to take, if at all. You think you are in the right place at the right time with the right vision, but nothing is happening and you do not understand why. You wonder if you are being impatient waiting for something to occur. Is the ball in God's court? Or, is the ball in your court and you are holding things up through your own inaction? Maybe you are meant to initiate the process in some unforeseen fashion you have not figured out yet. You need a plan for discerning the appropriate response and course of action.

Remedy: Depending on your vision and conditions, the ball is either in your court or in God's court. This is the most important determination you can make at this point if there has been no progress at all. You make this determination through a combination of communication with God, feedback from what is and is not working, and common sense. Here is the step-by-step course of action you should take:

1. Your Startup Plan

Given the nature of your vision, what would you be expected to do? This is a logical, common sense question. Many, but not all, visions come with well-defined tasks needed for manifestation to occur. For example, if you vision involves selling your home and moving, you need to put the house on the market. Do your research while in communication with your co-creative Partner. Interview agents, get recommendations, and look at the sales records of real estate companies in your area. Then discuss your findings and options with God before taking action, picking a realtor, setting a price, and signing a contract. Together, come up with a plan of action. Do your part first. If your vision has absolutely no recognizable start-up plan that you can initiate, move on to number two.

2. God's Plan

After you have done everything you can think of to start the process of manifestation, continue communication with God and discuss feedback you are getting from actions taken. Talk to God about what is and is not working. This helps to hone the plan of action. Co-creative time with God will also generate new insights. Through your discussions, further steps you can or need to take will be revealed. Complete all tasks. For example, you have your house on the market, but do not get any offers. While conferring with God, you might be drawn to place flyers around town or maybe you realize that the color on your dining room walls is not appealing. Augment your chances for success by expanding your options and taking corrective action in keeping with Divine communication.

If you had no conceivable startup plan, communication with God should yield some ideas on how to proceed. Complete those tasks. If after communicating with God, you still have no plan of action, you are expecting a lot from God. You are expecting results with no effort on your part. Hope for the best, surrender the results, and have a backup plan. The ball is definitely in God's court and your vision will either succeed or fail. For example, there was no way I was going to Sedona, Arizona without being given a ticket. (See Chapter 11: Example of Manifestation within the Flow.) I did not have the money or the means to earn the extra money at that time. I was out of ideas. After I made my request, I surrendered the outcome. My backup plan was to stay home. If you vision is totally dependent on God for manifestation and there is nothing for you to do, still stay in close communication with God until manifestation occurs or failure is obvious. The ball is in God's court.

3. Feedback Regarding Actions and the Need for Consistency

As you make changes in your attempts at manifestation through attraction and receptivity, pay attention to the flow. Are you aware of any kind of assistance? Are there any breakthroughs or positive signs? Are you gaining momentum? Can you see doors opening? Is there ease? These are signs of encouragement that should be consistent with positive indications in your communications with God. If so, keep going until you have done everything you and God think you should try. When you run out of things to do, the ball is in God's court.

On the other hand, suppose the feedback related to your attempts is consistently negative. You are not getting any assistance. You have no momentum and there is no ease. Everything you try fails immediately. You have to fall back on your communications from God for clarification. Are your exchanges encouraging? If so, then you can continue to discuss options and try new things; however, consistent negative feedback regarding your efforts coupled with encouragement from God is an inconsistency. At the very least, it is a call for a major review and perhaps a course correction. The danger is communication with your co-creative Partner is being distorted because you are not open to hearing the truth. Consistency between communications and your experience is a form of validation. Inconsistency denies confirmation and this can signal a problem. As long as new options and tasks arise in your communications with God, continue your efforts.

If the feedback related to your attempts is negative and communications from God are discouraging, or God is uncharacteristically silent on the matter, there is a major problem with your vision and you need to accept this. This is not a matter of who should be doing what. An explanation of the problem may or may not be given in your discussions with God and corrective action may or may not be possible. You should consider surrendering your vision completely.

4. Temporary Stoppage

Some visions span months or years. Periods of inactivity are not only possible, but likely. When progress is difficult or the flow is interrupted regarding a major project, be patient. Move forward when restrictions lift and the flow returns. Either you or God will need to take the first step, but before that, you will sense a change in conditions and movement in the flow.

If you are waiting on others who are dragging their feet, you can make contact and inquire as to when decisions might be made or supplies might arrive, etc. You can offer assistance, but if matters are totally out of your hands, then the ball is not in your court. You must wait unless you can find another source or avenue for manifestation. For those who are forced to wait, the delayed timing might be beneficial.

5. Testing the Waters

When you are stopped or delayed and unsure as to who should make the first move, you can test the waters by taking action. Adhere to the "Rule of Three" stated in Chapter 10: Communication Guidelines. After three attempts, rest and wait for conditions to change or improve.

11. Lack of Financial Support

If there is one factor that seems to delay or derail contracts and visions more than any other in regard to the avenue for manifestation, it is the real or imagined lack of money. A perceived financial deficit raises anxiety and weakens trust in your co-creative Partner. It is the major reason why some people throw in the towel and completely give up on their vision.

Money should never be the goal of your vision, though it might be the result of your efforts upon completion of your project. You are more likely to feel the pinch while you are working on your contract, especially if your contract is a long, involved process. If your vision will require a lot of your time, you have to figure out beforehand how to sustain yourself during the process. It is never wise to quit your job and cut off all financial support just because you have a dream. It is better to think ahead and plan for living expenses. You may have to quit your job if you need to attend school, move to a different location, or make some other drastic change, but do not leap off the financial cliff expecting God to catch you. Proceed with caution until you are absolutely sure what you and God have determined together is the best way to proceed and how to support yourself in the meantime.

Remedy: It is not the intention of Heart Journey for people to go into debt in order to manifest. One of the rewards of Heart Journey and an open heart is abundance which may include financial abundance both in the end and along the way. If it does occur, then it is a gift, but it is not to be expected or depended upon. It is also counter-intuitive to Heart Journey to sink into debt. It is true that some individuals will need to pay for education or training. Others may have to take on financial responsibilities in the form of rent or equipment costs if they are opening a business. The amount of money you must put in or generate is related to the path and vision you have chosen. Even in those situations it is best to first look for scholarships, grants, and financial assistance. In most situations, you will get some help if you are on the right track. If you are not receiving any assistance or financial breaks at all, this might be a sign that the flow is not with you at this time. In the ideal situation, you will have financial reserves or income (that you spend wisely) to sustain yourself throughout the process. This might be in the form of a job you continue to hold, a savings account, or trust.

If you are anxious about money, but you still have food in the cupboard, a roof over your head, clothes on your back, and money in the bank, keep going. There are numerous stories of spiritual seekers who got what they needed financially at the last possible moment. Your focus should be on whether or not you are on the right track and moving with the flow, not on the money. God will not ask you to be hungry, homeless, naked, and penniless. It is not a requirement and will not happen unless you mismanage your time, energy, and resources. The greater your dedication and effort to the manifestation process and the sooner you complete your tasks, the less likely you are to have financial issues.

12. Lack of Moral or Ethical integrity

It should be obvious by now that Heart Journey is a spiritual path built on moral and ethical integrity. You cannot manifest through attraction and receptivity until you are right with yourself, right with others, and right with God. It does not matter if you can justify your actions in your mind. Right is still right and wrong is still wrong. In most cases there is a very clear line dividing the two. If you have gone through all the items up until this point, and still have not found an answer, it is time to look more closely at moral and ethical integrity.

You cannot attract, receive, and manifest when you are less than honorable. This includes being honest with yourself, principled toward others, and virtuous before God. This is not to put ethics and morals out of the reach of most people, but it is to instill ownership. You are responsible for your actions. The simplest thing can lower your ability to manifest when you step outside the lines. For example, do you owe money that you refuse to repay? You cannot expect to receive abundance when you withhold what is due others. Do you download or share copyrighted material, (movies, music, or books) illegally? It is stealing and it does create a karmic debt. When you are frustrated or had a bad day at work, do you take it out on others, creating unnecessary pain, pain that did not have to exist? Do you take advantage of those weaker than you? Are you unfaithful to vows and promises you have made? Are you prejudiced? Are your business practices unfair, dishonest, or simply lacking full disclosure?

These are just a few examples of situations, thoughts and actions that might appear to be outside the realm of Heart Journey but can actually lower your ability to attract, receive, and manifest even when you have done everything else right. The road forks; choose wisely.

Remedy: Only you and God will know the truth regarding personal integrity. Enter the silence and take a moral and ethical inventory with your co-creative Partner.

The Delicate Art of Skillful Navigation

Manifesting through the power of attraction and receptivity is like assisting the process of birth. Think of yourself as the gentle midwife. Too little force and nothing happens. At the right moment you must encourage the mother to push the baby out. Too much force and trauma results. Pushing too soon can injure the baby or the mother. Appropriate action must be taken at the correct time and this may include a period of waiting and doing nothing. During labor and delivery, a gentle midwife practices the delicate art of skillful navigation, guiding the mother in the best way to bring her baby into the world, and honoring both the woman and the birth process which is unique to each labor.

In the same way, you are a gentle midwife when you seek to manifest through attraction and receptivity. You must honor the inherent uniqueness in each manifestation process by complementing and synchronizing all your movements to what is emerging. You must apply the right amount of force and effort at the appropriate time. Pay attention to subtleties. Continuously monitor what needs to be done, and counteract any tendency toward resistance, disruption, and stagnation. You must be aware of emotional undertones such as anger or fear, in self or others, that could impede the process. All inhibitions and resistances need to be counteracted, all traumas need to be gentled, and all stagnations need to be fueled. Keep the environment calm and minimize distractions. Your goal is to smooth the way by staying in the flow and in close communication with your co-creative Partner while completing the final steps.

The midwife involved with the birth of a child needs to be aware of the rise and fall of energy in regards to the birthing process itself. In most instances, birth cannot proceed without increased energy and intensity. Immediately before the baby is born, when the mother is in the stage of labor called transition, the mother's contractions increase in frequency and strength. The midwife knows the signs of transition and assists the mother most closely from this time until the actual birth, making sure everything proceeds successfully. As the baby descends into the birth canal, the mother begins the hard work of pushing the baby out. This is why birthing is referred to as labor.

The same is true of manifestation through attraction and receptivity. Generally, the energy increases in intensity and frequency shortly before manifestation and this shift characterizes the stage of transition. An increase in energy may appear as stress, tension, desire, frustration, anger, excitement, or any other emotion. Circumstances may become more chaotic. The intensity will last until the process is complete and manifestation is fulfilled, or the individual backs down in fear and abandons the project. The high energy transitional stage is the one most crucial step to the manifestation process, and the one subject to the greatest amount of resistance, disruption, or stagnation. Even if you have been watchful and steady up until this point, this will be your greatest challenge.

All the impediments mentioned in this chapter can appear or reappear during this transitional stage, the final steps toward manifestation and materialization. Recognize the signs and do not retreat. Also, do not cause trauma by rushing ahead, trying to get through the process quickly. Each manifestation has its own timing. Do not get distracted or discouraged at the most important moment of the journey. Remain focused. Gently guide your vision (through the birth canal) into manifestation. A steady pace during the transitional stage allows for maximum insight into the mystery of manifestation through attraction and receptivity.

Chapter Seventeen:
Health, Healing, & Death

Disclaimer

Although healing, health issues, and even death will be discussed in this chapter, in no way should any information in this book, and especially in this chapter, be taken as medical advice or a substitute for good medical care. I am not a doctor. I do not prescribe and I do not advocate any course of treatment over another. For my own healing, I have used both traditional and alternative medicine. I have sought help from medical doctors, naturopaths, massage therapists, chiropractors, acupuncturists, herbalists, and practitioners in a number of different modalities. I generally do not limit my treatment plan to only one form of care. I stay involved, ask questions, and make conscious health choices.

Furthermore, the stories of co-creative healing presented here are strictly my own and should not be used to treat anyone else. No recommendations are implied. I have specifically left out complete treatment information so others will not be tempted to follow my routines regarding any illness of their own. Though illnesses may appear similar, each case is different and each person is different. Healing is individualistic and can be as mystical as manifestation through attraction and receptivity. For this reason, it cannot be taught, only experienced.

In all honesty, my success with my own healing has not been 100%. Sometimes it has worked beautifully and at other times it has not. Some problems were easy to heal, some took a long time, others were impossible to heal without serious intervention. I cannot tell you why. Healing and the ability to heal differ from person to person, and illness to illness.

Bringing God into the Healing Process

One of the greatest comforts in my life has been the communications with God during times of illness. Co-creative efforts are never a substitute for seeking medical help with health problems, but I believe God should not be left out of the healing process either. Once you develop a strong co-creative partnership, use it in every area of your life, (not just for manifestation through attraction and receptivity), and especially in the process of healing. A strong exchange with God can be invaluable in times of illness. Don't just pray for individual healing. Pray that your doctors, nurses, dentists, and therapists will be guided to make the best recommendations regarding your care. Pray God will oversee and inspire their work. Invite God to your doctors' appointments and into surgery. Everything goes better with God! Work together as a trio, you, your co-creative Partner, and your healthcare professional to determine the best course of treatment. If there are options and decisions to be made, discuss the pros and cons with your provider and also with God. Then make the best decision based on all the information provided.

Illness and Causality

Some illnesses have known physical causes and some do not. Besides bacteria, viruses, toxins, smoking, alcoholism, drug addiction, genetics, and vitamin deficiencies, diet and a lack of exercise can be causal agents as well as contributing factors to physical decline and disease. But then, the origin of some diseases is unknown.

Some illnesses have emotional or psychological underpinnings and some do not. Our thinking patterns can have a direct causal effect on our bodies, but this is not always the case. Some individuals become ill in the prime of life when they are at their happiest and most fulfilled. There seems to be no causal agent; no rhyme or reason. Disease, like healing, can be a mystery that is not fully understood.

Physical Contributions to Disease

It is a great disservice to anyone who is sick to assume that s/he in some way caused an illness. Numerous factors contribute to disease including genetic and environmental factors as well as unknown influences. Many of us have an Achilles heel, an inborn organ weakness that frequently requires attention, especially when we are stressed. Maybe it's a weak stomach, irritable intestines, or a tendency towards heart disease. We all deal with something that may or may not lend itself to healing regardless of the attention we give it or the care we seek.

Personally, I was born with an enamel defect on my permanent teeth, a condition I inherited from my father. I can pray and practice healing techniques till the cows come home to no avail when it comes to my mouth. I brush, I floss, use mouthwash, and a waterpick. I have regular checkups and cleanings with limited success. Trips to the dentist are always surprise-filled adventures. I never know what new calamity the dentist will discover. He has discovered things I have never even heard of, technical names I barely remember. He takes pictures and probably discusses my teeth at conventions. I have had perfectly good teeth die without ever having had a cavity or injury. Sometimes procedures had to be done a second time. For some reason, the best dental care did not work the first time around. It is just the way it is with my mouth. I accept it and make sure I get good dental care and serious professional intervention to keep my teeth healthy. There is no emotional reason for these problems. They are not related to stress or nutrition. I can find no cause other than genetic roulette. At this point, I do not beg God for healing, but I always ask for God's help when I go to the dentist.

Sometimes disease just is, without a known physical cause, and occasionally without a known physical cure. If you are ill, certainly discuss this with your co-creative Partner. Healing may not be possible, but comfort is.

Emotional Contributions to Disease

Though one should never judge, it is true that some illnesses have a direct emotional correlation. Generally, the emotional influence is not the only factor, but a contributor to an already existing imbalance. It is the straw that breaks the camel's back and tips the scale over past imbalance into disease. The good news is that if there is a direct emotional connection to a health challenge, chances of healing increase if the connection can be ascertained and the complex dismantled.

Example of Physical Healing

It was the Ides of March many years ago when a spot appeared on my cheek. At first I thought it was an age spot, but over the next 30 days it grew to be the size of a pencil eraser, red and inflamed. In mid-April, a piece of this sore on my face fell off into the sink. I was very distraught and immediately made an appointment with my primary physician. He diagnosed the sore as skin cancer and said it needed to be cut out. Although I had not been to the beach or sunbathed in years, my grandmother had a cottage on the Connecticut shore, and I was a regular in my teens and rarely wore sun protection then or as an adult. I was referred to a dermatologist and a plastic surgeon. I left the primary physician's office knowing that I did not want to have surgery. I knew I formed ugly scars from previous surgeries and I did not want a scar on my face.

I went home and made an appointment with the dermatologist. I had to wait five weeks for the first opening. Then I called the plastic surgeon and had to wait three months to be seen. I was worried about the wait. If this sore had grown so big and ugly in 4 weeks, what would it look like by the time I got to the dermatologist or the plastic surgeon? How much of my face would have to be cut by then?

I was not well versed in the co-creative process at this time. In fact, this diagnosis might have triggered the beginning of my co-creative health exchanges. I felt lost and alone, unsure of what to do next. I did not know who to turn to other than God in Whom I placed my trust. So when I laid down that night, I said this prayer:

"I don't know what to do. I don't know how to call you. I don't know how to ask or what to expect. But I know you can hear me, and I am begging you now to help me heal. I do not want a scar on my face. Please come and tell me what to do."

The most beautiful vibration came over me and I slept in this vibration all night long. I have since come to recognize this vibration as a healing energetic pattern. It is not the only pattern I have ever experienced; there are many and some are uncomfortable. Sometimes pain intensifies before it is corrected. Sometimes healing is all mental insight without any physical sensation at all. But I open to it. I trust it and I am never afraid.

I saw many things during that first night. I was aware of the emotional contribution I was making to the presence of the cancer. I was hurt by a failing relationship and I had fallen into a victim mentality. I was literally wearing my hurt on my cheek for all the world to see. I realized this was foolish because the other party did not care one bit about my face, while I would be left with a scar. Seeing this folly, I immediately began to dismantle this counterproductive emotional complex I was caught in. As I have stated before in these pages, "Don't get angry, don't get even. Get enlightened and empowered! Would you rather wallow like a victim or create the life you want?" I needed to move on. I got it mentally, then emotionally, and inculcated the learning into my physical being by vowing never to go there again emotionally. I was not a victim. I was a strong and empowered woman. I would not let a failed relationship define my life, my fate, or my face. This turn around was fairly quick and easy to make on an emotional level.

Pulling the plug on the emotional element to my skin cancer helped, but it would not remove the growth on its own. Years of being a beach baby were also a factor working against me. During the night I worked out a plan with this intelligent healing force God was pouring through me that included nutritional changes and topical creams. I began my new routine the first thing the next morning. During the coming weeks, I checked in daily with God concerning my progress. Slowly the sore began to heal and change from raw red to healing pink.

Five weeks later, as I was walking into the dermatologist's office, I begged God,

"Please, I do not want to be cut. I would rather use a topical chemotherapy cream on the skin cancer. And while You are at it, I don't want to have skin cancer at all."

After the exam, the dermatologist stated I had solar keratosis, a pre-cancerous condition. She wanted to do laser treatments to remove the sore, but my insurance would not cover it. She wanted to cut it out, but I told her I formed keloid scars. She decided on a chemotherapy cream, thank God! She told me my skin would become very inflamed when I used the cream.

I left the office thrilled, and as I walked out, I thanked God, but mentioned that now I did not even want solar keratosis. "Just get rid of this sore, please!" I used the cream for the prescribed 4 weeks. Nothing happened. My skin never reacted to the topical chemotherapy as it should, there was no rawness, no weeping sore, but the growth totally healed and went away. When I returned, the dermatologist was dumbfounded and did not know what to think. She decided that she and the previous doctor must have misdiagnosed a case of eczema.

After three months, my appointment with the plastic surgeon finally came up. By this time the sore had disappeared completely, leaving no trace. I asked the plastic surgeon what course of action she would have taken had I come to her with anything suspicious. She said she would have cut it out or at least taken a biopsy. Either way, I would have had a scar.

I am very grateful to God for this experience, the healing, and also the delay. The delay in both appointments allowed my face to heal without surgery and a scar. At first I was very concerned about the long wait for treatment, but my mind was at ease after my communications with my co-creative Partner. I knew to be patient. After only two weeks, I was also able to see positive changes in my face from my new routine and the dismantling of the emotional hurt that underscored the skin cancer.

Health Warnings

Some diseases and symptoms manifest as warnings of present or future serious illness. These warnings are a blessing from God and need to be recognized and honored as such. They are meant to save you pain and suffering, and may even save your life. Sometimes the warnings lead you to discover a more serious hidden condition that must be addressed. Sometimes the warnings notify you that you need to take corrective action before it is too late.

For example, Tim had indigestion and heartburn. While investigating what was thought to be a case of acid reflux, doctors took an x-ray that uncovered an aortic aneurysm related to a genetic heart defect that needed immediate attention and surgery. Aneurysms occur when a blood vessel weakens and balloons. By the time the blood vessel ruptures, it is already too late. The individual bleeds to death within minutes. Aneurysms are silent killers. They have no symptoms or forewarning. Although some doctors recommend screenings for aneurysms in elderly patients, Tim was too young to be considered at risk. In addition, Tim had never complained of chest pain or shortness of breath, and he had regular checkups that included heart monitoring and EKGs. There were no cardiac symptoms and the aneurysm never would have been discovered were it not for the persistent indigestion and heartburn Tim complained of.

In Tim's case, the only option was corrective heart surgery, but Brian's warning symptom lead to a call for lifestyle and dietary changes. Brian was in his late fifties and very overweight when he began to notice changes in his eyesight. Brian's lifestyle was sedentary and his diet consisted of fast food, sodas, sweets, and snacks. He had not been to a doctor in years and had no intention of going. Instead, he decided to get new glasses. Fortunately, he went to someone who recognized the signs of diabetes in his eyes. This was a wake-up call for Brian. Not only was his health in danger, his vision was being negatively impacted. He saw this warning as a blessing. He scheduled a complete physical, consulted with a nutritionist and began an exercise routine. Brian knew he had to make major changes to avoid the serious consequences commonly associated with diabetes.

A Different Kind of Healing

Healing is not just about the process of recovering from illness, it is also about the healing professionals you draw to you for assistance. It is essential to have caregivers you respect and trust. It is also important to understand what your body can or cannot handle in regard to treatment. In addition to allergies to medications, know the techniques and substances that work best. Find a good fit for preventive and also remedial care.

Example of Finding a Healer

I struggled with perimenopause for many years. I suspect it's a family tradition. I hemorrhaged several times. The last time was excessive and I called my gynecologist's office and left a message regarding the hemorrhage before they opened on Thursday morning. My call was not returned by the next morning. I was aware that my gynecologist was leaving Friday afternoon for vacation, so I called my primary physician and left a message with the nurse explaining what had happened. Though things had quieted down a bit, I was still bleeding heavily and thought I should be seen. Five o'clock Friday afternoon I realized that no one had returned my calls and now everyone had left for the weekend. I was faced with the choice of going to an emergency room if needed, and if matters continued unabated, I would probably be hospitalized by Monday morning. I needed to take action.

So I walked into my home office, looked up at the ceiling and said, "God, I need an herbalist now. Now, God!" I requested an herbalist because I did not want to go to a stranger in an emergency room. I did not want to have surgery to remove my uterus, nor did I want the inside of my uterus cauterized. I don't do well with most medications or hormone replacement. Natural has always been better for me. Exactly two hours later, at seven o'clock, the phone rang. When I answered a voice said,

> "My name is Lynn Shumake and you do not know me, but I am a pharmacist and an herbalist. My daughter works with your son and he happened to mention the trouble you have been having. My wife had the same problem last year and I think I can help."

Lynn invited me to his home and gave me a tour of his medicinal garden. I came home with samples and instructions for various teas to make and sip. After twenty-one days of bleeding and two hemorrhages, the bleeding stopped completely in less than 24 hours after starting the herbs. My primary physician called Monday morning and I scheduled an appointment with him, but by then it was all over. He ran blood tests that confirmed the blood lost. Though weak, I began to recover quickly and the problem grew less and less serious from that point on.

Healers and Healing

I do believe in the power of prayer and I have seen its effect first hand. There was a woman in my neighborhood who was in a terrible automobile accident. She was in a comma and not expected to live more than twenty-four hours. Her husband arranged for a prayer vigil among family and friends. They prayed continuously for a number of days and nights. She eventually came out of the comma and began to recover. I would see her walking around the block with her husband during her rehabilitation. She had a slight limp and walked with a cane, but her survival was a testament to the power of prayer.

I also believe that some people have special healing powers and I have sought their assistance from time to time. I have had sessions with Reiki healers, attended Catholic healing masses, and experienced energy so strong my knees buckled and I slid to the floor. My advice is to seek out reputable people who are committed to healing, attribute their gift to God, *and* come highly recommended. Do not go into this kind of healing blindly. Know who you are dealing with.

Routines for Weight Loss, Addictions, and Good Health

You can use the co-creative partnership to assist and support you in any health matter including losing weight, however, you must have first established strong and clear communication with God. Follow a God-modified plan as long as it is a nutritionally sound diet and you are under professional medical care. Do not attempt to "go off road" with some crazy, lopsided, quick-loss eating scheme. God will only participate in a diet that is for your highest good and meant to improve your health.

For best results, start with a proven dietary program. There are many available. God can help you co-creatively choose the best program and medical supervision before you begin. Once you have both in place, seek God's input on how to customize the program to meet your individual health and dietary needs. Be prepared to stick with the program and only eat what is on the menu. I can remember reaching for a sugary soda while dieting and hearing the thought voice say, "Don't even think about it!" Discuss the shopping list with your co-creative Partner before shopping and then only buy from the list unless there is something vital you just did not think of beforehand. Co-create a daily or weekly menu based on your doctor's or healthcare professional's advice. In addition to selecting the foods to eat, also discuss the amounts to eat and when to dine or snack. Planning is everything. Follow up with regular professional supervision and discuss your results, successes, or failures with your co-creative Partner. Based on your progress, make further modifications to your weight loss plan.

Your desire to lose weight is your vision. Your focused and sustained thought is the daily routine you plan to establish and follow to reach your goal. This might involve eliminating certain foods from your diet, restricting calories, and exercising. A prayer increases God's moment to moment support and enhances the flow, making the process easier. Daily menu planning, food selection, behavior modification, and your new health routine are all part of the avenue of manifestation. Though you pray for God's assistance daily, and even regularly throughout your day, you still have to do the work and supply the will power. That ball is firmly in your court.

High calorie, fat laden, salty and sugary snacks probably won't be on the plan. They never were on my co-created dieting menu. God created nutritious and healing vegetables, fruits, grains and proteins for a reason and they are still favorites.

This co-creative health format can be used for a variety of more serious issues including smoking, alcoholism, or substance abuse, and has always been a part of many programs such as Alcoholics Anonymous, Overeaters Anonymous, Narcotics Anonymous, etc. You will find that spiritual influence is part of many healing programs which recognize the assistance of a Higher Power. Remember to always seek medical or professional guidance. God is a co-creative Partner, and "co" is the operative pre-fix here. God is not sole-creative Partner. The more professional expertise and trained medical assistance you bring to bear on a health issue or crisis, the greater the likelihood of success. Breaking an addiction is not something you can or should attempt to do on your own. Let God guide you in attracting the best doctors or professional team to develop a sound individualized treatment plan. Then pray for support and insight while on the program as you work toward recovery, healing, and good health.

On Death and Dying

When faced with a life-threatening illness or death itself, the co-creative Partnership can be a great comfort. If you have already established strong and frequent communication, God can assist you in the passage, guiding you each step of the way. The more established the relationship, the less frightening death will appear because of the trust and faith co-creative experiences have given you. The mystical journey of opening your heart and receiving abundance within a co-creative relationship will grow into a mystical union as you pass away and cross over to the next stage. Your co-creative Partner can assist you in a number of ways. Besides helping you cope with physical illness and discomfort, God can help you gently release worldly cares and connect to familiar or welcoming experiences on the other side. Benefits can be three-fold.

1. Physical assistance with the illness

Ask for assistance with your condition and any discomfort or pain. Be clear in regard to what will give you the greatest relief while you are still in the body. Discuss options with God and pray that your doctors, caregivers and hospice workers will be inspired and honor your transition as sacred. Tell God when you are in pain and where it hurts. This helps to focus the co-creative attention in the right area.

2. Letting go

When you know you are about to pass over, ask God to help you and your family prepare. We have birth coaches in this country, but we do not have death coaches. Ask God to enlighten you to your individual process. Release any regrets, guilt, anger, or negativity. You do not want to carry these with you. Seek to heal broken relationships. Know that you are forgiven regardless of what does or does not happen, and regardless of how others respond. If your heart is open and you are forgiving, then you will be forgiven and healed. God can help prepare your friends and family for letting go as you will need their support during the crossing.

3. Your journey to the other side

As you finalize your life here, begin to state your preferences regarding the passage. You may request a special person or being to greet you and lead you home. You may see and become familiar with this person in your final weeks. It is also common to see angels and spirits before crossing over. Ask for glimpses of what it will be like. You may go in and out of dream-like visions or have a dry run before you finally leave. Know that there is great beauty and an abundance of love on the other side. Different body sensations and tingling that you experience may be part of the transition.

Example of the Power of Love in the Afterlife

I have no fear of death since an awakening when my children were young. My oldest child was in school and I had just dropped my younger son off at nursery school. I was driving home when I was touched by the most beautiful energy. It shot right through my body and I knew with every fiber of my being that I was very loved. The love I felt at that moment was a million times greater than anything I could even imagine here on earth. I immediately recognized this love as that place where we exist before, between, or after life. We do not think of love as a place, but that is how I experienced it. I pulled off the road and began to weep with the beauty of it all, it was so overwhelming. Despite my wonderful life, despite my husband and children who I loved dearly, I said, "Take me now! I am ready." The pull was that great, that attractive. I was ready to give it all up.

It was not my time, but I hope that when I do surrender into death, that it is as welcoming and loving as what I experienced years ago. Those who pass on leave their pain, worries, and limitations behind to go to a glorious place. As painful as it is to see them leave, there should be great joy in the going and I believe it is important to give them permission to transition.

Example - Uncle Frank's Journey Out of Dementia and into Glory

I needed a new kitchen floor. The old one had been damaged by horizontal rain coming in under the doorway and through the key hole. While I was in the flooring showroom, speaking with a salesman I had just met, he looked up from his calculations and said, "Who's Frank?"

"Excuse me?" I replied.

The salesman repeated the question, "Who's Frank? He is standing right next to you."

There was no one standing next to me.

The salesman went on, "He says his name is Frank and he has something wrong with the right side of his face."

I suddenly realized who the salesman was talking about. There was no mistaking the description. My Uncle Frank had been hit in the side of the face by an airplane propeller during World War II. The blow had knocked him unconscious, off the aircraft carrier and into the ocean. Fortunately, another seaman immediately jumped into the water and saved his life. He had trouble with the nerves in his face from that time on. My uncle was 90 years old at the time and had lived with advanced dementia for the last ten years. My mother had called me the previous evening to tell me that her brother was in heart failure and not expected to live much longer.

I replied, "You mean my Uncle Frank."

"He is shaking his head yes," said the salesman. "He wants you to know that he is okay and happy. He is glad to be free."

My uncle passed away the next morning. It was a great comfort to me and my mother to know that even though he could no longer speak or communicate, he was already safe and on the other side before he stopped breathing. It was a gentle ending to a devastating disease.

When people get close to death, it is common for them to have a little extra energy just before they go. They may open their eyes and speak physically, saying goodbye, or they may project as my uncle did.

Example - The Nature of Choice at the Moment of Death

I was dressing for my son's graduation from college. As I dropped the dress over my head and onto my shoulders, the thought voice in my head said, "This is the dress I will wear to the funeral!" As far as I knew, no one was to die, but at the time my mother-in-law had been in and out of the hospital with an undiagnosed illness.

Several weeks later, I spoke with her in a dream. I don't dream much and rarely remember my dreams, but I remembered this one. My children, husband and I had come for a visit and were about to leave. Everyone was already in the car, but I was still on the sidewalk talking with my mother-in-law. While she was saying goodbye and how glad she was to see us all, she also spoke to me telepathically. Her message was, "I need to be alone to die." In the dream, I nodded that I understood, then I got in the car and we left.

When my mother-in-law entered the hospital again, I began daily long-distance Reiki treatments on her with her permission. I also prayed for her recovery. She was finally diagnosed with a life-threatening problem needing corrective surgery. She was given a 50% chance of survival which later dropped to 10% once she was being operated on. Before going into surgery she told her children that she had lived a good life and if the recovery would be difficult or if she would never fully recover, she would rather not wake up from the operation.

At the time of the surgery, I sat down to do another Reiki session on her and saw a seven foot angel of blue light hovering over her body. In that instant I also saw the array of choices she was being given. They were limited. I wept as I saw her struggle with a long recovery and knew she would never be the same. I saw what she saw in her superconscious state and then, as I watched, she chose death as the gentlest path. As she lifted toward the angel, she released all worries, all doubts, and everything that would hold her here. She was happy and free and I was glad for her.

This was the third and final confirmation of her passing, along with the thought voice and the dream. But having very little experience with death at the time, I went outside and asked God for one more sign. At that very moment a mourning dove descended on the roof of my house and began to moan. I thanked God and prepared for her passing. She came out of surgery in good health, or so we all thought. She seemed to rally, like many of those close to death, but then died several days later. She never recovered consciousness.

There is freedom in dying, choice in the process, and love as a reward for the crossing.

Example - My Father's Passage into the Hands of the Angels

My father died of vascular dementia. He had numerous small strokes late in life which primarily affected him physically. Though he seemed to be able to remember some things, he first lost the ability to walk, then the ability to move around in bed, and finally the ability to swallow. Communication was limited, but he was clear that he did not want a feeding tube to prolong his life.

He was in a nursing facility at the time of his death. I would visit daily and stay for long periods of time. He was very sick and weak for almost a year. He had good days and bad days. Periodically he would rally, but then he would start to fail again. My sister was away on business at the beginning of his last decline, but generally she was also a daily visitor. While home and asleep in the early hours of a November Thursday morning, my father called my name. I instantly woke up. Then he said, "Two days!" I knew he was getting ready to pass over, but I was horrified to think that he might pass while my sister was out of town. I watched him closely over the next few days and though he did not die, he took a major turn for the worse on Saturday. My sister returned from business later that night. The following Monday morning Dad again woke me up at one o'clock in the morning. This time I saw him in beautiful golden lights. Four golden angels were picking him up and lifting my father's golden spirit body out of his physical body. I quickly got dressed and rushed to the nursing home. My father was sleeping peaceful with my brother at his side. It occurred to me that, like my Uncle Frank, my father was already in transition. I like to think that he essentially left that night though physically he lingered until the early hours of Friday morning. He died with family at his side. It was not the easiest death to watch and we did our best to ease his passage. I take great comfort in the vision he sent to me and the possibility that he was not aware of any distress because he was already gone.

Part Three:
Spiritual Development
and Heart Openings

Chapter Eighteen:
Twelve Co-creative Thoughts

Introduction

Heart Journey is both mundane and sacred. On one hand, there is the manifestation process and on the other hand, there is the co-creative partnership with God. Taken together, these two teachings result in profound psychological and spiritual changes.

In Part One: The Initiation, you stated your desire, formulated your potent focused thought, and ritualized the signing of your contract.

In Part Two: The Co-creative Partnership and Manifestation Process, you practiced surrender, sustained your potent focused thought, established a co-creative partnership with God, and learned the key elements to manifestation through attraction and receptivity within the flow.

In Part Three: Spiritual Development and Heart Openings, there is still much to discover and master. In this chapter, Twelve Co-creative Thoughts, you will learn to alchemically transform limiting thought patterns into enlightened co-creative ways of thinking, feeling, and acting. The newly transformed thoughts will support and enhance the co-creative partnership, heart opening, and the process of manifestation.

In Chapter Nineteen: Eight Stages of the Heart Opening, the levels of heart openness will be discussed. Opening your heart more fully to the process of attracting and receiving eventually leads to the possibility of channeling and generating abundance not only for yourself, but also for your family, friends, co-workers, and the world. To attain the highest level of heart openness with the hope of generating abundance, you must maximize your ability to love yourself, others, and God. The three loves combined and in balance are accelerants in the process of manifestation through attracting, receiving, channeling, and generating. The ability to love completely and unconditionally sets the stage for true devotion to God.

> "Verily, I say unto you, inasmuch as ye have done it unto one of the least of these my brethren, ye have done it unto me." (Matthew 25:40, KJV of The Holy Bible).

Transforming your thinking and opening your heart completely are spiritual lessons innate to any mystical path including Heart Journey. They lead to a sense of oneness, human with Divine, and the experience of God as the Beloved. Although much of the journey has involved changing your thinking and perception, it is love that leads you to the possibility of a mystical union with God.

Twelve Alchemical Thought Transformations

This chapter focuses on the twelve limiting, negative, and counterproductive thought patterns common to most people. You will need to alchemically transform these "leaded" thoughts into "golden" or more enlightened co-creative and loving thoughts, in the same manner in which an alchemist was believed to transform lead into gold. The old ways of thinking, (and also feeling and behaving), are not suitable for Heart Journey or any journey into mysticism. They impede your heart opening and thwart spiritual growth. The twelve counterproductive and limiting thought patterns presented here underlie negative emotions and misguided behaviors. They support your right to feel jealous, angry, fearful, and many other forms of negativity, all of which are inconsistent with open-hearted lovingness. They justify actions that undermine the co-creative partnership. These thought patterns and their accompanying emotions and behaviors represent the efforts of the ego to control others and circumstances, while defending its right to exist separate and distinct from everyone else. In truth, you are not separate, but part of a whole, a dynamic whole, a Divine whole. The twelve limiting thought patterns are traps and if they are not recognized and transformed into their enlightened counterpart, they will foster resistance that blocks spiritual development, mystical insight, unconditional lovingness, and the potential for abundance.

In most cases, you will be letting go of lower thought patterns you do not need or want, and embracing corresponding higher, spiritual thoughts that will provide insight into your heart opening and enhancements to the process of manifestation. Some of the twelve thought transformations may seem easy for you; some will be more difficult. They are arranged in order from the easiest to the most challenging. Slight individual differences apply, but it is best to take them in the order presented and one by one. Work with one thought transformation at a time, keeping it foremost in your mind and counteracting negativity by practicing the new alchemical thought pattern for a month. Place cues in your home and work environment along with your contract and vision as reminders of the transformation you are seeking to make that month. At the end of the month, move on to the next co-creative thought. You are not expected to master any of the co-creative thought transformations in such a short time. These transformations are like life-long callings. There are layers and layers of spiritual insight and growth innate to each new co-creative thought pattern. In the beginning, awareness in and of itself is considered progress, a step in the right direction.

Work your way through all twelve over a year's time, and then begin again. Progress with one transformation supports progress with others as all twelve are interrelated. They build on one another and work together. Each round will awaken your heart further and deepen your experience.

1st Co-Creative Thought Transformation

Old thought: The Do-It-Yourself Fantasy
Alchemical transformation: Learning to Attract, Opening to Receive

This is the first alchemical thought transformation that turns mental lead into co-creative gold. The old thought pattern is the "Do-it-yourself Fantasy" or if you will, you have to earn it and go get it yourself. This process is straight cause and effect reality. You do the work and you get the results in keeping with your efforts and skills, period. This self-will manifestation program requires a step-by-step plan and a prioritized to-do list. Once you formulate your plan, you write up your list, roll up your sleeves, and work hard to get the results. But, straight cause and effect reality is not the only process available. It is the active mode for manifestation, but manifestation does not have to be solely active. There are also passive, attractive, and receptive means and modes for manifesting that you can learn, practice, and master.

In Part Two: The Co-creative Partnership and Manifestation Process, you learned that you do not have to do it all yourself. Manifestation does not necessarily involve a long to-do list that you push your way through item-by-item. You can manifest through the process of attraction and receptivity, sharing the load and responsibility with your co-creative Partner. You have already begun to shift out of the first old leaded thought pattern and into the new golden co-creative thought pattern you need to develop which is, "Learning to Attract, Opening to Receive." Through your Heart Journey contract and the co-creative Partnership:

> 1. You are becoming more passive and patient.
>   This is the beauty of surrender.
> 2. You are becoming more attractive.
>   This is the beauty of desire.
> 3. You are becoming more receptive.
>   This is the beauty of an open and loving heart.
> 4. You are becoming more mystical.
>   This is the beauty of a co-creative partnership with God.

It all works together as a coordinated whole. Desire fosters attraction. Opening your heart fosters receptivity. The co-creative partnership fosters spiritual development. The combination of all three processes fosters abundance in one of its many forms. What you need and/or desire can come to you in accordance with your highest good and the highest good of all involved.

Example of Attracting and Receiving

I wanted an abundance Hotei, a laughing Buddhist statue that represents wealth, wisdom and happiness. He holds a gold ingot over his head and has a huge belly. You rub his gold for abundance, rub his head for wisdom, and rub his belly for happiness. I never made a direct request for this statue, but I do remember looking for one for over a year and not finding exactly what I wanted. I was waiting for the right statue. One day, I was driving through Ellicott City, near my Maryland home when the thought voice spoke,

> "There's a Hotei at the Antique Depot."
> You would think by now I would not question the voice, but I replied,
> "They do not have Hoteis at the Antique Depot. They have antiques."
> The thought voice spoke, "There's a Hotei at the Antique Depot."
> I continue in disbelief, "They have small individual antique kiosks there. None of them are Asian."
> The matter of fact thought voice spoke, "There's a Hotei at the Antique Depot."

This was the third time, a significant number. What patience God must have with me! The Antique Depot has four floors of individual kiosks. I had not been there for a year or two. I searched all four floors and was in the second to the last kiosk where the most beautiful Hotei I had ever seen was for sale. He was 17 inches tall, with a large gold ingot, hand painted in full color. Not only was he inexpensive, but a friend and house guest had just given me enough money as a thank you gift to purchase him. He did not cost me a thing. I cannot tell you how happy this Hotei makes me. I smile and laugh every day when I look at him and he is a reminder of God's love and caring available to everyone.

The Process of Attraction

Expand your abilities into the passive, attractive, and receptive modes for manifestation by finding and developing this muscle. It lies in the heart. You can receive by allowing rather than doing. In some situations, reception is not only more effective than action, it is the only process that will work. For example, you cannot force a higher love or spiritual partnership. A relationship of this quality is always associated with attraction and greater lovingness. You can only open to it and flow with it when it comes to you. You cannot make it happen. Attracting a higher quality spiritual friendship, partnership, and/or marriage occurs when you are loving to others and open to receiving love. Doing this regardless of the response from others, regardless of the return or lack thereof, regardless of the person or people involved, and regardless of the situation is the signature of a heart that stays open and loving, come what may.

As part of your Heart Journey, temper your aggressive approach to receiving, and practice attraction through an open heart and the delicate art of skillful navigation. This process involves patience, especially in the beginning. You have to give the etheric intention for material manifestation time to emerge into form. You cannot predict in advance the timing needed for manifestation to move from spirit into matter. Formation may happen in an instant; or it may take years.

Once you develop your passive, attractive, and receptive abilities, abundance will flow to and through you, as long as you remain open-hearted. The more pure love you pour out, the more abundance you give to others, the more magnetic and attractive you become. You can begin to channel love and abundance in all of its various forms. Continue in this manner, staying open when you would close, receiving when you would refuse, and giving when you would deny.

2nd Co-Creative Thought Transformation

Old thought: Even Steven Reward System
Alchemical transformation: Receive More than Your Fair Share

In regard to abundance and manifestation through attraction and receptivity, give up your need for fairness and the envious response that inequity can evoke. There is nothing fair or unfair about what you receive or do not receive. God is abundantly creative, loving, and giving. While on your Heart Journey, the amount you receive is in accordance with your own ability to attract and receive and not according to God's ability or willingness to provide as long as it is in keeping with the highest good for all involved. Abundance can be as plentiful as the air you breathe.

There is plenty of oxygen to sustain life on our planet. The amount of oxygen you have in your lungs is directly proportional to your lung capacity and nothing else. It would be silly for you to be jealous of another who seemed to have more air in his or her lungs than you. If would be silly for you to become angry thinking that this person was stealing your air, even if s/he were hyperventilating. No matter what, s/he could not suck away your air. Given normal, open air conditions, you would never feel a shortage even if the two of you fought to hoard all the oxygen in the area. As soon as you take a deep breath, you will have all the air you want or need, and then some. In this regard, fairness has nothing to do with who has more or who has less air. The amount of air available is abundant and totally independent of your or another's actions. The amount of air you personally take in is subject to your individual lung capacity and your desire to inhale more or less.

If you open yourself to receiving, you will always receive more than your fair share. This will be true for others also. As illogical as it sounds, everyone can receive more than their share as shares are unlimited. Though you do not have to earn the right to manifest through attraction and receptivity, you must be open to receive. This involves a loving heart. Divine abundance, though unlimited, is like a series of radio stations that transmit at various unseen, unfelt, and unnoticed frequencies. You have to have a receiver tuned to the correct frequency to hear the music or news. If you do not have a mode for reception, you will be unaware of the transmission around you. Even if you have an appropriate receiver but live in a low-lying valley, the number of radio stations you can pick up might be limited in comparison to those living on a hilltop. Mountains can obstruct the radio signals causing reception to be weak, intermittent, overwhelmed by static, or nonexistent.

Likewise, if you live in difficult, traumatic, or spiritually adverse circumstances, you can be in a valley so to speak, and less able to connect with and respond to loving and abundant co-creative insights. Higher frequencies can be beyond your reach. Your ability to attract and receive becomes limited as soon as jealousy and other negative emotions cause you to be less than open-hearted. It is your response to events and not necessarily the circumstances themselves that handicap you. A jealous response to another's good fortune or abundance will preclude heart openness. All negative emotions are heart restrictors. Open hearted, unconditional love and negative emotions cannot exist in the same place at the same time. Negativity of any kind sucks you down into a valley and limits you to the lowest frequencies of reception, if at all. Abundance, love, attraction, and receptivity are all of the highest frequencies and are more harmonious with co-creative and Divine input. Once jealousy over unfairness or any negative emotion arises, your heart will begin to close and your ability to attract and receive will drop. You lose your attunement to God and each degree of closure costs you dearly.

On the other hand, those who are able to remain open-hearted and loving despite difficult situations and experiences, whatever they might be, gain the most. Their spiritual development actually becomes accelerated and enlightened. They have freed themselves of circumstances beyond their control and become masters of their inner state. They are not victims of their environment or their own misguided thoughts and emotions. They maintain their position as open hearted, co-creative partners and continue to receive assistance despite events and their circumstances.

You cannot afford negative thoughts and feelings related to fairness regardless of the stimulus. The cost is too high; the loss of potential too great. In reality, fairness or the lack thereof is a myth when applied to Divine abundance. You can have more than your fair share at any time by opening your heart more completely, loving unconditionally, and increasing your attractive and receptivity ability.

3rd Co-Creative Thought Transformation

Old thought: The Mental Ghetto
Alchemical transformation: Silence and Reflection

Energy follows thought! What you think, creates your reality. You do not want to reside in the Mental Ghetto where negativity roams the streets. Lower thought-forms such as gossip, prejudice, vulgarity and/or crudeness lower your frequency and are all inconsistent with opening to the higher mental states and communicating with your co-creative Partner. Compassion is the antithesis of disapproval and insensitivity, and will not arise under these conditions. You cannot truly open your heart while disrespecting others.

Perhaps the most common and damaging form of chatter in the Mental Ghetto is negative and nonproductive gossip about an absentee. It's called, "Let's you and me talk about him or her." In this situation, there is no desire to help or understand, only defame or vent. The conversational structure, by its very nature is a breeding ground for inaccurate information since there can be no rebuttal or clarification. You only get one side of the story, a story meant to further someone's personal agenda and feeling of superiority. Everyone loses in this situation. The promoters of the gossip subsist on a daily diet of judgment, criticism, and dislike. They become put-down artists with closed hearts rather than masters of manifestation and abundance. The listener, as a willing participant, is no less culpable. S/he is caught in the middle by the dysfunctional exchange and is dragged down simply by listening. It takes two to tango, or in this case, two to defame. The target of the gossip is tried, judged, sentenced in absentia, and victimized. None of this is conducive to heart openness.

So, it follows naturally, that if you want to co-create and sustain your focused thought, you must clean up your thoughts to live in a more pleasant environment. You can start by refusing to participate in gossip. If you have a problem with someone, have the integrity and honesty to deal with him or her directly. Never say anything behind someone's back that you would not say to his or her face. Make this your policy towards everyone and state your policy whenever and wherever you are confronted with the issue. Be clear with your family, friends and co-workers by voicing the following:

> "I promise that I will not be discussing you in a disrespectful way behind your back, nor will I be listening to such conversations. If I have a problem with you, I will come to you directly. If someone attributes negative comments about you as coming from me, call me on it. The truth will come out. If someone else says negative and disrespectful things about me behind my back, don't tell me. I do not need to know what is said unless and until this person comes and discusses matters with me directly."

The act of making this statement and detailing your intention is life altering. If you want to end some of the dysfunction and drama in your life, this is a way to do it. Refuse to participate in gossip, third party roasts, and any conversation which disrespect another. You set a standard by being direct and being clear about your methods and motives. In time, this standard will have a positive effect on others. By uplifting your thoughts and holding to higher principles, the consciousness of those around you will also be affected.

You are on a mystical journey. You have learned to deal directly with God and not solely through a designated and trained professional. Now learn to deal directly with humans. Do not triangulate conversations through a third person and expect to address problems or solve issues. Going through another party dilutes your personal power, muddies the water, and confuses the issue. This is counterproductive and a totally ineffective attempt at resolution.

If you need to have professionals present for particularly difficult or violent situation, so be it. Certainly insure your safety. Third parties who are present as witnesses or for support, protection, clarification, or mediation, such as counselors, lawyers, police officers, doctors, employers, authority figures, friends, or family members are acceptable and even advisable for serious issues and interventions. You do not have to handle situations entirely on your own and sometimes a third party, whether invested in the outcome or disinterested, lends credibility to what you are saying. But unless the third party is a trained professional, do not expect him or her to address issues for you or without you.

Become aware of the kinds of conversations, jokes, and comments you hear or might get involved in. Do they serve a useful purpose? Are they consistent with your spiritual goals? Do they support your heart opening? Will they contribute to the process of manifestation through attraction and receptivity? Are they creative exchanges that seek to understand, assist, and instruct? Or, are the thoughts and words meant to demean, punish, blame, hurt, justify, or distance? The road forks here. There is only one course of action open to those who wish to rise above emotional debris and progress spiritually. If you want to sustain your potent focused thought and manifest through an open heart, cut out misplaced attention. You only have so much time and so much mental energy. Choose wisely. A mind is a terrible thing to waste!

In Part Two: The Co-creative Partnership and Manifestation Process, you established communication with your co-creative Partner in meditation, quiet moments in your home, or walks in nature. You learned to listen to God. This increased your sensitivity to subtle communications and the thought voice. Now you need to clean up your mental environment by listening to your own thoughts in addition to co-creative exchanges and interpersonal communications. All three are important to spiritual development, but the inner exchanges are a true measure of your progress. Others may never see the real you. You can censor what you say and do while still thinking and feeling negatively. Only you would know the truth. Through internal monitoring you can become aware of areas needing cleansing or refinement.

What are the messages conveyed by your inner thoughts regarding your contract? Are they the kind of thoughts that contribute to your Heart Journey? Are they supportive of your hopes and dreams?

What is your thinking in regard to others? Are your perceptions laced with compassion and understanding? Are you truly openhearted towards those you meet? Do you look for opportunities to be helpful and kind?

What are the messages you give yourself? Are you optimistic? Encouraging? Or are you plagued by hypercritical and demeaning inner messages? Do you berate yourself regarding your body image, intelligence, or financial limitations? Are you repeatedly reminded of past failures, poor decisions, and shortcomings.

There is a potential dark side to our thoughts whether we express the negativity openly or conceal it, whether it concerns what we are attempting to accomplish, our perceptions of others, or our perceptions of ourselves. Negative thoughts in any form and on any level impede.

There are layers and layers of cleansing and advancement in Heart Journey which are beyond the scope of this book to define or teach. It is through cleansing your mind of negativity and listening in the silence that insights leading to amazing experiences occur. Silence is a classroom, your teacher is your co-creative Partner, and the material you study is the thoughts and workings of your own mind. Silent reflection is a necessary key to entering mystery. When you listen in the silence with an open heart and mind, truth is revealed and mystery made known.

Example of Inspiration in the Silence

I was in Maui, Hawaii, off shore, snorkeling for more than an hour. I was swimming back to my starting point where the car was parked when I spotted a sea turtle just ahead. My mask was a little foggy at that point so I raised my head and cleared the glass. When I looked back under the water, the sea turtle was gone. I was near the rocky shore and was hoping the turtle had not gone far, perhaps just around and into the rocks. It was dangerous for me to enter the rocks and disrespectful of the sea turtle's need for distance to infringe on its safety zone. Instead of approaching, I tread water in the silence. Only then was I inspired to hum "Amazing Grace" as loudly as I could under water. The turtle immediately came back around the rock to investigate. Soon a second turtle joined the first one. As I watched, the two began to dance, swimming almost upright toward one another, but then sliding past, barely touching extremities. They did this again and again as I sang. It was a beautiful sight.

4th Co-Creative Thought Transformation

Old thought: Disabling Need or Dependency
Alchemical transformation: Self-sufficiency Moving to Wholeness

This is your Heart Journey built on your desire, born of your co-creative partnership with God. Though you might be in a Heart Journey group and even if you are part of a group contract, your process is unique. The experiences you have, the techniques you master, the teachings you learn, and all the insights along the way are specifically handpicked for your edification. They are meant to complement your personality, enable the realization of your goals, and the fulfillment of your needs. Your specialized Heart Journey program is customized by your co-creative Partner. Dependency on others to either show you the way or travel with you alters the formula, distracts from your individualized program, and can delay or derail your progress.

There are several forms dependency can take. Part of any spiritual path is the hope of becoming whole. For this reason, many pilgrims start out with a complementary companion, someone who embodies the missing character traits and hoped for abilities. Though the two may travel together for a period of time, the main goals of this kind of relationship are sensitization to what is previously unknown, development of new abilities, and the embodiment of previously unrealized strengths for the purpose of becoming whole. This does not mean that the relationship is anything less than loving. It may actually feel like a soul level union, but the goal of any spiritual relationship is *not* to continue to depend on another. The true goal for each party is individual wholeness and self-sufficiency. The true goal for the spiritual relationship is equality through a commitment to each other's growth. You outgrow the complementary and symbiotic partnership so a more mature relationship can emerge.

The bottom line is that in order to progress on your Heart Journey, you must proceed at your own pace and in your own manner. Do not delay your journey to match step with another no matter how well s/he complements you. Do not expect someone to slow down so you can catch up. It is important for everyone to participate in the individualized experiences innate to his or her path.

In the same manner, do not depend on anyone else to do for you what you must do or master yourself. There will be plenty of people to assist you along the way, but there may come a time when a stepping stone is no longer helpful or becomes an impediment to your progress. Should this occur, you need to go it alone. Find another avenue for manifestation or pathway for spiritual development by moving on, around, or through. There are always alternatives if you think and act like water running downhill. No stone or log will ever prevent rushing water from reaching the bottom of the hill. There are always ways to continue on, and many times they involve simple side-stepping maneuvers that avoid conflict or heartache.

This is your mystical journey. Depend on your co-creative Partner to guide your steps. You should not surrender power to any one person and expect to be shown the path or told the truth. Many different people, at different times, will help you on your journey, but ultimately you are your own witness to God's presence in your life. If you limit your experience to one person and become emotionally or psychologically dependent on him or her to answer all your questions or fulfill all your needs, you will weaken your direct connection to God. On the other hand, be open to all teachers, in all forms, from the smallest to the largest, from the grandest to the most humble. There will be many teachers, every day and from many walks of life, even common people with stories to tell and bits of wisdom to convey through word or symbol. Learn from the child at play or a beggar in the street, watch the birds as they fly, or see a rainbow in the sky. Listen openheartedly to all.

You have a responsibility to yourself and others to be the best you can be. Do not be afraid to move ahead and do not be afraid to be left behind. Your journey is unique; honor it. Your position on the path in regards to others is unimportant. Your position on the path in regard to the guidance received from your co-creative Partner is the only significant measure of progress. No matter where you are on your journey, have compassion for those who seem less fortunate or struggle with insights you already have. You were once there. Have gratitude for those who helped you along the way. They gave you their best so you could continue on. Give back in recognition of your many blessings and pay it forward.

5th Co-Creative Thought Transformation

Old thought: Reality Deception
Alchemical transformation: Multidimensional Perception

Delusions about reality are holding you back if you believe there's only one reality and it is basically limited to the physical world you see and feel. There is more, much more than meets the eye. There is an invisible spiritual realm that can remain cloaked because of its subtlety. The visible material plane and the invisible spiritual dimension coexist as an interwoven reality that is rich, diverse, pliable, and multidimensional. When you limit perceptions to your five senses, you are deceiving yourself and selling yourself short. There is so much more than the physical world and your potential is so much more than what you can physically manipulate or accomplish.

It is in the invisible spiritual realm wherein God resides and creative energy exists. We live in this unseen world too, whether we know it or not, and this world lives in us. There is no segregation. Rather, a vibrational continuum exists from the higher creative frequencies to the lower physical frequencies leading to solidification into matter.

Creative energy is the building block of the invisible world and also the building block for everything in the visible realm. Creative energy has unlimited potential. It is the beginning, the precursor to all forms, and some people simply refer to creative energy as God the Creator. Almost every religion and tradition talks about an unseen force, whether labeled God or not. It is the force that creates our world as we know and see it, and other dimensions we have yet to discover.

Because the seen and unseen worlds are interwoven, contacts are ever present and influences bleed through. This crossover allows for Divine communication, making symbols, signs, coincidences, ease, God whispers, lucid dreams, and visions meaningful and significant. The connection enables the co-creative partnership you seek to establish with God and the guidance you receive.

There is still more going on between the visible and invisible worlds than just communication and Divine guidance. It is the creative energy in the invisible realm that supports manifestation in the physical realm. Desire and thought, (or Divine word), define the manner and form that manifestation will take. Desire is the emotion; thought is the translation. Love and attraction initiate the concentration and compression of creative energy. Love is the emotion that opens the heart; attraction is the resulting power that functions like a magnet drawing the appropriate creative resources together, making them available for the process of manifestation. As creative energy is compressed through the process of attraction, space becomes limited. Movement is restricted, oscillation slows, and the vibrational frequency is lowered. At this point, condensation begins, the process of changing from one form to another. We normally associate condensation with a vapor becoming liquid. In the process of manifestation through attraction and receptivity, you can think of creative energy as spiritual vapor that condenses to a fluid state which can then be poured into a form. Surrender is the emotion that augments receptivity by holding open and empty the form in which solidification takes place. While desire and thought create the form, surrender creates the emptiness that makes the form receptive. The process of formation proceeds from the initiating desire and thought by way of attraction and receptivity to manifestation. Manifestation results from the flow of creative energy to wherever there is receptivity, acceptance, compatibility, or need.

1. Desire and thought (establish definition)
2. Love and attraction (initiate concentration and compression)
3. Frequency limitations (result in condensation and fluidity)
4. Surrender fosters receptivity (allowing formation and manifestation

Admittedly, this is a simplified attempt to define a very complex spiritual process that remains cloaked by design. Miracles happen for unknown reasons. The process of manifestation through attraction and receptivity fails for unknown reasons. There are no guarantees and no formula is foolproof. The workings of God and creative energy remain a mystery. The important point to remember is that there is a vibrational continuum. Matter is nothing more than creative energy oscillating at a slow vibrational rate. The undefined, unformed, abundant creative energy innate to God and the invisible realm can manifest in a process that goes from higher vibrational frequencies to lower.

One of the characteristics of the invisible world is that it is pliable, more pliable than the visible world. The visible world appears to have varying degrees of solidification. There are solid elements such as the rocks, vegetation, animals, humans, and man-made structures such as houses, roads, bridges, and buildings. Water is certainly more fluid than any of these forms and can readily take the shape of any container or freeze solid. But water is not nearly as changeable as air which can expand and contract. The creative energy of the invisible world is even less tangible and more pliable. It can assume any form, and under certain circumstances, (which cannot be fully explained), is able to change instantaneously. Because the physical world embodies creative energy, some flexibility and responsiveness exists though there may be limits to the amount of change that can occur at any one time. The process of transformation generally moves at a much slower pace. Still, change does occur in the most stable of forms. We know that even continents shift over time.

Your reality is comprised of the visible world, the invisible world, (to the extent that you are aware of it), and your interactions with experiences in both. Though your reality may appear fixed, it can actually be affected by your thinking patterns in cooperation with God. Solid structures tend to remain the same physically, though sensual distortions are possible and can be meaningful.

Example of Shifting Realities

I went with a friend to the Herkimer Diamond Mines in New York State. Herkimer diamonds are really double terminated quartz crystals. They are clear glass-like crystals with points on both ends. They can be found on the ground at the mines. The best time to go crystal hunting is after a hard rain, when the water has washed away the dirt and exposed the Herkimer diamonds. You can just walk along and pick them up.

The experience was very surreal for me. I would squat down and stare at the ground and see absolutely nothing. Then suddenly the earth would drop down and the Herkimer diamonds would pop up sparkling. As soon as they appeared I would race to pick them up because before long and always before I was done, the earth would rise up again and the diamonds would fall back into the earth and disappear. This process was great play for me and occurred numerous times over the span of several hours. It was like shifting between two dimensions, both real, interwoven and interchangeable. This had nothing to do with the light. The day was heavily overcast and there was never any direct sunlight to expose the crystals. The changes in my ability to perceive were a mystery to me, but showed me that there was more here than meets the eye.

By focusing your sustained thought and desire, you already know that you can initiate shifts in the visible world by the process of manifestation through attraction and receptivity. The more consistent and compatible your thoughts, feelings, and actions are with guidance from your co-creative Partner and the highest good of all involved, the faster a change might occur and the more dramatic the result. Over time and with experience, your communication with God, your connection to invisible creative energy, and your recognition of subtle influences involved in manifestation will strengthen. This is an important point to remember. Like your reality, your spiritual development is not static. You do not get to some point and think you have arrived, no matter how many experiences you have or what you have been able to manifest. Your relationship with your co-creative Partner and the invisible spiritual realm is meant to be ongoing and continually enlightening. Every insight, understanding, or experience you have will eventually fall away as a new insight, deeper understanding, or recent experience arises regarding your mystical relationship with God, the visible and invisible worlds, and the process of manifestation through attraction and receptivity. There are numerous tiers of discovery and wonder.

On a mystical journey such as Heart Journey, individualization is to be expected. What you previously believed about God and the spiritual realm may have been a product of or reaction to your religious education and upbringing. At this point, your former beliefs are being affected by your direct experience of God as your co-creative Partner. You are moving beyond rhetoric to a heartfelt connection. This may cause you to review what you have been taught in light of what you are experiencing. Profound changes are possible. This is your journey; you choose what to believe. You may or may not begin to experience other realities, etheric beings such as angels, spirit guides, ascended masters, your soul, or higher self. In your mind's eye, faraway lands might appear or different time periods, as space and time barriers fall away. Open your mind as well as your heart. As your inner senses become more and more attuned to subtleties and your co-creative partnership with God, it is up to you to make sense of what you experience and decide what you believe.

Example that Spans Distance and Space

Like most sons and daughters who go away to college, my son would bring home laundry, even if he was only home for the weekend. He was good about doing the laundry himself, folding everything into his basket and hanging up his shirts. Once when I was returning him to school after being home, we attended a late night event. I dropped him off at the dormitory at about one o'clock in the morning. He was concerned about me driving home alone.

> I asked, "Do you want me to call you when I get in?"
> He replied, "No, you will just wake up my roommate."

I said, "Then I will just send you a thought message"

The trip home was short and uneventful. I walked into the house, put down my purse and sent the thought message, "I am home." As I turned I noticed all of my son's shirts hanging in the laundry room. He had packed the laundry basket into the car, but forgot the hanging shirts. I sent a second thought message, "You forgot your shirts."

Meanwhile, back at college, my son was climbing into bed when the first thought message came in.

He thought, "Good, Mom is home."
His next thought was, "Duh! I forgot my shirts."

The unseen world is rich with the potential for creating, manifesting, supporting spiritual development, and healing those physically and emotionally challenged. The invisible world is God's realm and God is your co-creative Partner. Any belief in a fixed physical reality belies God's power, limits your ability to manifest through attraction and receptivity, inhibits your progress on the spiritual path, and blinds you to assistance with physical, emotional, and mental healing. When you are short-sighted, you become partially alienated from God and your potential as a true co-creator.

6th Co-Creative Thought Transformation

Old thought: Mental Constructs
Alchemical transformation: Open Minded

As you grow and learn, your mind begins to organize information into mental constructs. Organization facilitates both acquiring knowledge and comprehending what is learned. Much of the information you store is second hand. You are told it, taught it, or you read it. Firsthand knowledge arises when you process and store your understanding of direct experiences. Either way, it is the nature of the mind to make sense of what is or is not happening. Knowledge, facts, information, and even truth, (as you perceive it), becomes formatted and established. New information and experiences are expected to complement what is already known and add to the existing data base and mental constructs. With time and age, these thought patterns become ingrained. They can also be highly rational, logical, and anticipatory.

As long as you think you already know and understand, or have established a pattern of interaction with your experience, you will miss the evolving intelligence innate to the mystical path and the arising insight and wisdom. You become a closed book, finished before you begin, resistant to divergent information that is incompatible with your mental constructs or contradicts your rational assessment. Preconceptions delay your mystical edification. You cannot learn what you think you already know. You need to suspend knowing, remain open minded, and feel your way along while in communication with your co-creative Partner. Direct interaction is an essential component of the mystical journey. Mystical intelligence is not a static knowledgeable state, but a moment to moment process, an evolutionary way of interacting with each and every experience as it arises that allows for continuing spiritual development.

While on your Heart Journey, an open mind is as essential to insight as an open heart is to love. It is better to assume that you do not know. You can also assume that you do not know that you do not know. It is only when you are surprised by a mystical revelation that you discover what has been missing. Realizations, when they emerge, can be far afield from your expectations and mental constructs. For you to progress and develop spiritually, something entirely new should arise and enter your consciousness. You cannot think the "ah-ha" that needs to occur. It is not linked in any way to what you already know. You can only ride the rising tide of awareness as it is happening. What is forgotten, hidden and unknown will gradually emerge in you, and from you, but only after you eliminate preconceptions of what might actually be forgotten, hidden and unknown. Mystical knowing comes as an unfolding mystery and leads to insight and wisdom.

Example of Preconceptions Resulting in Resistance

There is an ancient story of a master trying to teach his students about the mysteries of life that go beyond the obvious that only they can discover for themselves. He knew that there were things that could not be taught or put into words, even by a master. The best he could do was point. From there, the students were to progress beyond his pointing.

He took his students out into the night to look at the sky. He said that all of his teachings were nothing more than a finger pointing at the moon. The students were not to fixate on his finger. They were to look beyond his finger to the moon.

In Chapter Nine: Energetic Example, I told of my time sitting before a poster of a Tibetan mandala. I wanted to unlock its mysteries and I thought by studying it closely, noting the placement of this or that or the number or amount included I could crack the code and learn the mandala's secret. Actually, the mandala was more like a finger pointing at the moon. All my theories were for naught as I became fixated on the poster itself. It was the energy that spontaneously arose out of the mandala and literally hit me between the eyes that woke me up. I had my ah-ha moment, but it did not arise from my mental gymnastics. I thought I knew; I had a plan, when actually I was thwarting any chance I had of having an experience of awakening.

So, give up any adherence to truth as you know it, whether you label it with a small "t" or a capital "T." Your truth, whatever it is, is always in the past, while you are in the now. In this sense, established knowledge and understanding can prevent you from seeing anew and experiencing fresh. Also surrender your need for rational or logical experiences and explanations. They will not exist on the mystical path.

Example of a Mystical Hawaiian Journey

On my first trip to Hawaii there was a particular heiau my friend and I wanted to see. A heiau is a Hawaiian place of healing made from stones. We were not sure exactly where this heiau was. The guide book was not specific, so when we got to the area we asked several people in the nearest town. Everyone said they had no idea where the heiau was or how to get to it. Since the heiau was well-known, we suspected that we were not being given directions for a reason.

We went on our instincts anyway, following God whispers, "turn left, then right, down the road a stretch, now another turn," etc., and eventually came to a place with numerous Hawaiian "keep out" signs. We thought this might be the place, but did not want to intrude without permission. We had no idea how to get permission so we reluctantly turned around and began to drive home. Less than a minute down the road we saw a woman mowing her lawn. I felt drawn to stop and ask one more time for directions to the heiau. The woman came over to the car and told us that the heiau was not a tourist attraction. It was considered a sacred site for ceremony only and declared off limits by the local kahuna.

We had spent several days with a kahuna on a different Hawaiian island. When we told the Oahu kahuna we were interested in seeing this particular heiau, she gave us a hand-written introduction on the back of her business card. We showed this to the woman and indicated that we had come with a lei and sweet potato as an offering. To our surprise, she replied that she knew who to ask for permission. She could make no promises, but if we did not mind waiting, she would go in the house and call.

We remained in the car, but no sooner had the woman entered the house when we were scanned. Neither of us that ever had this experience before, but we both recognized it simultaneously. A slight radiation feeling started at the top of our heads and slowly descended to our feet, then rose back to our heads. We knew the local kahuna had just looked us over etherically to check us out. Within seconds the woman came back out of the house, gave us directions, and told us the name of the kahuna granting permission. We returned to the keep out signs, parked the car, and walked in.

We were not given directions on where to find the heiau once we were on the property, but again we followed God whispers. Within ten minutes and without much wandering, we arrived at a lava path. My friend immediately took off her shoes and continued on barefoot though the lava rocks were very sharp. She felt it was important for her to do this. I kept my shoes on. The path ended at a huge heiau and just as we got there the owner of the property came out of the entrance and said we were trespassing on sacred grounds. We mentioned the local kahuna by name and said we had been given permission. The owner looked at my friend with the offerings and bare feet and said, "I see you have come in the sacred way." She stepped aside and let us pass.

My friend entered the heiau, I never did. Just as I approached the doorway, the thought voice said I was not to enter. I obeyed even after all we had been through. Maybe it was the shoes. Maybe it was just not my path. In any case, I remained outside. When my friend emerged crying, I half carried her back along the sharp lava path. To this day, I have never seen that heiau though I have been in the area several times.

Your moment to moment experience and direct communication with God are invaluable learning tools. The process of going with what it arising and staying in close contact with your co-creative Partner is essential to the evolution of mystical intelligence and spiritual development. Mystical moments will only emerge when you stay open minded without restrictions, conditions, or preconceived expectations of what should or should not be happening and what it might mean.

7th Co-Creative Thought Transformation

Old thought: Judgment
Alchemical transformation: Compassion

The wise person wishing to travel the mystical path delays and even avoids judging others or experiences as good or bad. Like mental constructs, judgment is a close-ended process meant to terminate investigation so the mind can assume understanding and move on. Characterizing people, events, or circumstances as either good or bad leads to an established pattern of interaction or avoidance. Although no one needs to remain in a dangerous situation, characterization in positive or negative terms is commonly swift, arbitrary, over used, and self-limiting. Judgment is the antithesis of mysticism which is an open-ended inquiry into the unknown where black and white fade to gray and all patterns of response are useless and counterproductive. When you judge, you label people, places, things, events, and circumstances in accordance with your degree of comfort or discomfort. Based on your assessment you determine your involvement or distance. Mystical experiences, by their very nature, can make you uncomfortable and they don't always come through bright minds and pleasant surroundings. If God cannot reach you through someone's goodness, God will reach you through someone's craziness, and mystical experiences can sometimes appear to be unbelievable and crazy.

Judgments are frequently based on preconceived notions colored by emotional content and past experiences. They are not just a product of your moral or ethical upbringing. They are also influenced by prejudices, social influences, the need for rational understanding, personal history, individual preference, and a myriad of other factors. Judgment is a simplified ending to a complex conscious and unconscious process. The good or bad, black or white, positive or negative label can lull you into thinking you know the person or the situation. You think you understand; you probably don't. But once categorization is established, rightly or wrongly, responses can become stereotypical and automatic. How can you follow a mystical path when your mind is steeped in the practice of making judgments that stop the process of insight and growth?

The judgmental mind judges again and again. This becomes a well-established route to understanding in your mind, though many times a false understanding spawned on a short-sighted route. When faced with mystery, the tendency will be to make the unknown or unknowable appear known as quickly as possible. Divine mysteries defy definition and cannot be adequately conveyed in words. Nor do they come with proof of their spiritual value. The truth is that as much as you quest for experiences on the mystical path, the unknown will make you uncomfortable, especially when the unknown remains unknowable over a period of time. Your mind is used to tidy packages that have names and experiences that make sense. Mysticism is not tidy; it does not make sense. Your unconscious goal will be to make sense of it all in any way possible, as quickly as possible. You have to get used to not knowing and not fully understanding. You do this by first delaying and then avoiding judgments entirely.

Judgments are a reaction *to* rather than an awareness *of*. When you make a judgment, you are refusing to look deeper. This has implications not just on the mystical level, but also on a mundane level and in regard to human relations. When you judge another, you distance yourself from a meaningful interaction and connection by drawing premature, stereotypical conclusions. The individual can be characterized as being this or that, rather than experienced as unique. The label prevents any meeting of the hearts and minds. You do not have to work to know or understand this person and you do not have to be concerned with unknown personality elements.

When you judge a person for his or her actions, whether terrible, inadequate, or misguided, you eliminate the possibility for compassion. The truth is we all commit offenses. If you are evolving spiritually, you can probably look back on some past situation and realize you could have handled it better, even if you made the best of a bad situation and learned from it. We all grow and learn. I am forever grateful to those who tolerated my past transgressions and those who will tolerate my future ones, and still regard me with love.

I am aware that I have been faced with a decision or dilemma of my own in regard to almost every past judgment I have ever made. Not wanting to face too many more tough situations, I prefer not to judge. I suggest you learn to see the total picture by allowing extra time for understanding, corrections, apologies and a paradigm shift.

You probably have established personal limits, lines you have drawn in the sand and will not cross. Those lines are there to protect you. You will go only so far. You are not going to be hurt, used, duped, or (insert your own verb here) again. But what is it that exists beyond that limit? What lies on the other side of the line you have drawn? I am not talking about placing yourself repeatedly in compromising situations or dangerous circumstances. I believe an ounce of prevention is worth a pound of cure. You need to protect yourself from predators, for your own sake and for the sake of the perpetrator. But I am talking about those new situations where presenting elements *appear* similar to past difficulties and a pattern of condemnation and avoidance is established. It is only when the heart and mind are left open, that you cross this artificial line you have drawn to travel beyond your present level of comprehension toward compassion and healing. That line in the sand is your growing tip and you only grow by crossing it.

Additionally, the process of judging will have a negative impact on your own psyche.

> *"Do not judge, that you may not be judged. For with what judgment, you judge, you shall be judged; and with what measure you measure, it shall be measured to you."* (Matthew 7:1, KJV of The Holy Bible).

"As you judge, so shall you be judged," does not necessarily mean that you will be judged by the same standards or for the same offense by others. It means that as long as the apparatus for judgment is in place in your mind and the pattern reinforced again and again, it can turn on you at any moment. The thought pattern you have ingrained in your mind to judge others will judge you whenever it is idle and needs a target. There is no separation. When you cease to judge, you will cease to feel judged.

You can reach across the gulf that separates one person from another when you set aside your critical eye and seek to truly understand and connect with others despite differences. If you wish to enter mystery, grow beyond your present understanding and heal, always delay interpretation and judgment. The longer you delay, the longer you will go on learning. As long as the file is open, insights and learning will continue.

Example of Judgment

When I lived in Maryland, my house was out in a rural area. When I would go into Baltimore City, I always took the same route. There was a stoplight just before getting on the highway going home. Many times a man or woman would be on the corner begging for money. If the light was green, the traffic was such that it was difficult to stop. However, the red light was a long one and I always gave something to whoever was there.

One day, I was coming up to this corner and the light turned red. There was a man with a homeless sign. The thought voice said, "Give him a twenty." I had never given out this much money before and was a little embarrassed by the offering so I folded the bill up and tried to conceal the denomination as I handed it to him. He immediately looked at it and asked, "Why did you give me so much money?" I answered truthfully, "The voice told me to." I expected him to laugh or question me further about "the voice," but to my great surprise, he said, "I know you!"

Now I rarely went into the city, maybe once or twice a year, and I was certain I did not know any homeless, toothless, middle-aged black men. My judgmental mind immediately decided that this was a line or gimmick for more money. In that instant, the conversation became understandable to me and I was no longer uncomfortable with how this man might know who I was. My end to this mystery was that he was bluffing and didn't know me at all!

Then he said, "Your name is Mary." I was flabbergasted beyond belief and stammered, "How do you know me?" I did not have a name tag on and there was nothing in or on my car that would in any way indicate what my name was. Turns out, he knew me from thirty years ago when I was a waitress earning extra money for college at a local restaurant and he was a busboy. He remembered me even though my hair had turned gray and I looked very different.

The inequity of our lives was heartbreaking. As the light changed and I drove away I started to cry. I was an American princess in the land of opportunity and he probably never had a chance. Though I remembered the job and situation, despite all my education and intelligence, I had forgotten this person completely, his name and his face, while he had remembered me. He never forgot who I was even after thirty years and he never judged me according to my clothes or condition. He met me without pretense. But though I acted generously, I know in my heart that I judged him as I drove up to that corner. Was he really homeless? Would he go on a binge with the money I gave him? Why didn't he get a job? I acted like part of the solution, but my judgment made me part of the problem.

8th Co-Creative Thought Transformation

Old thought: Possessiveness and Control
Alchemical transformation: Honoring

Possessiveness towards others implies the delusion of ownership and the right to dominate. You cannot and should not own, and you do not and should not have the right to dominate. Controlling others, even for their own good, implies that you know best. Not necessarily! The tragedies innate to possessiveness and control are numerous and far reaching both for you and the object of your attention.

Attempts to possess another are misguided and doomed to failure. Possessiveness kills the very beauty you seek to own and the relationship you covet. A caged bird will not sing. A butterfly trapped between your thumb and finger will rip and shred its wings in a quest for freedom. The love you crave is the antithesis of ownership and the two are mutually exclusive. You are deluded if you believe you can make it work. You are living a lie if you think it is actually working.

Possessiveness is as detrimental to you as it is to the object of your affection. The more conditional your love, the less open your heart. Your attempts to do the impossible, (and it is impossible to truly love yet seek to possess), seriously impact your ability to attract and receive abundance. While your heart is closing, you are spiritually regressing, whether you sense it or not, and your attractive and receptive ability is waning. You risk a continuing downward spiral wherein communications with your co-creative Partner become more difficult, distorted, and sporadic as your vibrational frequency declines and emotional distractions increase. Without steady guidance, life becomes harder and more of a struggle. When you feel the need to be possessive of your loved one, your relationship is already in trouble and in danger of dying. It is better to face the issues head on with love. In reality, it is your only hope.

You cannot make someone love you. You can only open *your* heart to a higher level of love, understanding, and compassion. If your relationship is in trouble, you have two very different choices, each requiring its own strength.

> 1. If you still love this person and the relationship the two of you have built together, keep your heart wide open and choose to stay through thick and thin. Do not fall into the trap of "least common denominator love," wherein you will only love another as much as you feel loved. It has already been established that your partner's love is waning. Low balling your love to match another will only make matters worse. It is better to love openheartedly if you wish to turn things around. You may be unevenly yoked for a while, but then one of two things will happen. Either your partner will be uplifted, eventually following your lead and become more loving also, or s/he will slip farther and farther behind, eventually falling away completely, emotionally and/or physically. Sometimes you can out love and out last difficulties, and sometimes you can't, but at least you will know that you gave it your all. A relationship that does not and cannot heal ultimately dies regardless of what you do or how loving you are. It will go to the grave faster if you are possessive.

> 2. If you feel like you have exhausted all options and the situation is both very difficult and having a negative impact on both of you, perhaps the more loving and compassionate thing to do would be let this person go. It is either time for a temporary break or time to move on. To continue in a sham relationship with limited options is not in anyone's best interest. You would be living a lie. It is far better to survive the change and love again than to let your heart become hardened by a dysfunctional and dishonest daily interaction.

Attempts to manipulate and/or control another deny his or her free will, cloud his or her path, and thwart his or her co-creative interaction with God (regardless of whether or not the individual appears conscious of the interaction). There is beauty in everyone waiting to bloom. It has been programmed from the beginning by the Divine We all carry a spiritual gift to be manifested in our lifetime, a unique dance that can emerge when the conditions are right and efforts supported even if only by one person or only for a moment. The chances that this potential will be realized increases when you honor the best that each person has to offer. Honoring calls forth this spark and fans the flames of Divine inheritance. No matter the starting point, honoring is a beneficial option, especially when you are hoping for improvement. Even the most hardened criminal can grow or gain insight when there is support. This does not mean that s/he should be released from prison or will be completely rehabilitated, but any progress is a step in the right direction. The alternative is that the spark never ignites or dies out completely and all potential is lost. It is to everyone's benefit to work with God by honoring or supporting the best in another.

The tragedy for you is that attempts to control others narrow *your* focus and limit *your* options. There is a direct, negative effect on you because you must stay vigilant that the target of your attention is behaving in a specific manner according to your wishes, needs, or expectations. When others don't toe the line to make things happen according to your expectations, you have to be ready to step in and take up the slack. When you end up doing the dirty work for others, you enable their dysfunction and lack of responsibility, or become codependent yourself. Meanwhile, you are distracted from your own life and path. You lose awareness of better options, your co-creative potential, and Divine Partner Who will never participate in a possessive or controlling venture.

Possessiveness and control bind you to finite small expectations and blind you to infinite possibilities and limitless abundance. You grasp at one particular option or outcome, when in reality many options exist, all of which may be more beneficial than the one you are currently struggling to maintain. You suffer from a poverty mentality, believing that there is only person, one situation, or thing that can make you happy. While you fight to maintain control, the ego and small self-will become stronger than Thy Will. You will no longer trust God to provide and will try to make things happen on your own. Your behaviors and thoughts will manifest through the channels of conditional love and conditional hate, fostered and sustained by fear. It is an all-around losing position for everyone involved, the possessive and the possessed, the controlling and the controlled.

Realistically, you have no power to control another adult. It is an impossible task that always ends in failure. You may for a time control the body, but you won't control the mind. And if you learn to control the mind, you won't control the heart. You might think you control the heart, but will never break the spirit which belongs to God. All control is temporary. The greatest power you have lies within you for the purpose of your own personal growth and fulfillment. The weakest, least effective use of personal power occurs when you attempt to control another. The strain and drain is so great, eventually you become dis-empowered. It's a losing proposition.

Instead, picture yourself placing the out of control person in the arms and care of your co-creative Partner. Let go and let God. God works in strange and wondrous ways! Even when God cannot work through someone's best characteristics, God will work through other qualities and avenues. All beings are on a journey to God, some sooner, some later.

Everyone has the right to come and go, learn or not learn, succeed or fall flat. This is a hard lesson to learn when it is your loved one who is tripping or lost along the way. You can offer guidance and speak your mind. Providing information, making suggestions, and giving assistance can be helpful and welcomed behaviors. These actions seek to empower and enhance, not overpower and control. Intervention when someone has totally lost their way with drugs, alcohol or other addictions is appropriate when it provides accurate feedback and support, but not force. Even in these situations control will not work. The individual has to want to be healed. If he or she is not willing, it's not time. Until then, as painful as it is to watch, there is little you can do. Regardless of the situation, an attempt to overpower or control, (even in another's best interest), is generally useless and detrimental to you own spiritual development. Sometimes allowing someone to fall or fail is the only thing that will open the door to recovery.

When it comes to children and parenting, control should not be confused with guidance and the need for structure. You do not own your children and should not shape them according to some preconceived image. They have their own little Divine sparks to fan and gifts to manifest. But they do need your supervision to grow into responsible and productive adults. Guide your children by allowing them to develop naturally in an enriched and loving environment that fosters positive character traits. Support their strengths. Seek to fortify the Divine spark in them by honoring the best they have to offer.

When it comes to relationships, possessiveness should not be confused with commitment. A stable marriage or fulfilling relationship actually broadens horizons rather than narrows them. In situations where partners are mutually dedicated to each other's growth, trust reigns and honoring is a way of life. It is a sign of true love and there is no need to control.

When it comes to elderly parents who are no longer able to make good decisions or care for themselves, control should not be confused with caregiving. With the growing cases of dementia and Alzheimer's disease we must care for our parents as we would care for our children and keep them safe. Responsibilities for an elder may be part of your spiritual journey. After you learn spiritual concepts, you may be called to practice and demonstrate what you have learned through service to others and acts of kindness.

When you honor, surprising things happen. Like the turtles who danced before me while I sang "Amazing Grace" under water, (see "Example of Inspiration in the Silence" earlier in this chapter), honoring reveals the essence of God in everyone and everything in a way that could not be anticipated.

Example of Control

The first day that I moved into my new house, there were bluebirds in my backyard. These were the first bluebirds I had seen since I was ten years old on a field trip. I was thrilled and immediately put up a bluebird box, hoping they would nest and they did the following year. Unfortunately, spring came early and was followed by a period of bitter cold. All five babies died during the cold snap. I had no idea what had gone wrong. There was a local bluebird rehabilitation group and when I contacted them for information, I was put in touch with "Mr. Bluebird" who monitored many of the county's bird boxes and rehabilitated sick or injured birds. I was told that my case was not unusual as bluebird nests all over the countryside yielded frozen babies that Spring.

I started helping out, monitoring boxes in my neighborhood and assisting Mr. Bluebird with his rounds. I learned a lot about caring for these birds and their rehabilitation needs. Bluebirds are very gentle birds, but they will protect their young at the cost of their own lives. They will not leave the nest when attacked. Their major predator is the house sparrow which is not native, but an accidental import from Europe. House sparrows complete with bluebirds for nesting boxes. They will jump into the bluebird box and carry off the smallest babies or peck the mother and fledglings to death by pounding on their heads. The mother will usually die on her young as she will refuse to move. The house sparrow will then proceed to kill the babies. It was common to find severely injured bluebirds while making rounds. Mr. Bluebird did his best to rehabilitate those birds.

One day two three-day-old bluebirds close to death were brought to my home. They were not expected to live, their heads were so badly pecked. One bird was paralyzed on the left side of his body. Mr. Bluebird was going out of town for the weekend and there was no one else to take the birds. He asked me to fill in. I cared for them as I had been taught, but I also did Reiki on them, an energetic healing technique. One recovered quickly and I called him Godzilla. I had to put him in a separate box to keep him from stomping all over his sibling. After two days Mr. Bluebird was back on town and Godzilla was taken out to a nest with similar aged baby bluebirds for adoption by the parents. The second bird was recovering slowly. He was no longer paralyzed, but did not seem to have the same will to live. Though I noticed this, I kept healing and feeding. My ego needed to pull off a miracle.

On the third day of care and after a feeding, the baby bird gave a huge sigh and in that sigh I saw my folly. I was willing this bird to live and he wanted to die. So I gently said, "You don't have to do this, you know. Just stop your breath!" With that the bird took a second breath in and a much longer exhale. As it exhaled, his head rolled to the side, his wings dropped down and open, his legs went limp. His third and last breath was shallow. I realized that I was witnessing death. The Tibetans say "three breaths and you are out," (meaning out of body and passed over). But I could see the bird's heart still beating inside its tiny chest. So I said, "Now stop your heart."

With that the baby bird opened his eye for the first and only time in his short life. Baby bluebird's eyes are sealed shut at birth and do not open until they are older than my young friend. The open eye stared straight into my heart and we were instantly one. I can never put into words the connection he and I made at that moment, but I am forever changed by the experience of letting him go. Once I stopped controlling and began to honor his dance, I saw his life as he wanted it to be. I witnessed his intelligence, wisdom, and total lack of fear. I glimpsed the reflection of God in him. I was touched by this tiny being. With that, his eye closed and his heartbeats followed the same pattern as his former breaths. Three beats and he was gone. He died in my hand, within seconds of my release, and left me with an understanding I will treasure all my life.

9th Co-Creative Thought Transformation

Old thought: Ego Armada
Alchemical transformation: Egoless

Judgment, possessiveness, and control are all products of the ego. Transforming these old thoughts into co-creative thought patterns related to compassion and honoring should prepare you for ending your reliance on and identification with the ego. Dismissing egoistical wants, needs, defenses, offenses, and fabrications is the next step in opening your heart more fully to the Divine and allowing God to guide you into a deeper mystical experience.

The ego is a component of the personality that maintains and promotes self-interest and self-importance. For the spiritual person on Heart Journey, the ego is a false frame of reference for growth and insight. God is, and should be, your point of reference. While you may understand this intellectually, rooting out the emotional response patterns perpetuated by the ego is a difficult process that requires insight and vigilance.

The ego both loves and hates you. The ego is that part of the small self which defends you against all attacks, no matter how slight, but also criticizes you for the smallest infraction. It is a double-edged sword intent on control, both controlling you and controlling others. The ego "loves" and protects you through ego defense mechanisms which ward off and respond to criticism from others. The ego "hates" you by setting unrealistic standards akin to perfectionism. Lowering your ego defense mechanisms and counteracting negative self-images not only opens your heart to greater love and understanding for others, but it also allows you to love yourself more completely just as you are.

The ego seeks to gain power by convincing you that you need to be defended. Others may disapprove of you, censure what you say, denounce what you do, mock what you believe, or devalue what you have. Haven't you been hurt in the past? Proof positive that you need defending! The ego develops a repertoire of defense mechanisms that will keep negative comments at bay and/or counter any challenge. On the other hand, a good defense can be an offense. Why wait? By criticizing others or putting them down, your position and status can be assured before any assault, so let the ego fire the first shot! Either way you look at it, whether defending or offending, the goal is self-protection. What you do not see is that defense mechanisms result in the illusion of separation, or the misconception that you and your adversary have nothing in common and your paths are not linked in any way or for any reason. He or she has nothing to show or teach you and there is nothing you need to understand about him, her or yourself.

The ego also critiques you and your performance. In order to minimize criticism by others and the potential for any future emotional repercussions, you need to be perfect or at least better than your critics. If you do not stand up in comparison, you are sure to hear of your faults sooner or later. The ego acts as the inner critic and will waste no time pointing out real or imagined flaws. Perfectionism is the gold standard, but being better than others will do in a pinch. Either one insures your higher status, moving you beyond reproach, and warding off future faultfinding by others. Image is everything and the emphasis is on the external manifestation. Sometimes the voice and standards of the inner critic echoes those of a parent or authority figure. Regardless, it is yours to deal with now. In all situations, just do your best, given the circumstances, time limits, and resources available. Realize that this is all you can or need do. Perfection is not an option for anyone. It is unreasonable and unhealthy to allow the ego to push you to adhere to unrealistic expectations.

Offensive attacks on others, defensive techniques, and self-criticism are meant to keep you and others in line. The ego wants you to believe that all this is essential to you when in reality it is not. It is the ego that needs to be needed in order to survive. You, on the other hand, do not need the ego at all.

Control is not of the heart and neither is the ego. Both are the antithesis of love and openness. The two modes of interaction, control and love, are mutually exclusive. If you wish to be openhearted, to attract and receive abundance while continuing on a mystical journey, surrender control and drop your defenses. Once the ego is no longer in control, it will cease to be relevant and empowered. It is at this point that God comes most relevant. God should be your spiritual compass, empowering your life.

The ego is a passe'personality remnant from "fight or flight" days of old. We used to have to fight for survival or flee to safety. Since the majority of us are no longer in danger and needing to run away quickly or stand our ground and fight valiantly, the ego could be out of a job were it not for the inflation of far less damaging situations. The slightest, unintended comment can elicit a defensive response and emotional reaction. It is the negative emotion, whether it be anger, fear, or doubt, which repeatedly ignites a self-protective response that initiates the ego's return to power and usurps God's influence and guidance.

The ego propagates the illusion of separateness. Despite what the ego might tell you, you are not a separate and distinct entity needing a strong offense or defense. Instead, you are part of a whole seeking oneness and connection, something the ego tries to prevent. The ego keeps you from knowing and experiencing yourself and others at a deeper level by erecting an artificial barrier composed of slights, injustices, fears, doubts, lack of confidence and anger, much of which is fabricated or blown out of proportion.

Because of the ego's offensive and defensive tactics, you can lose sight of your connection to others, God, and even yourself.

Have you ever seen someone open up when you loved him or her beyond expectations? Have you noticed that good deeds are infectious? Or that negativity can spread? Whatever you do or focus on is contagious. There really is no barrier or separation, but by being lulled into thinking you are better than others, or being beaten down into believing that you will never be good enough, you end up isolated, alone, and separate. There is no equality, no meeting of the minds and hearts. It is a trap to feel proud, better than others, impenetrable, and totally in control. It is also a trap to self-flagellate. Both tactics are ego driven and meant to divide, conquer, and isolate.

To progress quickly on your spiritual journey, appreciate who you are and be grateful without being prideful. At the same time, lower your defenses and allow yourself to experience vulnerability, humility, and personal folly. There is no need to defend or explain yourself. Instead, take time to honestly listen to what others have to say. You might learn something when you see yourself through their eyes. Sometimes the image will be true and helpful, sometimes the image will be distorted by the messenger's own ego defenses. But if you at least listen, you can connect with another, understand his or her position, address misconceptions, and sometimes resolve disagreements. Saying you are sorry for a given situation even when you are not totally at fault indicates that you recognize another's disappointment. There is no need to react, defend, or counter in many instances. The egoless person in touch with God listens to what is being said and seeks to build bridges instead of walls.

In the same manner, learn to listen to what your co-creative Partner has to say. Ask to be shown and invite God's review. When the response is gentle but more loving than you would have imagined, you know you are being shown spiritual wisdom. Keep in mind that God will never berate you or make demands. God will never condemn you or others. The level of love and wisdom innate to the exchange keynotes Divine insight.

A great asset for getting around the ego and progressing spiritually is your ability to look at yourself honestly and laugh at your own folly. You are human. Sometimes your missteps will be intentional, sometimes they will be accidental, but if you knew better, you would do better. Humor gentles your eyes, whether you look at yourself or others. The wise person sees everyone's shortcomings, including his or her own with gentleness, then uses the information to grow spiritually. We are all naked really; just some of us still think we have clothes on.

Example of My Own Egotistic Folly

Maybe I was feeling insecure or maybe I was prideful. I was definitely nervous. I was about to speak at a conference on a new topic. I wasn't sure how my lecture would be received. I turned to God for reassurance and casually said, "Gee, it would be nice if I got a standing ovation for this talk!" That was my ego talking!

When I was introduced, the announcer suggested everyone stand and give me a warm welcome and standing ovation *before* my talk. I had a good laugh at my own folly as I walked onto the stage. God has a great sense of humor! I was being shown how misguided my ego was. And just to complete the lesson, after I spoke, no one stood up.

10th Co-Creative Thought Transformation

Old thought: Guilt
Alchemical transformation: Forgiveness

Guilt can serve a useful learning purpose when it leads to awareness, growth, restitution, healing, and eventually, forgiveness. But guilt is more commonly experienced as a negative emotion that justifies further punishment or self-flagellation even after apologies or attempts at reparation have been made. All negativity leads to heart closure and guilt is no exception, whether you feel guilty long after it is productive, or you keep guilt alive by withholding forgiveness from others. The lead to gold alchemical transformation for guilt is forgiveness which can promote healing for both the perpetrator and the victim.

When you are the guilty party, transgressions, crimes, mistakes, and slights whether intentional or unintentional usually lead to feelings of regret and guilt in all but the sociopath, child, and those mentally ill or intellectually challenged. It is normal to feel guilty when you have caused another pain or difficulty, but the goal is to learn from your mistakes and make a regretful situation better. In the most positive manifestation, guilt can be a stepping stone to healing and forgiveness if you take the following steps regardless of the nature of your offense, from a serious crime or injury to a derogatory comment or joke at someone's expense.

1. You must accept responsibility for your actions.
2. You must be contrite and apologize.
3. You should make reparation, as best you can.
4. You need to resolve to change in the future.
5. Ask for forgiveness and forgive yourself.

Step one

Recognize that guilt is your doorway to insight when you take full responsibility for your actions or behavior. You cannot begin the healing process, for you or the victim, until you take this first step. Owning what you did or did not do, intentionally or unintentionally, leads to insight and understanding. It allows you to grasp what you have done and the impact you have had on others. When you take full responsibility for your actions, you open the door to both psychological and spiritual growth. If you don't take responsibility, you will never fully relate to the damage you have caused or empathize with the victim. Instead, you maintain or develop a blind spot. By avoiding accountability, you thwart your own growth and healing for the victim.

Step two

You have to truly regret your actions or behavior and feel sorry for any injury, pain, or negative effect they might have had. If possible, return to face the difficult situation you created and apologize to the victim for your past transgressions or ineptitude. If you feel that a direct apology would be inappropriate or impossible for one reason or another and the offense is a major one, confess to a religious figure, healthcare professional, therapist, friend, or law enforcement officer depending on the nature of the offense. Giving voice to your apology deepens your sense of responsibility and insight into the impact of your offense on the victim.

Step three

You are required to make amends to the victim if possible. It is not enough just to say you are sorry. Apologies are hollow when there is no reparation, restitution, or compensation. You must help the victim return to the former state if achievable. You can make amends either directly or indirectly, depending on what is best for the other party. If interaction is ill advised or amends impossible, lend assistance to victims of similar circumstances or other causes. Do some good somewhere for someone. This is for your own personal healing and will help you realize the full effect of any injury or pain you caused. Honor the process of restitution in an appropriate manner. When you pay for the damage you create, or work to correct the problems you have caused, you are not only less likely to offend again in the future. You become part of the solution rather than the problem.

Step four

Make a firm commitment to change. Learn all you can from your mistake and resolve to do things differently hereafter by investigating your motives and developing a positive strategy for the future. What led you to that situation? What caused you to respond the way you did? There had to have been other, more appropriate responses. What were those options? What kept you from choosing one of them instead? How would others have handled this situation? Is there a role model you can look up to? Consider what you would do differently now if you could turn back time. Come up with a game plan. Gaining insight into what you did and why you did it along with what you can do differently can help to prevent future occurrences. Your apology and reparations mean nothing if you continue to behave in the same manner, creating new offenses.

Step five

You may or may not be lucky enough to be forgiven by the victim, but regardless, you need to forgive yourself. You are a student of life involved in a learning process. You may make decisions you later regret and sometimes terrible mistakes, both intentional and unintentional. If you have conscientiously gone through the other four steps, you have the right and responsibility to forgive yourself. This is a necessary step in your own healing.

If you have committed a crime or more serious transgression, you will probably experience a lifetime of insight from this traumatic event. The more serious the offense, the more times you will relive the event and have to go through the five steps. For you, this will be a repetitive process. Healing will involve shedding layers and layers of counterproductive behavior and establishing new rehabilitated social skills. You may never be forgiven by the victim and find it difficult to forgive yourself, but as you shed each layer and reform yourself, honor your progress. Forgive yourself bit by bit with each round if that is all you can do. Find a way to give to others so the healing process can continue and your heart can open.

If you are plagued by guilt in regard to a petty offense, you probably have not been through the five steps or been conscientious enough as you accomplished them. You need to dig deeper and try harder. If you have made sincere and repeated efforts over a slight offense without positive results, it is time to move on or see a counselor. Guilt is a useless and wasteful emotion when it lingers like an old house guest who is no longer welcomed. Once you have done everything that can or need be done to make amends and prevent future reoccurrences, forgive yourself and put the matter to rest even if others do not or cannot. You should not wallow in guilt any more than the victim should remain stuck in self-pity. It is time to rise above the negativity and begin to recreate your life for yourself and others.

The less guilt you experience over the past or carry in the present once you have gone through the forgiveness process, the more likely you are to look at yourself and your actions honestly. Awareness can lead to preemptive corrections. You won't have to live mistakes in the future if you stay alert and proactive. You can begin to project your possible actions forward, see their probably effects and responses, and then make appropriate adjustments before proceeding. In this way, foresight replaces hindsight and enables increasing self-mastery.

The other side of guilt involves the victim withholding forgiveness and getting stuck in victimization. This can be both psychologically and spiritually damaging and makes no sense when the offense is minor and unintended and the offender is truly sorry while attempting to make reparations or correct the situation. Refusing to forgive and holding onto pain in this situation suggests a psychological pattern of victimization that might be best addressed in counseling if it is a repetitive life occurrence. Even if the offender refuses to apologize, is incapable of understanding the pain he or she caused, or simply unaware for one reason or another, you should endeavor to rise above the situation and move on. If nothing can be gained from trying to inform the perpetrator as to his or her transgressions, bypass this person completely and recreate your life. Don't get angry, don't get even, get enlightened! With God as your Partner, you are more powerful and creative than anything that has happened to you.

Forgiveness is much more difficult, but not impossible, when the offense is major, long lasting, and/or permanent. But regardless of the offense committed and the pain experienced, the inability to forgive the perpetrator, or to channel the hurt and anger into a positive pursuit or cause, extends and magnifies the damaging impact of the original offense. When you refuse to forgive, you continue to replay the offense and carry the pain with you on a daily and even hourly basis. This not only effects your heart openness, but also your spiritual growth, as well as your mental and physical health. In this way, the original offense is extended well into the future and far beyond the initial incident.

Withholding forgiveness negates any possibility of compassion or understanding for the perpetrator. This may or may not be possible for you given a major offense, and might seem unreasonable when a crime is truly senseless, the effect permanent, and/or there is no justice. The important point to keep in mind is that forgiveness is not primarily for the benefit of the offender, it is for your benefit. You do not have to make a statement of forgiveness to the offender or even see him or her face to face. This may only increase your pain and sense of victimization. Forgiveness is for you the victim because the inability to accept and forgive will stunt your spiritual growth and close your heart, even if only a little, to all those you love and all the joy in being with your loved ones.

When you refuse to accept and forgive, depression or anger usually sets in. Depression is very different from grief. Grief is an immediate reaction to a serious offense that involves painful sadness. Grief tends to bring people together, forming or strengthening interpersonal bonds as others rally around with offers of support. Grieving individuals may also draw closer to God for comfort or assistance. Grief can lighten with time and eventually be commingled with fond memories of the past and resolve, if not hope, for the future.

Depression, on the other hand, is very different from grief. Depression deepens and darkens with time. It separates and isolates as the individual withdraws from interaction with others and may even become mentally, emotionally, and physically unreachable. Any and all positive emotion can be overwhelmed by negativity. Life slows down for the depressed individual as there is no attempt to move forward. A truly depressed person cannot see positive choices or contemplate constructive actions. He or she prefers to do nothing and ceases to truly relate to anyone or anything.

Refusing to forgive can instead result in anger. While depression lacks movement, anger can be a call to action. Hopefully this will be corrective action related to a purpose or cause instead of a reaction or retaliation. Allowing anger to rage without a creative or productive outlet for expression will be detrimental to your physical and emotional health as well as you spiritual growth. Relationships may suffer, even relationships with those you love. Anger can separate and isolate as effectively as depression. Creating a means to effect positive change for yourself or others that will prevent unfortunate events or harm in the future makes the best of a bad or even horrible situation. Sublimating your anger and pain into a push for change is an act of caring for others that allows the heart to remain open and heal. If you cannot forgive, make a difference, somehow, somewhere, and some way, otherwise you will feel helpless against injustice and weakened by your inability to respond. You are not helpless and weak. With the help of your co-creative Partner you can channel your anger in a positive and productive manner.

If you are or have been a victim, you have to find a way to come to terms with what has happened so you can live a full life with an open loving heart. You cannot stop living and loving because of someone else's mistake or transgression. That is giving them too much power. You have to move on for your own sake and for the sake of those you love. Victims who become courageous and inspirational when faced with a major challenge or injury remain openhearted because of their beneficial effect on and interchange with others.

Confer with your co-creative Partner if you want to do something constructive and transformational. What sense of purpose can you lend to a painful event? How can you effect a positive change for the future? If you cannot forgive, then at least respond in a creative or artistic manner for the sake of your own healing. I realize this is easier said than done, especially when the offense is serious, but perhaps it is your best option for the future and essentially what you are here to do.

Even if you are truly creating the life you deserve and want, the inability to forgive in one small area of your heart can weaken your lovingness and result in a heart less open to all regardless of whether you are forgiving yourself or another. You cannot harbor guilt, depression, anger, or a lack of forgiveness and not be tainted by it. Refusing to forgive defines you as either a perpetrator or a victim. You carry the label with you, identify with it, and relive it. You need to put this burden down. When you fail to respond effectively to an offense, you change physically, mentally, emotionally, and spiritually. A positive response is every bit as important as forgiveness. The best healing comes when you thrive in spite of and because of whatever you have been through and transform guilt into forgiveness. If you are able to accomplish this, you will be rewarded with a completely open in-flowing and overflowing heart.

11th Co-Creative Thought Transformation

Old thought: Distrust
Alchemical transformation: Trust and Faith

There is a reason that these last three alchemical thought transformations are at the end of the chapter; they are difficult to attempt, let alone master, even in a lifetime.

They represent the final stages of heart openness, surrender to God, and selflessness that lead to the ability to attract, receive, and even generate abundance for yourself, others, and the world.

Distrust and trust in this context have nothing to do with partners, spouses, children or other family members. They are not God and they are not perfect. You need to use your own judgment in these relationships and in regard to mundane matters. Distrust and trust as presented here are only in relation to God. You might be thinking that you have built a strong relationship with your co-creative Partner and you totally trust God in guiding your life. You may have experienced one or more Divine upgrades at this point. In upgrade situations it is easy to step back, loosen the reins, and let God recreate the situation. It is easy to surrender when something better is occurring.

The real question is, "Does your trust and faith in God include whatever happens to come your way?" What if your desire is never fulfilled? What if the thing you fear and dread most is for your highest good? Are you willing to accept denial or adversity? Illness? Loss? Your commitment to God, the co-creative partnership, and your spiritual growth may be tested at some point. This is not to say that negative things will happen, but every life has its ups and downs. When the chips are down, will you blame God? Will you lose faith? Is your trust so fragile that it cannot withstand even the smallest life challenge or adversity?

In addition to adversity, do you lose faith whenever you don't understand why things are the way they are, or conversely, why they aren't different? Do you look for guarantees regarding the outcome or success of your endeavors? Do you expect to know the rhyme or reason for any event or course of action ahead of time? Sometimes the reason is not evident for months or even years after the fact and only revealed in hindsight. Will you insist on knowing exactly where you are headed and how you will get there before you proceed or can you trust that God knows the way? Can you follow blindly God and "put this bead here?" (See Chapter 11: Example of Following Blindly.)

The need to understand in advance or along the way is a control issue that indicates an inability to surrender completely. The implication is that once you understand you will give your approval and proceed. When you have complete faith in God, you trust God's guidance even if pieces of information are lacking. The mystical journey is irrational at times. It is given that you will not always understand the how, why, where, and when, but must proceed by simply placing one foot in front of the other. You cannot claim to trust in God when there are prerequisites to your faith. There cannot be, nor should there ever be, preconditions to your faith and trust in God.

A lack of trust and faith can arise in a completely different situation. Perhaps there is no adversity, but there is also no communication with your co-creative Partner. This takes a lack of understanding to a new level. Not only are you lacking complete information, you have a sense of abandonment. Can you continue to believe in the co-creative partnership and trust in God if communication seems to dry up and stop?

What if there are no visions, no signs or symbols, and the thought voice in your head falls quiet? Can you carry on in the manner God has revealed to you without apparent Divine support and guidance? The reality is that this is likely to happen sooner or later. This period of silence is common in the spiritual progression of the mystic and has been called, "The Dark Night of the Soul" by Saint John of the Cross, a Christian mystic. At some point, it may be your task to carry on in a vacuum and demonstrate the knowledge and principles that you have learned. Your trust and faith in God is not tempered until it has been tested.

The questions presented above are important because they query your commitment to God and the path you have chosen, both in good times and in bad, in sickness and in health, for richer or poorer, and when is direct communication or in silence. You co-creative partnership with God is like a betrothal. As in any engagement leading to marriage, the relationship needs to grow in love, trust, and faith. There are challenges innate to spiritual development just as there are challenges that strengthen a commitment to marry. If or when adversity, a lack of understanding, or silence arises, you need to hold your ground in regard to your beliefs, experiences, and devotion to God. Continue on in the manner inherent to the teachings, practices, wisdom, and guidance already revealed in past communications.

Example of Trust in God

There was a firewalking lecture and experience near my home. It was clear to me that I needed to attend though I was not convinced that I wanted to firewalk. Before we went into the lecture, we were shown a cord of wood, fifteen feet long and five feet high. It was set on fire and allowed to burn down during the lecture. While sitting in the lecture for the next two hours, I saw a bird flying back and forth in the rafters of the building. I kept thinking, "I do not want to be trapped and limited like that bird. I need to free my thinking, my beliefs, and ultimately my life."

When we came out after the lecture, the coals were spread out over a fifteen foot path. As we formed a circle around the coals, you could feel the heat and see the glow. I know there is some controversy regarding whether or not the coals are really hot or can actually burn you, but logic says you should be able to feel something!

Before I walked, I made a plea to God.

> "Please, do not let me get burned. I do not want my feet to get blistered walking over the coals. In fact, I do not want to even feel the heat of the coals under my feet. I wish to ride on a cushion of air, never touching the lumps of coals at all."

This was my request to God and I trusted that it would be so. Halfway down the fire pit, I discovered to my shock that I actually could not feel the coals under my feet. I looked down. I could see the solid, fat, glowing chunks I was stepping on. I could *hear* them crunch, but only *felt* softness as I walked the length of the fire pit. I remember thinking how amazing this was.

12th Co-Creative Thought Transformation

Old thought: Self
Alchemical transformation: No-Self

At this point, you might think that there is not much left to transform. You have been through eleven alchemical thought transformations. You have been surrendering self-will and following Thy Will. You have become more heart-centered and open. Cleansing has occurred as you practiced releasing judgments, control, and anger. You have been emptying yourself of personal agendas that interfere with being a representation of love. Because of your efforts, the co-creative partnership is now strong. Perhaps you attract and receive abundance, or even channel it to others. The whole process of practicing the alchemical co-creative thought transformations is leading you toward transparency wherein you shift from self with personal agendas to no-self with only Divine agendas. You are beginning to act as God would have you act and live as God would have you live.

While progressing through the first eleven alchemical co-creative thought transformations you made significant emotional changes. Anger has abated, at least somewhat. You are now less judgmental, defensive, and controlling. You have learned to let go and let God. Along the way, some life issues or psychological complexes may have been resolved. This should allow you to look forward to the future rather than back at the past. You embody feelings of love for yourself, others, and God. Hopefully, this has become your primary emotion with all of its variations of empathy, understanding, compassion, and forgiveness. When you feel the pain of others, you can respond as God would respond with offers of support. You practice kindness toward all living things and encourage others to be the best they can be. You are becoming an emissary for God on earth, feeling as God would have you feel, loving as God would have you love.

The alchemical co-creative thought transformations have also led to intellectual development. You have grown while on your Heart Journey. At this point, decisions should not be made just from a practical, rational, or emotional perspective. They should be based on contemplation and collaboration with your co-creative Partner. This adds a whole new dimension to the decision-making process. As a result, your choices are more on target, insightful, and highly effective even in stressful situations. The way you think and reason is now more cohesive and consistent. You have conviction because of a deeper understanding of how and why things work. Choices are good for you, but also good for others. Based on the insights gleaned from your co-creative exchanges with your Partner, you think wisely as God would have you think and choose wisely as God would have you choose for yourself and those around you.

Spiritually, you see with the eyes of compassion and offer assistance where it is needed. Your co-creative partnership with God gives you the strength to follow your passion. Your beliefs are evolving as insights arise from your interchange with God. These beliefs are now the backbone of your ethics, morals and philosophy of life. When you make a commitment, you keep it. You are becoming a silent spiritual warrior for God. There is no need to preach, no need to tell others what to believe or what to do. You only need to become as God would have you become, an example to others.

Your body, mind and spirit are more harmonious and coordinated. There is a consistency between all three levels. What you intuit and believe becomes what you think and feel. Together they are the basis for action in accordance with the co-creative process. In this way, you come to be a clear channel, a vehicle for the manifestation of Divinity on earth in all of its forms, in addition to being a vehicle for the manifestation of abundance. Essentially there is no difference between manifesting love and manifesting abundance. They follow the same pathway through an open heart. By practicing all that you have learned up to this point, you manifest abundance as God would have you manifest.

All this might sound like a tall order, but it does not have to be so. The "no-self" fits neatly and even efficiently into everyday life. It is the dedication to the process of conferring with your co-creative Partner and then following God's lead instead of self interest. Your individualized niche in the scheme of things has all been worked out within the co-creative partnership. You are where you need to be doing what you need to do for yourself and others. It is not a static position, but an evolving path intended to foster spiritual growth.

The concept of no-self has a range of manifestations from simply listening and heeding, to dissolving all personal agendas and surrendering everything to God. A mother foregoes her own needs so her baby can be comforted. This is no-self. A father goes to work to support his family. This is no-self. But then, so too is self-denial or sacrifice for the good of the whole. The level you function at and the degree to which you ignore self-interest is between you and your co-creative Partner. It may change from situation to situation or from one time to another.

Example of Shape-Shifting

I was traveling with a friend and we were staying with her teacher for a few days, a Cherokee medicine woman. It had not occurred to me to check out the accommodations ahead of time. I was glad to experience Sedona and have a place to stay. Unfortunately, the home had between four and seven resident cats, depending on the time frame, and I am extremely allergic to cats. I develop severe asthma when I am around them. There is no medication that helps with this and I have tried them all including inhalers, antihistamines, and anti-allergy medications. The first night of my stay was the closest I have ever come to being hospitalized for not being able to breathe.

My host was aware of the problem and during that first night and every night of my stay, she shape-shifted and came to my room in the form of an eagle, hawk, or owl. I never saw the bird physically, but clearly felt its five foot wingspan hovering over my body. The beat of the large wings sent rushes of air onto my face and neck as they flapped back and forth. I was never frightened by the visits. I knew my host was there to heal me.

I awoke early in the morning after my first night and only the lower left lung was clear enough for me to breath. I got dressed and went out walking. The fresh air always seems to clear my lungs and by the time I returned an hour later, I was feeling much better. The medicine woman was up and having breakfast. She told me she had done her best the night before, but was only able to clear the lower part of my left lung. Her description was exactly what I was feeling when I awoke.

Final Words

The transformations listed in this chapter have many levels of mastery. Each time you work your way through them, new insights and skills will arise and your experiences will be different. There are layers and layers of teaching associated with each one. They all have one goal, to open your heart to greater love for yourself, others and God while attracting and receiving abundance. Progress with these twelve steps will be reflected in progress through the eight stages of the heart opening described in the next chapter and advancement on the mystical path. My recommendation is that you focus on one co-creative thought transformation each month, for a time period of one year. After a year you will have practiced, but not mastered, each one of the twelve thought transformations. At that point, you may choose to return to the first alchemical thought transformation, the "Do-it-Yourself Fantasy" and begin a new cycle of discovery, insight, and spiritual growth. Each time your repeat the cycle or return to a particularly difficult co-creative thought transformation, new insights will arise fostering further spiritual growth.

Chapter Nineteen:
Eight Stages of Heart Openness

Introduction

Awareness and recognition of the following stages of heart openness arise as you work through the Twelve Co-creative Thought Transformations and the spiritual wisdom communicated directly to you by your co-creative Partner, God. You will most likely start with the first stage, "Cognizance of Heart Closure." This does not mean that your heart is entirely closed, but that some part of your thinking, feeling, or interaction with others is limited. Heart Journey is meant to shine a light on areas of constriction and most beginners withhold love from someone, even from his or herself, or in certain situations. It is possible to start out at some other stage, but your placement will most likely be in one of the first four stages included in "Signs of an Opening Heart." As you continue to work with the Twelve Co-creative Thought Transformations and grow spiritually, your heart will open more fully, remain open longer, and begin to harmonize internally and externally. Thoughts and feelings will reflect your spiritual maturity and your actions will be consistent with Divine input and heart openness. Once that has occurred, you may begin to experience the four later stages of heart openness included in "Signs of an Open Heart." This is where the greatest amount of abundance can be received, channeled, and also generated for self and others.

You probably will not progress through the Eight Stages of Heart Openness in a linear fashion. At different times, in different situations, and with different people you will be at various stages, sometimes simultaneously. You may master some stages quickly, but struggle with others. You may jump ahead or fall back at any time. Just because you have reached a certain level of heart openness does not mean you will stay there. Openness can be very erratic, especially in the beginning, and can change several times during the day depending on who you are with, events, and circumstances. With time and practice, you will rise to higher and higher levels of heart openness and spend longer periods in the later stages. Eventually, you will remain open at all times, in all situations, and to everyone you encounter. The ultimate goal is to stay in the state of Acceptance and Generation, accepting what God has in mind for you and generating abundance and happiness for yourself and others. Only a truly open and loving heart can do this.

The value of knowing the Eight Stages of Heart Openness comes from recognizing where you are in the process of opening your heart and comprehending the corresponding task before you. Each stage is linked to a specific lesson which must be completed in order to move on to the next higher level. Mastery in one situation does not necessarily mean mastery in all situations. Success in one relationship does not necessarily mean success in all relationships. Heart openness can be situation and relationship specific in the beginning though the goal is to always remain openhearted. It is possible to skip levels, but only if you have previously mastered the tasks associated with the interim level or levels in one or more areas of your life, and can then quickly comprehend and instantaneously complete intervening steps. Skipping comes with time and experience.

You should be aware that cleansing will be part of the process and is meant to strengthen your ability to remain open. Once you commit your heart to openness, love, and compassion, any hidden and ignored latent issues will come to light. Relationships and situations from long ago will return, or modern day replicas will arise. Reliving the emotional trauma associated with hurt, injustice, mistakes, poor decisions, or tragedy is painful, yet intended to heal your heart and liberate your ability to love. Welcome the option of rewriting your responses and seeing things differently this time around. The other person might not change, the situation may remain the same, but you have the freedom to choose, see, or understand differently. That may be all you can do, but it will be enough to maintain heart openness.

After you have mastered all of the stages of heart openness, you may be in none of them. This is not meant to be a complete list of all possibilities. It is simply the beginning of the process. The Eight Stages of Heart Openness can fall away to new levels of understanding and experience beyond words and symbols. The way of the mystic eventually transcends all communication and teaching, becoming individualized and ineffable. Heart Journey is meant to lead you in the process of heart openness with the understanding that a deeper love of self, other, and God is still possible.

Signs of an Opening Heart

Stage One: Cognizance of Heart Closure

There are three main reasons why the heart is closed, either partially or completely. One is related to past wounds and pain. The second is associated with training and prejudice. The third is the result of inattention and dissociation from emotions, relationships, and life in general through a shift in priorities. For example, internal awareness and interpersonal involvement can be replaced by an emphasis on money, possessions, career, or any other activity that isolates the individual, numbs the emotions, monopolizes time, and ignores the heart. Many times the three reasons for closure are interrelated. A past wounding can result in prejudice and lead to a shift in priorities and avoidance of heartfelt interchanges.

Our hearts, like our relationships, atrophy when ignored. What we do not use, we lose. A wounding in the past can lead to avoidance of issues, situations, and people in the present appearing similar to previous injuries or pain. Evasion usually works for a period of time, but only because something in the heart dies or lies dormant. Sooner or later someone comes along who, either through attraction or revulsion, reopens the past hurt and awakens the heart to the love that is lacking. This is the moment when one becomes cognizant of heart closure.

The process is similar when one has been trained to fear or hate a particular segment of the population. Prejudice and indoctrination result in at least partial heart closure, and are likely to generalize to other groups and situations. With time, intolerance and discrimination grow beyond the initial sensitization and may be passed on from one generation to the next. It is only when someone in the line of succession is seized by an interaction or experience that does not fit the distorted belief and counteracts the ingrained perception that change begins. When one person becomes cognizant of his or her heart closure and makes a change, the chain is broken.

Isolation and inattentiveness are many times the result of past pain and conditioning, but the resulting shift in priorities is not normally seen as avoidance. The individual gets caught up in life, job, acquisition, and time restraints. Responsibilities replace interpersonal connections and while the individual may be very dependable and mature while carrying out duties, this does not necessarily translate into joyous interactions or a fulfilling lifestyle. Despite the daily interaction, the individual is more focused on doing than being, burning the candle at both ends. A generalized lack of emotion is a major coping mechanism. Inattentiveness of this nature can be far reaching in its effect on heart openness. Awakening, when it comes, is usually accompanied by regret over the time and opportunities ignored and missed.

In any of these situations, the lack of heart openness is not necessarily conscious or intentional. It is easy to drift away from pain into forgetfulness, closing the door and the heart to any and all experiences, unpleasant or not, and getting busy with work or daily living while failing to connect with anyone in a heartfelt way. Dissociation can last for years or even decades. Stress adds to the separation by depleting emotional energy and the urge for renewal. Relationships and connections that are complicated and demanding get even less attention. When you are stressed out, low on energy, money, resources, and time, you tend to avoid involvements that include problems, particularly complex, multifaceted problems. In your ideal insulated world, everything needs to run smoothly.

Task: There is a moment of awareness when you heart awakens to the lack of openness and the need for greater lovingness. It can be like an insight dawning, a feeling rising, a pull to something outside of yourself, the consciousness of something greater, or the realization that something is wrong or missing. Regardless of your history, regardless of how many times you have passed this point, or even if this is your first awakening, you know there is more, more than you have been aware of before. Whatever the spark, it calls you like a moth to a flame and you are moved to open your heart, even if only a little, even if only tentatively.

With the knowing generally comes an issue of love, or the lack thereof, for someone. The person may be close to you, a family member, neighbor, relative, business partner or spouse. Conversely, the person might be your nemesis or a perpetrator of painful or criminal activity. You may be called to open to the possibility of love or compassion and asked to forgive. Perhaps you need to love or forgive yourself. A situation that rouses your heart from sleep may be part of your immediate experience, something seen or heard in the media, or an old memory rising from the depths. Regardless of the stimulus or circumstance, you know you have been deeply affected by a heartfelt insight and called to change. The only correct course of action is to surrender to the journey, acquire the skills necessary to open your heart more fully, and respond with love and compassion.

If you have been on Heart Journey for a while and have passed through this stage of heart openness before, issues will evolve over time and pertain to higher and higher levels of acceptance and unconditional love. It is possible to return to "Stage One, Cognizance of Heart Closure" again and again while still growing in your ability to love. Each round will be built on past openings and eventually move you to complete heart openness that is sustained over time. Only this, and nothing less, will allow you to permanently move on.

And so, your Heart Journey through the Eight Stages of Heart Openness begins. Recognize where and when you are less than loving, prejudiced, or unforgiving. Question your feelings, actions, and intentions. Do you demean, judge, avoid, hate, discriminate, control, deny, or ignore? Do you withhold love in any way whatsoever? Do you lack connectedness, meaningful relationships, and emotional fulfillment? Do you value things more than people, doing more than being? These are all signs of closure. The degree of closure does not matter. Any hesitation to loving well indicates some degree of closure and is the signature of "Stage One: Cognizance of Heart Closure."

Stage Two: Heart Vulnerability

As the heart begins to open, the first sensation to arise is vulnerability. Vulnerability is the signature of Stage Two. It originates from two conflicting dynamics: the willingness to move beyond some degree of closure; and the apprehension associated with doing so. The act of opening can be exciting in some situations, especially in regard to a new romantic relationship, but hesitancy and fear are also possible and common. After all, how many times have you loved and lost or been hurt? Your sense of anxiety and feeling of vulnerability can be related to a painful awareness of your own limitations as a lover on any or all levels, or your resistance to trusting in love again. Either way, you must step outside of your comfort zone to move through and beyond this stage.

Other circumstances are not new and compelling, but instead pre-existing. Perhaps your feeling of vulnerability is caused by a loss of control or threat to an existing relationship or situation. Your sense of security and stability can be undermined by a lover, spouse, partner, parent, or child. Your initial reaction might be to regain control. This will not resolve the problem in the long run and you will be forced to return to this stage of Heart Vulnerability again and again until you master the task of letting go and loving unconditionally.

If you are called to forgiveness, you might be wondering how you will protect yourself from similar situations in the future. Perhaps you need to develop skills and plans for security and safety. If present circumstances are immanently threatening or dangerous, you should protect yourself both physically and emotionally. Immediately remove yourself from the situation. This is not only the wise thing to do, but the spiritually correct way to proceed. Take minors or others in danger with you. Removal can be permanent or temporary depending on the situation. In either case, time away will allow you to regain your strength and to accurately perceive how to proceed in the future. You do not have to embrace the offender. You can have compassion and forgiveness for perpetrators from a distance and you might accomplish this more readily from a position of safety.

By letting go of blame or regret over past transgressions, whether yours or another's, you do not dishonor the pain and loss you or others have experienced. You are merely growing spiritually and moving past difficulty into more enlightened territory so that you might thrive. By learning from your experiences and rising from the ashes, you are strengthening your ability to love others in the future and opening to a more fulfilling and rewarding life.

Task: Vulnerability is a key to growth at this stage and it is essential that you remain awake, aware, and out of your comfort zone as much as possible. Mentally follow the trail back to the point of origination to discover the issue or issues which prompted heart closure in the first place. Is the reason for closure in the past? Is it an old excuse for missing present day healing? Is it the wise choice for the future? Closure occurs for a reason. The reason might be understandable given the circumstances or totally illogical, but is never the enlightened response.

Also examine the stimulus that initiates the call for openness. The reason for closure and the stimulus for openness are generally linked in some way. The stimulus might be specifically designed for you by your co-creative Partner to counteract your heart closure and encourage openness. An understanding of what the stimulus has to offer will help you move forward. What is the incentive? Is it hope, insight, compassion, longing, forgiveness, enlightenment, peace, or love? Is it success, a job or career you have always wanted, a partner, family, or child? How much promise and value do you give to the opportunities you are being offered? How much promise and value do you give to closure?

The course of action available to you regarding openness might seem illogical, and frequently a leap of faith is required. The stimulus and the feeling of vulnerability will coexist and persist until you make a decision and take a step forward. Should you choose to remain closed, the stimulus will lose impact and fade away temporarily, but fading is never permanent. If you are truly on a Heart Journey, your co-creative Partner will up the ante and call your hand again and again. In addition, visions of missed opportunities will weigh on you. The easiest and simplest course of action is to override your fears and the sense of vulnerability to open your heart.

If the stimulus calls for a mutually loving exchange, everyone involved can benefit. It is to your advantage to be open-hearted. If the call is to let go and let God, you really have no viable course of action. You do not own and cannot control. Sooner or later all attempts to manage or manipulate a person or situation will fail. You can only choose your response, either to love and move forward, or to close and then regress. If the call is for forgiveness, growth will be primarily for your benefit and may have little or nothing to do with another person. Those who find it in their hearts to forgive gain a lot more than those who are forgiven. Being forgiven is not a free pass and still mandates a lot of hard work and dedication to both psychological and spiritual growth. But the person who forgives immediately demonstrates a level of maturity which allows the heart to heal.

There is much to be gained from opening your heart despite feelings of vulnerability. Even an incremental increase can infuse your heart with joy, peace, wisdom, personal love, and/or Divine devotion. Any positive heart felt emotion is a strong sign that you are moving in the right direction.

Example of vulnerability

Many years ago I was in a challenging relationship that had serious flaws. I was doing my best to stay with this person and address issues, but I was not fully aware of the negative effect the relationship was having on me. One day, when I was alone, I began to sob uncontrollably. I must have cried for at least forty-five minutes. Waves of sadness were washing over me. In addition to my tears of sadness, my chest hurt. I was young and I was sure I was not having a physical heart attack, but I was very aware of the emotional pain causing a physical sensation. My heart was breaking. In my mind, I wanted the pain to end and so I pictured myself squeezing the pain into a smaller and smaller ball. When it reached the size of a walnut the pain completely stopped, but to my horror I realized I could not feel anything at all, no love, no joy, and no hope.

I cried out, "My God, what have I done?"

I immediately endeavored to open up the heart and asked for God's help. I remember saying, "Blow it back open. I do not care what it takes."

Now I have three children, one delivered by natural childbirth. I know what transition labor is like and the process of reopening the heart was very similar. I began to experience heartfelt contractions that would last for approximately thirty seconds. I would then have about three seconds to catch my breath before the next heart contraction began. The squeezing sensation went on for several minutes. I was never afraid. I trusted in God and the process. In the midst of the final contraction, I felt a snap in my chest as the bonds encircling my heart on some level seemed to break open. I took a deep breath and for the first time in this life, I breathed free and clear. Never had I taken a breath like that before.

At that very moment, this thought arose in me: "I will never again limit my ability to love, to someone else's ability to love me back." I had been both a victim and perpetrator of least common denominator love. I would love someone to the extent that that person loved me in return. I matched others step for step, but never loved beyond their limitations or abilities. This may have sufficed in the past, but because I was now in a difficult and unloving relationship, my ability to love my partner and all others was growing steadily smaller. To my dismay, I realized that I was letting another set the standard for love in my life. I was conforming to a distorted pattern that promoted rejection, pain, limitation, and fear instead of love. On that day, I chose heart openness across the board and in all situations without reservations, restrictions, or qualifications.

I faced my fears by overriding my feeling of vulnerability. My fear was that I would be rejected. The thought voice had a comment about that, "Mary, you have already been that!" This was so true. My greatest fear had already happened, repeatedly, I just did not want to believe it. I coped by closing my eyes, my ears, and my heart to the pain. The heart vulnerability I felt arose as a deterrent to recognizing this fact.

The stimulus for openness was the potential for a stronger bond of love with others in my life, my children, my family, my friends. "One bad apple does not spoil the whole bunch." I needed to dwell on what I had and not on what I had lost. The person I was estranged from was no longer my lover, no longer my provider. Realizing this freed me from repeated attempts at connection and allowed me to love unconditionally, without expectations of either of us. I could step back, view my situation clearly from a distance, and begin to heal.

Stage Three: Spiritual Input, Thoughts, Emotions, and the Physical

The heart is complex. It is not just a physical organ in the body. It is a multidimensional component with connections to the other levels of experience. For example, the heart is linked to our emotional nature. We know what it is to be heartbroken and experience a physical sensation in the chest of loss and missing. Love loss can literally lead to heart disease, as in "he or she died of a broken heart." We also know that the thrill of a new love can elicit a physical sensation of lightheartedness. Older committed couples in love relationships experience less stress. The joy and peace established over many years of togetherness lowers blood pressure and fosters good health.

But the heart does not just *respond* to stimuli; the heart can be the initiator of physical, emotional, mental, and spiritual change. When we pray, the heart opens and healing impulses are sent to the person prayed for. Studies show that patients prayed over do better than those who are not. Physical healing of the body, not just the heart, can be augmented by prayer. When we meditate, an open heart can foster a climate of love and peace that flows through the meditator as well as to others. This is why some prefer to meditate in groups. Thinking also changes during and after meditation. Insights arise as one draws closer to God. Just opening your heart and communicating with your co-creative Partner introduces you to spiritual concepts, intuitive perceptions, and compassionate responses. As insights trickle down and generate mundane applications, thinking evolves, emotions are calmed and uplifted, while actions become loving, meaningful and productive. All this arises from an open heart.

Spiritual Input and the Spiritual Level

The spiritual level of awareness includes any and all spiritual, philosophical and religious beliefs you have along with wisdom and insight gleaned from your communications with your co-creative Partner. Keep in mind that first and foremost your beliefs must be kind and have a positive influence on your life and on the lives of those you touch. Fanatical beliefs meant to justify harming or controlling others are incompatible with Heart Journey, unconditional love, and heart openness. Regardless of their source, judgmental beliefs that condemn others need to be purged as they restrict openness and thwart compassion.

Spiritual beliefs are meant to guide you in becoming a better, more loving person who leads a productive, fulfilling, and sacred life. The support you receive from your communications with God can give you a sense of purpose. Why are you here? What is your path? Are you leading a purpose-filled life and making a contribution? If you are here to do something, what are you meant to accomplish now or in your lifetime? Who can you help? You may have a life-long calling or be in a position to provide occasional assistance as needed. Your focus may be on family or extend out to the community or beyond. The point is to understand your calling, whatever that might be. It is the nature of spiritual growth and maturity that you see how we are connected and perform good works or acts of kindness that assist others or have a positive impact. Each contribution is important, no matter how small or infrequent. Through the co-creative partnership, God will encourage you to respond accordingly.

Your happiness and fulfillment are also God's concern. You are not meant to hammer yourself into something you are not. You are meant to manifest the innate beauty and joy within you. Divine communications can guide you when dealing with mundane choices, problems, and issues. This will ease the decision-making process and improve your results. Spiritual principles have practical applications to daily living situations that can sanctify your actions. Your co-creative partnership with God and your beliefs on a spiritual level are your touchstone for right action, right living, and positive choices. They provide structure and guidance through the good times and bad.

Task: Follow a routine of reflection and awareness of spiritual beliefs and principles through meditation and prayer. Regular contact with your co-creative Partner fosters internal and external peace and spiritual cohesiveness. Consciousness that is developed and maintained at this level is an important asset on your Heart Journey. This is the spiritual headwater which can flow into your life, impacting your thoughts, feelings and actions. Awareness of the heart connection at this level is crucial.

Thoughts and the Mental Level

While the spiritual level may consist of beliefs and Divine communications, the mental level consists of thoughts. When you are young and in school, your thoughts primarily consist of what you have been taught, what you have read, studied on your own, or been told. The mind does not endeavor to believe, it needs to know, and keeps a catalogue of both useful and trivial information. Thoughts naturally gravitate to logical information and rational comprehension. Sometimes scientific investigation and/or proof is required, depending on indoctrination and experience.

The mind also learns by figuring things out. Understanding cause and effect reality arises from the intellectual ability to analyze the connection between actions and results. "If I do this, then that will happen." This process is an innate form of learning and acquiring knowledge. It is how we grow mentally from a toddler who experiences gravity by dropping toys and watching them fall to the floor, to an adult who understands consequences and knows what actions, experiences, and situations are advantageous and those that are not. "I will never do that again!" The goal is to establish behavioral patterns that lead to successful outcomes through knowledge, good decisions, practical applications, appropriate actions, and an understanding of causality.

Thoughts also enable communication, whether it is communication between individuals or communication between levels of experience. This leads us to the most important task of the mental level in regard to Heart Journey and heart openness. Thoughts enable the translation of spiritual beliefs and wisdom gleaned from the co-creative partnership with God into appropriate applications, responses, and actions. This is a crucial step in the process of adhering to your beliefs. You must apply spiritual input to issues you face in life, make wise decisions, and construct an appropriate plan of action. The mind is the translator of spiritual principles and thoughts can be the translation of those principles.

Task: Awareness is the key. In those quiet moments of reflection, pay attention to your thoughts. Are they representative of higher input from the spiritual level or are they anchored to emotional debris and physical needs? This all important question determines the probability of spiritual growth or the lack thereof.

The mind is the builder and thoughts are the building blocks. Being aware of your thoughts means being aware of what you are building. This is an important link in the chain of command to living a sacred, abundant, and loving life. In the same way that a focused, sustained thought translates your desire for the purpose of manifestation through attraction and receptivity, the mind also translates spiritual principles into thoughts that reflect co-creative intentions and open-hearted lovingness that can impact emotional responses, relationships, and actions.

Emotions and the Emotional Level

When it comes to emotions, separate the needy, codependent, jealous, angry, and controlling emotions from those that are joyful, helpful, loving, and rewarding. The distinction is essential. Emotions are not all created equal. Some are constructive and some are destructive. The best emotions connect us with others and life in a meaningful way. Emotions like love foster strong bonds and stable relationships. They allow us to connect to one another and enable intimacy. Compassion leads to understanding others, and perhaps forgiveness. Passion and joyful productivity lends purpose and fulfillment to profession and life. Depending on you spiritual path and directive, any and all of these positive emotions can be in keeping with input from your co-creative Partner.

On the other hand, negative emotions such as jealousy and anger are never in keeping with spiritual input. Negative emotions create distance between friends and family members, and can destroy relationships. Blame and guilt deny compassion and understanding, eventually leading to isolation and loneliness. Depression robs life of meaning while hopelessness thwarts the ability to create positive solutions and change. It is the negative emotions that steal our potential and hold us captive in detrimental, counterproductive life-cycles.

Unfortunately, for most of us, emotions simply are and are not subject to control. You can be happy one moment and angry the next. Both positive and negative emotions tend to rise spontaneously. You might be feeling great until you get stuck in traffic on a hot, sticky day. You might cry watching a sad movie even though you know the story is make-believe. Conversely, you might cry at happy occasions like weddings or the birth of a child. Emotions are fluid. They can change quickly from one feeling to another and rise spontaneously without any conscious choice from you. Attempts to control emotions generally fail and suppression is not the answer. What you feel is what you feel, but what you do with the feeling is what counts.

While translation of spiritual principles occurs at the mental level, transmutation of negative feelings occurs at the emotional level. Translation is the spiritualization of thoughts; transmutation is the spiritualization of feelings. Transmutation is an alchemical process that raises one form to a higher manifestation, for example, the transformation of lead into gold. On the emotional level, transmutation changes a negative emotion like guilt into forgiveness, or anger into creativity. This is only done through training of the mind and emotions through the assistance of your co-creative Partner. It is a skill that is not easily taught, but is ascertained through insights gathered in the gap between thoughts and breaths in meditation and reflection. Don't hesitate to discuss negative emotions or difficult situations with your co-creative Partner. There will be no condemnation or rebuke, only insight.

This is the power attributed to the spiritualization of the emotional level. Rather than control or suppress the energy of a negative emotion, it can be channeled into a higher, more positive, and powerful expression that has a practical and productive application. Someone who is angry about a particular situation can create an effective solution to a personal or professional problem. For example, think of the changes in our consciousness and changes in state and federal laws that have been created by Mothers Against Drunk Driving, or the National Center for Missing and Exploited Children. These organizations were established by grieving parents who experienced personal tragedy and needed to do something positive for the sake of all children and in memory of their lost loved ones. These two examples are extreme cases of the transmutation of anger into a creative and positive response, but any act of forgiveness, even for the smallest transgression, is also a transmutation of a negative emotion into a positive one.

Task: Awareness is vital, so be cognizant of emotions as they arise. Do not attempt to suppress or control them. Honor your feelings and they will teach you, eventually. It will be difficult to let go and let God while scenarios replay again and again in your head and self-talk occupies you mind. This is common with a new transgression or wounding. Suspend judgment for the moment and allow feelings to cool a bit. Be gentle with yourself. When you are ready, take the situation to your co-creative Partner. At first, you might not get a response, or a response you are willing to accept. Time is on your side and insight will come when you are truly ready. It might arrive in a rush or be revealed slowly over daily exchanges. If you are persistent, and this is needed, especially with your first attempts at transmutation, you will see ways to grow and create from negative emotion to move ahead in a positive and productive manner. As you gain perspective and repeatedly reach for higher ground, negative emotions will be brought into closer alignment with your spiritual intent.

Body and the Physical plane

Translation of spiritual principles occurs at the mental level, transmutation of negativity occurs at the emotional level, but implementation is the process associated with the physical plane. This is the level at which manifestation occurs, where creative ideas are brought into form, where emotions are expressed for better or worse, where bodily needs are met, and actions produce either positive or negative results that have consequences. All actions are motivated by factors on the physical, emotional, mental, and spiritual levels. The all important question you need to ascertain is: what is the source of the motivation? Is the next step you are taking part of a logical progression? Is it instigated by an emotional reaction to an event or comment? Is it an ingrained habitual response? Or, is it inspired by spiritual input from communications with your co-creative Partner? Awareness of the motivating source for any action contemplated or taken heightens your understanding of why you do what you do, feel what you feel, say what you say, and believe what you believe. Although knee jerk responses seem to occur without thinking, they are not without causative emotions regardless of how involuntary they appear to be. Understanding motivation puts you in touch with the purpose, goal, and projected outcome of your actions, important pieces of information. If you wish to keep your heart open, you need to monitor thoughts, emotions, and actions.

Task: As with the other three planes, awareness is the key. The physical level is every bit as important as the spiritual, mental and emotional levels. This is where it all begins to come together . This is the bottom line manifestation. You can want to pay off your debts intellectually and feel that the emotional stress over unpaid bills is detrimental, but still go out and buy a big ticket item. You may need to lose weight, want to lose weight, and feel depressed over clothes that do not fit, and still eat too much of the wrong foods. Your actions need to reflect your beliefs, thoughts and feelings.

Stage Four: Harmonizing the Four Levels of Experience

Once you have become sensitized to the four levels of experience and their functions, the goal becomes one of inner harmony. The spiritual, mental, emotional, and physical levels need to function as a cohesive whole for the heart to open fully and remain open. Each individual level needs to be aligned with spiritual input and communications from your co-creative Partner. Harmonization is a step by step process that begins on the spiritual level, proceeds through the mental and emotional levels to be fulfilled on the physical level. Along the way, there can be no disagreement or resistance.

Spiritual Input and the Spiritual Level

The spiritual level is a wellspring of the best and brightest insights you can bring into the world. It is the standard bearer of positive incorporation of Divinity into humanity. Through times of meditation, prayer, and reflection you have been establishing strong and clear communication with God which you can now use this direct connection to seek guidance on any and all major and minor issues you face daily. Your connection to God as your co-creative Partner and your spiritual beliefs are meant to filter down to the mental, then the emotional, and finally, the physical level where appropriate action takes place. Congruency and consensus between you and God facilitates movement from one level to another and determines the best course of action. As you follow spiritual principles more closely, you begin to represent God in earthly matters.

Thoughts and the Mental Level

Spiritual principles and wisdom akin to the situation or issue at hand must be translated into the most appropriate application. You can have enlightening spiritual input, but unless you apply it in the most appropriate way and in a timely manner, results will be unsuccessful. It is the duty of the mental level through coordination with the spiritual level to comprehend pertinent principles and then translate them into a useful format that can both address issues and guide individual actions. Understanding principles and refining the course of action comes from close communication with your co-creative Partner. The back and forth, question and answer period is crucial when dealing with an important issue. Your feedback and insights into what is and what is not working clarifies directions and refines applications. The process may seem slow at first, but eventually, through awareness and reflection, it should become quicker, smoother, and more effective.

What makes this transition most effective is the logical reasoning on *why* a particular spiritual principle was chosen and *why* a particular application is the best option. This bit of information is a selling point the mind can use to convince the emotions that the plan is a good one. In this manner, the mind helps spiritual input convey both a lofty motivation and a concrete, beneficial result.

There are times when the spiritual input is totally based on faith and defies all logical explanation. This does happen, and unfortunately, at times like this, the mind can be swayed by what it has been taught or told, even if the information is false. This is where trust in your co-creative Partner is invaluable. It enables you to make a leap of faith when necessary. Important too are the communication guidelines around what is, and what is not, a communication from God. Though decisions might be based on faith, they should always reflect loving spiritual principles.

Emotions and the Emotional Level

Once spiritual input has been accurately translated into a constructive thought or course of action, the task becomes one of acceptance and adoption at the emotional level. The mental level as the go-between helps to facilitate this. As frequently happens, especially during trying times or in regard to serious matters, agendas are different once the emotions are involved. Communications may bounce back and forth between the mental and emotional levels until an accord is reached. Feelings are either innately compatible with the translated spiritual intent or must be transmuted to a more open-hearted form of expression and higher understanding. In this way, congruency is established between the spiritual, mental and emotional levels. Each step has its own transition to master, but as you work with the awareness of spiritual input, motivation, and the factors associated with the various levels, it is possible to arrive at the physical level with what amounts to a spiritual mandate.

Body and the Physical Plane

Even when a spiritual mandate has progressed to this point, there are still physical hurdles to overcome. Hormones, especially sex hormones can defy all logical and spiritual input. Though it is true that the body should follow and not lead, this is not always the case. Illness or fatigue can derail the ability to act. Rational analysis can seem irrational when it comes down to taking action. "You want me to what?" You have to ask yourself, are you living from the top down, (spiritual principles guiding thoughts, emotions, and actions), or are you living from the bottom up, (physical needs and emotional reactions directing life and possibly overruling rational thought and spiritual principles). Who is in control here or what is out of control? In the best of situations, the body carries forth the plan and behaves in a manner that is consistent with spiritual input, mental translation, and emotional commitment.

Task: The body is your spiritual vehicle while you are in physical form. It is the means by which you can live a sacred life. Exemplifying spiritual principles while harmonizing the four levels of experience allows the heart to open fully and an open heart increases one's ability to attract and receive abundance.

The unifying commonality associated with all four levels is love, and in this sense, the open heart is the melting pot of physical experiences, feelings, thoughts, and spiritual insights for the purposes of conscious, sacred living. It is the antithesis of fear and the doorway to enlightenment. In the Theosophical tradition, the heart has been called "The Rainbow Bridge," the connection between earth and Spirit, between human and Divine. In the Catholic tradition, the faithful are taught to meditate on the "Sacred Heart of Jesus." In the Buddhist tradition, the compassionate "Way of the Bodhisattva" is seen as the pursuit of enlightenment for the sake of all sentient beings. The heart is central to all spiritual traditions built on love. It is the means by which inner harmony is attained and sustained when thoughts, emotions and actions evolve to truly represent spiritual input. An open and loving heart is also the means by which abundance is attracted, received, channeled, and generated.

Your task for this stage of development is to harmonize the four levels of experience in accordance with communications from your co-creative Partner. Spiritual principles which have been translated into applications at the mental level and supported by feelings at the emotional level should be acted upon in an appropriate and timely manner. The end product should be loving and should result in a truly open heart. This stage is the last step in the process of opening the heart. The next four stages focus on the abilities innate to a loving heart that is fully open.

Signs of an Open Heart

The goal is not just to attain heart openness, but to remain open-hearted in all situations and to all people, come what may. You have crossed the great divide, so to speak, and you need to stay on this side, in one of these four stages of heart openness. This means you must continue to love others, love God, and also love yourself. Nothing less will keep you here.

Of the four stages associated with an open heart, only two, "Stage Five: Receiving Abundance," and, "Stage Six: Channeling Abundance," involve abundance as previously defined. The nature of abundance changes with "Stage Seven: Spiritual Stress Test and Surrender" and, "Stage Eight: Acceptance and Generation." The process of manifestation through attraction and receptivity also changes in these two final stages because you transition to a higher level of spiritual growth and co-creative maturity. In Stage Seven, there is a materialistic dry spell which can occur for a number of reasons, both internal and external. It is meant to foster complete surrender to Divine intent. All spiritual paths end in surrender and Heart Journey is no exception. By "Stage Eight: Acceptance and Generation," you will have transitioned to a level of peace that you could not have desired, could not have dreamed up. The contentment you experience has nothing to do with material possessions, acclaim, or worldly pursuit. You are simply resting in God's arms.

Stage Five: Receiving Abundance

This is the stage at which everything comes together. The steps needed to combine diverse elements might seem complicated at first. Can you master the ability to pat your head while rubbing your stomach? Even if manifestation occurs spontaneously, you will still need to retrace your steps to understand how the process works if you wish to manifest repeatedly. Let's start at the beginning with a review of the skills you have attained and proceed step by step. Everything you have done up to this point has a purpose related to manifestation.

You have opened your heart to deeply loving self, others, and God deeply. Abundance occurs through an open heart. Trust and interaction with your co-creative Partner must be maintained during the manifestation process so you can adhere to spiritual input. Spiritual input needs to be translated and applied in a descending manner from the spiritual level, to the mental, emotional, and finally the physical plane. Internal harmony creates consensus and conductivity. Any disagreement between levels inhibits the descent.

In addition to inner harmony between levels, spiritual input, thoughts, emotions, and actions together as a coordinated effort must be synchronized to the flow. The flow is still one of the four major components needed for manifestation through attraction and receptivity. You cannot manifest without it. As you have learned, seizing control and forcing things through with a to-do list is not the same. The flow has periods of ease and periods of difficulty and even absence. While opening your heart and developing a strong, co-creative interaction with God, your intuition and sensitivity to subtleties increased. Your new found abilities should help you anticipate and understand both positive and negative flow. You need to float downstream, not paddle against the current. This is a crucial distinction in the manifestation process. You have to recognize ease if you are to act in a timely and appropriate manner. You also have to understand difficulty or lack of flow to avoid wasted effort and dead ends. Shifts in the flow are constantly occurring and indicate when to act, what action to take, and when to wait. Flow is like spiritual wind and your heightened awareness developed during Heart Journey has sharpened your perceptions. You can now sense the flow on your own, get cues from your co-creative Partner, or interpret ease versus difficulty.

Translation of spiritual input at the mental level and an awareness of the permeations arising during the descent through the emotional level to the physical plane also has benefit. Your original desire was translated into a focused and sustained thought which must now be tracked and modified accordingly as it descends to the physical plane. One might assume that there is only one focused and sustained thought during the entire Heart Journey and to some extent this is true; however, during the process of manifestation through attraction and receptivity, constant adjustment and refinement of the translation must be made according to changes in the flow, input from your co-creative Partner, and transitions from one level of experience to another.

The establishment of both internal harmony between levels of experience and then external synchronization to the flow is essential to the process of manifesting desire through attraction and receptivity. Ascertaining desire at each level of experience helps you track the descent. Desire descends from spirit into physical formation in the same manner spiritual input and communication from your co-creative Partner descends to physical applications. The process is exactly the same. This defines the skills and elements needed for manifestation through attraction and receptivity. They are:

1. An open and loving heart
2. A co-creative partnership with God
3. Harmony on four levels of experience
4. Synchronization to the flow
5. Desire tempered by surrender
6. A focused and sustained thought
7. Avenue of manifestation

Strong awareness of all these factors hones one's ability to midwife the process of manifestation through attraction and receptivity. Although manifestation can occur in the blink of the eye, this is not always the case. Instead, there may be a constant need for adjustment and navigation on your part. "The Delicate Art of Skillful Navigation," presented in Chapter 16: Troubleshooting the Avenue of Manifestation, is a manifestation technique that depends on your ability to facilitate translation on each level of experience while clearing all resistance discovered during the descent. Manifestation is not a slam dunk; it is a process. Sometimes it moves instantaneously with no effort on your part, and sometimes the process demands attention to detail and constant adjustments.

Translating spiritual input into practical applications is akin to translating your desire into your focused and sustained thought. Modifications made in accordance with communications from your co-creative Partner are akin to adjustments made in accordance with changes in the flow. Transmuting negative emotions into spiritual gold is akin to elevating your desire to reflect spiritual principles. Implementation on the physical plane is akin to lending your skills and efforts to the avenue of manifestation. Nothing has been lost in your Heart Journey training. Each skill, meditation, sensitization, and awareness is valuable in the process of manifestation through attraction and receptivity.

Everything up to this point has been preparing you for teachings that cannot be taught. "Stage Five: Receiving Abundance" is the jumping off point. The process of manifestation through attraction and receptivity is actually beyond words and teaching. Despite all the information given in regard to troubleshooting the process, manifestation has to be experienced firsthand to be understood. When you are able to track the process of manifestation from desire to materialization as it moves through the spiritual, mental, emotional levels into the physical plane while staying in touch with your co-creative Partner and the flow through an open and loving heart, you are truly prepared to attract and receive abundance. Beyond that there is nothing you can do and nothing you can be taught.

Stage Six: Channeling Abundance

There are two important tasks associated with "Stage Six: Channeling Abundance." You should express gratitude for the gifts of abundance you receive, and then you need to let abundance move through you to others. Channeling abundance to others increases your ability to attract, receive, and manifest.

Although you have set the stage for attracting and receiving, and even though you made a specific request stating your desire, in essence you are not the primary force behind manifestation through attraction and receptivity. Despite all the integrating, balancing, guiding, and heart opening you have done, this is still very much God's co-creative handiwork. Flow is, in many ways, the grace of God, the extra special boost that makes it all happen. Some factors associated with flow are a product of the physical plane, (such as seasonal climate, travel time, distance, etc.), but the ease that comes from doors flying open, or being at the right place at the right moment, and manifestations that occur instantaneously without rhyme or reason, are more than just flow, this is also the assistance of Divine grace. The four elements needed for the process of manifestation through attraction and receptivity can now be understood as:

1. Desire tempered by surrender
2. A focused and sustained thought
3. The avenue of manifestation
4. Flow and grace

Be grateful for the grace and assistance you have received. It does not diminish the hard work you have put into your Heart Journey mastering skills for the purposes of cleansing (eliminating negativity), involution (infusion of spiritual input from your co-creative Partner), evolution (becoming more enlightened), sensitization, (to the invisible realm), and facilitation of the process of manifestation through attraction and receptivity that still depends on the grace of God.

Working with God as your co-creative Partner over these past weeks and months has allowed you to enter into a personal relationship with God and receive God's love and grace directly in the form of manifestation. You have been blessed and you need to express your gratitude for each manifestation you have received and continue to receive regardless of the amount of effort and skills you contribute to the process. The manifestations you have been experiencing are likely to be miraculous in some way. See this process for what it is and be grateful.

Also, be grateful for the less obvious, nonmaterial blessings you have received. You have grown and matured spiritually through the establishment of the co-creative partnership with God. This direct relationship has initiated you into the path of mysticism. Mysticism can be defined both as a spiritual discipline aimed at communion with God and the belief in the existence of realities beyond perceptual and intellectual apprehension that are accessible by subjective experience, such as intuition. As stated from the very beginning, Heart Journey is a mystical journey wherein the ordinary person living an ordinary life can experience God the Beloved. As stated in the opening line of this book, "Heart Journey is first and foremost a love affair with God." Be grateful for how invaluable it is to have God's love, insight, and guidance in your life.

At this point, you should be a happier person than when you began your Heart Journey. The process of manifestation necessitates cleansing your thoughts and emotions of negativity to create congruency and lovingness. The co-creative partnership with God has been inspiring and enlightening. As a result, you have changed. Heart openness has enabled you to experience more love for others in your life, especially those you are closest to, family members, partners, and friends. Perhaps you mended a relationship or two along the way, forgave someone and healed an old wound. You might have eliminated a lot of the unnecessary drama. Interactions can be more rewarding and fruitful. If you have more joy and peace in your life, this is also a gift. You may have worked to get here, but you did have help. Be grateful.

And finally, your reality has also changed markedly. The landscape used to consist of what you could see, hear, smell, taste, and touch. That is no longer the case. There is so much more. Be grateful for your expanded, integrated, enlightened experience. You are not alone.

This stage is called Channeling Abundance with good reason. As you attract, receive, and manifest, you probably have more love and abundance than you can contain. Don't even try. It will and should naturally spill out of you and become abundance for those around you. It may take a material form or it may flow to others in the forms of joy, peace, enthusiasm, kindness, healing, and/or love. Abundance and grace from God is meant to flow into the world. You are meant to be a conduit, not a vessel. In fact, the more you give at this stage or allow to flow through you to others, the more you will receive.

Grace takes on form by becoming abundance in all of its permeations. It becomes contagious by infecting others with hope. It can spread like wildfire without preaching or religious commitment. It travels on the wings of kindness and uplifts those around you. It is your task to stay whole, balanced, harmonized, synchronized, open-hearted, and in touch with your co-creative Partner. Remember to open when you would close, receive when you would refuse, give when you would deny, and surrender the results. Do not limit your ability to receive for any reason. That may sound obvious, but in practice you might put up subtle barriers to abundance. Accept all that is coming to you and then pay it forward.

Example of Receiving

Just as I was a victim of least common denominator love, (see "Example of Vulnerability" earlier in this chapter), I also believed in equalizing all gifts with comparable giving. I felt the need to give back in kind for everything I received and to the very person who had gifted me. Accepting abundance was more like borrowing it for a short period of time and then returning it. I saw my abundance as a lending library. I could have abundance out on loan for several three weeks, but then I had to return it. This was not always possible given my resources, so I endeavored to only accept and receive what I could repay.

It occurred to me one day that I did not need to do this. I was playing "even Steven" with everything I was offered. I was limiting my ability to receive to my ability to repay in kind. Gifts are not really gifts when you treat them as mutual exchanges. Upon realizing this, my new mantra became, "I will no longer limit my ability to receive to my ability to repay. Nor will I limit my ability to give, to another's ability to give back. I will be as open to receiving as I can be, and as generous to others as I can be without any expectations." This freed me to receive and give more than my fair share. I saw my abundance as unlimited and a product of God's grace and generosity.

Stage Seven: Spiritual Stress Test and Surrender

Every spiritual student is tested while on the path, and every spiritual path ends in surrender. It is the natural course of spiritual development. Heart Journey is no exception in this regard. The test at this stage is one of open-hearted surrender. Nothing unusual or extraordinary has been added to Heart Journey; nothing important to your spiritual maturity has been left out. Testing is highly individualized and specific to the spiritual needs of the student. It is pre-programmed from the very beginning by one's personality, level of desire, ability to surrender, and spiritual development. Essentially, the test is a reflection of yourself and your coping mechanisms. It is a product of the choices you have made, the actions you have taken, and the ones you have avoided. Think of it as a spiritual stress test. There is no malice intended. No one wants to see you fail, least of all God, and in reality, no one ever fails outright in their journey to God; some travelers are temporarily delayed. Sooner or later, in this life or in another space, everyone surrenders.

Testing can occur on the physical, emotional, mental, or spiritual level, and any combination thereof. By their very nature, some tests span more than one level. Testing is not meant to be difficult though it can be if you forget what you have learned and stray from the path. The adjustment being made is in the balance of desire and surrender. Previously, you have clearly stated what you wished to manifest through attraction and receptivity. Regardless whether manifestation in cooperation with your co-creative Partner did or did not occur exactly as hoped, complete surrender is now the task at hand. Desire is no longer tempered by surrender; personal desire of any kind is superseded by surrender to God and with good reason. By surrendering and accepting what God has in mind for you, you can be abundant again, though in a different way, in a way you could never have imagined. Complete surrender can ultimately lead to a Divine upgrade and a new way of being in the world.

These are the four tasks you will be tested on: lovingness, spiritual principles, trust in God, and surrender. During the time of testing, you will be asked to remain open-hearted and remember the love you experienced since beginning your Heart Journey. You are to exemplify that love and pass it onto others by being kind, caring, and compassionate. You are also expected to adhere to the spiritual principles you have learned so far. Do not stray because conditions change or your ability to manifest wanes. Trust your co-creative Partner, God, come what may, even if communication stops. Continue according to plan, meditating and reflecting, putting one foot in front of the other. Finally, surrender to the process. It is meant to prepare you for a mindset of acceptance. You will not be tested on your ability to manifest through attraction and receptivity which you may have already experienced in previous stages of heart openness. You may continue to manifest, but you are more likely to fail at manifestation at this stage of spiritual development, or at least hit a dry spell for various reasons. This can be a real problem for those who have grown to depend on this ability.

Inability to manifest

One format the spiritual stress test can take occurs when the ability to manifest abundance becomes an overwhelming ego trip. Early successful manifestations can be followed quickly by acquisition and financial over-extension. The assumption is that if you can do this now, you can do this always and eventually manifest bigger and better benefits. If you fall into this trap, at some point, the pressure is on to maintain an abundant lifestyle at all costs. This is a precarious position to be in. Gone completely is the, "Not my will, but Thy Will," commitment to surrender. God is reduced from a co-creative Partner giving guidance to a mere provider or worse. God will not bend to your will nor will God support an ego trip.

Sooner or later everyone hits a manifestation dry spell. If you are financially over extended at that time and a manifestation junkie, anxiety will set in, followed quickly by the urge to take control. Spiritually, you can regress and begin to ignore ease versus difficulty signals; you just want to get your abundance fix. Spiritual principles and practices will be dropped along with a commitment to surrender. In the developing panic, you won't recall the love you experienced with God or the trust and guidance established in the co-creative partnership. Instead, you will feel alone, abandoned, and angry over the inability to manifest.

If you take God and the process of manifestation through attraction and receptivity for granted, thinking you have mastered some formula, you will fall from grace. You cannot take God out of the equation and continue to attract and manifest. If you have seriously overstepped your financial limitations, the dry spell will have serious economic consequences. Fortunately, few people will be tested to this extent, and as expected, the testing is of their own making. It is the ego-driven individual who creates unsustainable circumstances that magnify the testing of surrender. Do not be seduced by your initial ability to manifest. It is not likely to last. It was never the goal of Heart Journey and will never be the goal of any spiritual path. Communion with God is the true and final goal.

Situational test

Some tests seem purely situational. It is not uncommon for a person with strong spiritual assets to end up in a place that could use some uplifting, positive energy. This can occur in either your professional or personal life. You might have recently relocated for one reason or another, or your new awareness of spiritual input and cleansing of emotional negativity could have opened your eyes to the truth already around you. Suddenly, dysfunction seems to be the norm. You develop an aversion for gossip and drama and find it frustrating when time, energy, and resources are wasted on pettiness. You long for a more enlightened venue with like-minded spiritual individuals. Where is the love? Creativity? Kindness? It lies within you and you need to show it. It is hard to spread love and joy in a black hole, but that is probably what you are meant to do. It might be your task to carry light into that dark place and hold that space sacred. Your test is to express love and kindness when there is anger. Can you stand your spiritual ground and not fall into the trap others have already succumbed to?

A situational test frequently comes with a holding pattern. You get stuck in a set of circumstances, unable to move forward. You are where you are for a reason; the reason may or may not be of your own choosing. Perhaps you stay because your job provides much needed security, or you are due to retire soon with a pension. You might yearn for a different profession, but feel your family responsibilities would make a transition difficult or risky. If you are in a failing relationship, you might decide to stay for the children or until the finances are worked out and arrangements can be made. Sometimes, the reason you are stuck is unknown or totally beyond your control. You don't understand why you cannot sell your house and relocate, or transfer your job from one office to another. Trust that your co-creative Partner knows the why and wherefore. If it feels like you are stuck in a holding pattern, you are being called to surrender to the situation, especially if difficulty arises whenever you try to leave. This is your spiritual path for the time being. Be loving while you are here and adhere to the principles and practices you have learned. As soon as ease arises and doors fly open, move on.

Test of service to others

Testing can come in the form of service to others. You may get involved in a cause or respond to a desperate need arising locally, nationally, or internationally. You or your family might be faced with a crisis that demands you immediate attention. In these cases, the test of surrender takes the form of subjugating your plans and desires to the needs of others. It is your time to give back and perform acts of service willingly and with love.

The trap many fall into while serving others, especially when illness of a family member is involved, is one of distraction from spiritual practices like meditation and prayer. External demands can completely monopolize your time and energy causing you to disconnect from your co-creative Partner. In addition, it is extremely difficult to attract and manifest under these circumstances. There is no time or space for creative ideas or navigational corrections. You become so focused on doing and providing that you stop being. The result is you drift without an anchor.

Example of Service to Others

In 2005, both of my parents were diagnosed with debilitating illnesses. My youngest child was just graduating from college. Several of my siblings and I banded together to buy and renovate a home in Connecticut for our parents so they could move north from Florida and get the help they needed. At the same time, I relocated from my home in Maryland to Connecticut.

My parents' needs quickly became overwhelming. Caregiving shifts grew to twelve hours a day for a week at a time until twenty-hour care became necessary. Even though good caregivers were hired and both parents spent time in a nursing home, the demands for my time and attention were great. After my father passed, my mother still required twenty-four hour care when she left the nursing home and returned to the community.

Besides my parents' decline and the disabilities my father faced in the last ten months of his life, the most upsetting development during this time was that communication with God fell away. Did I meditate daily? No. I felt bad about this, but after twelve hours of caregiving, I was exhausted and needed to shop for food, pay my bills, do laundry, and attend to business as best I could. I felt lucky to have been able to sleep. I had no time to create or even think creatively. My brain was numb and I definitely felt adrift. The best I could do was hold to the spiritual principles I had learned and be loving and kind to my parents even during the toughest times of caregiving. I did not lose sight of the purpose associated with this time and the reasons I had chosen this path, but I felt disconnected from God.

God had been my touchstone and co-creative Partner for many years in my life. Without the unwavering support and guidance I had grown used to, I became confused. I honestly did not know if I was doing the right thing. Was it my path to spend years caring for my parents? Had I lost my way spiritually by being overwhelmed by their physical needs? Sitting in meditation or even prayer while my parents were not cared for did not seem spiritual. I begged God repeatedly to tell me what to do. There was no detectable response, no ease or flow, only a new caregiving task and a new health crisis that demanded my time and attention.

Meanwhile, I had arrived in Connecticut with a substantial saving account. Since I did not know what the future would bring or how my parents' needs might escalate, I had been financially conservative when purchasing a home and setting up a budget. Still, the manifestation dry spell hit hard. I was never in danger of losing my home or going bankrupt, but I was dismayed by the depletion of my savings. Business all but stopped and I had no time to focus on career endeavors or generate new business. Each attempt was met by an immediate caregiving task. Financial stress only added to my sense of the abandonment and loneliness which was both spiritual and emotional. Since moving north, I had not had the freedom to participate in groups or cultivate new friendships. I became isolated and at times even found it difficult to visit my out of state grown children.

The good news is that everything comes to pass. Eventually, my caregiving responsibilities lightened enough for me to go back to work. Ease reappeared and difficulty fell away. The flow of abundance slowly returned even though I did not push it or make requests. I was content to let it be whatever it intended to be without desiring. Finally, I am climbing out of debt. After I renewed my meditation practice I was back in communication with my co-creative Partner. God still did not answer my burning question, "Did I do the right thing in caring for my parents for so many years?" Perhaps it wasn't God's to address. This was all just my test of surrender, a test of my own making. I am in a different place because of caregiving, and it is a good place.

Health issue test

Sometimes the test of surrender comes in the form of your own health issue, especially if you have been burning the candle at both ends and not taking care of yourself. As mentioned before, tests are of your own making and can reflect an innate weakness or spiritual immaturity. If you have been ignoring your body and any warning signals that arose, you will be faced with a health challenge sooner or later and this might be your surrender test. Regardless of how you handle the health developments medically, it is especially important in this case to remain in contact with your co-creative Partner.

Relationship issue

As you progress spiritually, relationships need to be renewed regularly to remain current. In the best situation significant others will grow with you psychologically and spiritually as you cleanse and adopt principles and practices. Any relationship that is a major deterrent to the path you are on might fall away or become meaningless as a gulf develops over time. It may be difficult for your partner to understand your experiences, but if the love is there, the relationship will survive and even thrive. In this situation, it is crucial that you express unconditional love for others. It has been said that relationships are the hardest yoga you will ever practice and this is especially true when one has a spiritual growth spurt and the other partner does not. This does not preclude compatibility or others catching up later on. If love is truly there, trust that the relationship can be sustained and renewed.

The important thing to remember is that Heart Journey or any spiritual path is not the cause of misfortune. Sooner or later, challenges arise in every life. Heart Journey and the spiritual path are also not the cause of testing. The transition from desire tempered by surrender to complete surrender is innate to developing spiritual maturity. It is to be as expected as a baby learning to crawl or walk or an elder aging. The test is not the hardship. The test is what you do under less than ideal or stressful circumstances.

I have said it before, God uses good bait. Abundance is good bait, but the ability to manifest abundance through attraction and receptivity is not indicative of spiritual attainment, nor is it the true spiritual lesson. It simply means that you are able to open your heart, work co-creatively with God, and understand the process needed for formation. A sign of true spiritual growth is the ability to remain open-hearted and loving when the abundance stops, communication is interrupted, and you are never sure if you are on the right path, doing the right thing. You can only put one foot in front of the other and proceed in a loving manner, trusting that God is with you. After you have surrendered completely to your situation while adhering to the principles and practices you have adopted, you will have reached a level of spiritual maturity that allows you to slowly begin to move forward and onward to "Stage Eight: Acceptance and Generation."

Stage Eight: Acceptance and Generation

The most distinguishing features of this stage of heart openness are acceptance and the ability to generate love in any environment and for anyone. You are able to do this because you walk with God and exemplify the principles you have learned.

When you reach this stage of heart openness, you are at peace and your surrender is complete. Rather than enlist God's help in manifesting a personal desire, you are content with whatever God has in mind for you. You willingly accept the path you are on and simply follow ease wherever it might lead you. You are comfortable with who you are, where you are, and with what you are doing. Your co-creative partnership with God is strong and if communication was interrupted in the past, it has now returned. Your spiritual practice is part of your daily routine and you easily adhere to the spiritual principles you have learned.

While not exactly lacking desire, you are also not filled with desire. You may not feel the need to write another contract. Instead, you are open to following God's lead, willing to see what develops. Doors open, opportunities arise, and your path is made known step by step. You follow the flow of ease and it all makes sense. You trust that everything will be revealed to you in time. Despite what you might think, this is not a static period. It can actually be very dynamic and exciting as events unfold. You have reached a point where you are truly living life from the top down, from the spiritual co-creative interchange with God to the physical.

You carry sacredness within you. You exude love and light wherever you go. You not only channel love to others, you are able to generate love in dark places. This is because the Divine shines through you regardless of the environment and it comforts everyone you meet. You are in love with the world, with God, and all beings. You understand your place in the scheme of things and willingly accept responsibilities and tasks as they arise.

In the midst of all this, you are still abundant, but the manifestation process is different. This is not the flashy, desire driven materializations of the past, but a gentle, stable process of continuing manifestation. There is no pressure to manifest and no navigational issues. The process of manifestation through attraction and receptivity tends to occur spontaneously on its own. It seems like it is automatic and perhaps it is.

The nature of abundance has also changed. Abundance may or may not be material at this point, but there is enough material support regardless. In some way, you are sustained or taken care of. The presence of nonmaterial abundance is obvious. You experience insight on a regular basis. You have spiritual adventures and may travel to sacred sites or educational events. God moves through your life creating wonderful surprises, leading you to your highest good in each situation. Because you are a clear and open channel for God's grace, you are happy, hopeful, and fulfilled. Your joyful mood lifts the spirits of those around you.

Beyond Stage Eight

The movement through the Eight Stages of Heart Openness is not a one time, straight-line, end product progression. You may move ahead quickly in some stages and drop back in others. Even though you complete the progression through to the eighth stage, this does not mean that at some point in the future you will not return to a lower stage or formulate a new desire based contract. You can recycle at any time. Every life period has its own calling.

It is also true that the Eighth Stage of heart openness is not necessarily the final stage and end product of your spiritual journey. There may be more stages or transitions to come for those who continue on spiritually. Whatever comes next cannot be defined in these pages. Once you have reached this level of spiritual development, you and your co-creative Partner will ascertain what comes next and it is likely to be individualized and ineffable.

For now, it is important to note and recognize how far you have come since creating your original desire based contract and beginning your Heart Journey. Should your spiritual journey continue, you have what you need to go on:

1. An open and loving heart
2. Spiritual principles you adhere to
3. A spiritual practice
4. A co-creative partnership with God
5. An understanding of the manifestation process
6. A commitment to surrender

Journey well!

Chapter Sixteen:
Spiritual Evolution

It should be noted how goals, definitions, and processes have evolved since you started your Heart Journey. In particular, the goal of desire has now become demoted and with good reason. The definition of surrender has been refined to include complete surrender without conditions. It is not just a counter balance used to temper desire. Abundance is no longer strictly material but includes positive emotions, connections to others, and spiritual fulfillment. The process of manifestation through attraction and receptivity has shifted from a conscious process of attracting and receiving to an automatic process of attracting and receiving. And finally, the duality of desire and surrender has led to both manifestation and higher consciousness. These transitions result in major lessons regarding love and spiritual maturity.

Desire versus Desireless

When the importance of desire was first mentioned, there were two types of desire discussed. Desire was either a heart-felt personal passion or the surrender to God's desire, whatever that might be. In the final stage of your Heart Journey, you ceased to work on personal desires and instead desired only what you and God together wished to co-create. Desire is no longer about you; it is about God, or you and God working together. Material abundance is no longer the issue or the goal. Things, per se, don't seem to matter so much. Desire is not about what you can have; it is about what you can be or give. People matter. Service matters. God matters. Your love affair with God is a central force guiding in your life. You are committed to your spiritual growth and evolution more than any material goal or possession.

Ideally, you reside in a state of joyful abundance and use the processes of desire and surrender to stay there. Life is full, yet peaceful. You are not attached to good fortune, but you live it on your own terms. Desire is a positive asset you use wisely and skillfully to participate in life's co-creative process and to foster manifestation into physical form when needed.

On the other hand, you are able to become desireless. This is a step beyond surrendering desire to God's Will. This is more than, "Not my will, but Thy Will." This is truly stepping back with no restrictions and preconceived notions to see what God creates. The beauty of being desireless is that you get to see God move in your life. If you are doing nothing, not wishing, hoping, or asking for anything, but simply waiting and watching for God's move, you create a void. If you hold that space, sooner or later something will emerge, and that thing is of God. You get to see God create and to follow God's lead. This can be a very revealing, life changing moment in your life.

Definition of Surrender

In the beginning of your Heart Journey you were asked to compose a contract around your desire. You were to temper your desire with surrender, "Not my will, but Thy Will." Surrender was essentially an adjunct to your contract while desire took center stage. By the end of your Heart Journey the tables have turned and now your surrender is complete. Surrender no longer qualifies desire; surrender replaces it. You have grown to discover that God is better at creating than you are at desiring or even imagining. It is to your advantage to follow in all situations rather than attempt to lead or set goals. Divine upgrades are amazing and can take you to some surprising places. It is the wise person who stops making requests, surrenders completely, and instead follows the flow of ease while avoiding the frustration of difficulty. In this sense, the definition of surrender has changed dramatically since you started your Heart Journey. It can now be known that complete surrender is actually a method for attracting and receiving.

Definition of Abundance

In the initial stages of Heart Journey, abundance is usually defined within the context of material desires. Contracts are written for goals that reflect economic gain and acquisition, whether it is a home, car, great job, or money. Nonmaterial contracts might include good health though some spiritual contracts center on a relationship with God and spiritual development.

With time and experience, the definition of abundance expands beyond the strictly material to the ability to see purpose and goodness in every situation. Abundance takes on positive emotional characteristics like joy and peace. Abundance is being authentic, expressing your core self without fear of criticism or rejection. Abundance becomes an attitude, a perspective on life and a way of living fully with or without material wealth. In this sense, the definition of abundance matures along with spiritual growth and extends beyond economics.

The Process of Attraction

It has already been hinted that when you stop desiring and instead surrender completely, the act of surrender becomes attractive. Heart openness associated with complete surrender increases one's ability to attract at an unconscious level. This new found ability changes the components necessary for manifestation through attraction and receptivity and actually simplifies the whole process. You no longer need to desire or translate you desire into a focus and sustained thought. Concentration, navigation, and attention to detail are no longer essential. You simply follow the flow of ease and the prompting of your co-creative Partner while lending your skills and efforts to the process of manifestation as needed. In this way, attraction has become less of an active process and more of a passive one that you contribute to rather than initiate.

Duality and Consciousness

Great desire coexists with great surrender in Heart Journey. This is a duality that spiritual seekers have used for eons to promote spiritual growth as an alternative to suffering. Suffering as a spiritual path was personified by the Crucifixion of Christ, but there are other paths to understanding and enlightenment. Whenever you hold two mutually exclusive qualities in balanced dynamic tension, two things must occur:

1. There should be manifestation.
2. There should be a rise in consciousness.

For example, whenever a man and a woman have sex, there can be the conception of a child (manifestation) and the arousal of a deeper love and commitment (consciousness). The man and the woman are very different. They approach and experience the sexual act differently, but still they come together in balance and in dynamic tension. This creates the dual possibilities of manifestation and higher consciousness.

And so it is with desire and surrender. When you hold these two mutually exclusive dynamics in equal and balanced tension, the effect is both manifestation and higher consciousness. These are the two results you have experienced on your Heart Journey and this is why from the very beginning desire was tempered by surrender. It was a lesson to get you to see that what appears to be a mutually exclusive duality can actually be or evolve into a non-dual pairing that fosters manifestation and raises consciousness.

Love and Non-duality

The same is true of actions you take on behalf of others. You and another are dual forces. When you hold your needs and your neighbor's needs in balanced dynamic tension with love and compassion, you create a non-dual situation. Actions you take to benefit another are also beneficial to you because in many respects, there is no difference. You and others are one and the same. You cannot give without being generous. You cannot love without being loving. You cannot mature spiritually without honoring all life. As the Native Americans would say, "Mitakuye Oyasin." We are all related.

Your task is to seek the middle ground in all exchanges, the midpoint that leads to the manifestation of abundance in all its material and nonmaterialistic forms for yourself and others. That same midpoint leads to the generation of higher consciousness when there is a commitment to love. These midpoints are mystical doorways. Along with the principles and techniques introduced in Heart Journey, they are the tools you need to continue on, beyond what can be taught, spoken, or written, and can only be experienced and understood through your relationship with God, the greatest Teacher of all.

Index

A

abandonment 216
absence of manifestation 12
abundance xxiv, xxix-xxx, 3, 5-6, 245, 248
  as an attitude 248
  beyond economics 248
  channeled abundance 221
  generate abundance 107, 221
  limits 42
  material desires 248
  receive abundance 40, 221
  sharing abundance 55, 126
accelerated spiritual development 188
acceptance xxx
accountability 212
achievable 35–36
acts of kindness 206
acts of service 242
adjustments 151
adversity 216
agendas 41, 218
alchemically transform 184
alchemical team 100
amend 134
angels 177, 180
  angel of blue light 179
anger 22, 83, 85, 124, 168, 177, 209, 214, 215, 230
anxiety 104
apologize 212
appropriate actions 229
Aquarian Age 4
artificial barrier 209
asking xxv, 3–12
  asking for assistance 10
  asking for material possessions 8, 11
  asking for money 8, 9
  asking for wisdom 10, 11, 96
astral projection 139
attract xxviii, 11
attracting 32
attraction xxiv, 40
  follow the flow of ease 249
  passive process 249
  stop desiring 249
attractive
  beauty of desire 185
attunement to God 188
avenue for manifestation 104–108
avoidance 200, 201, 223
awareness 133, 134, 213

B

backup plan 164
becalmed 132
be careful of what you ask for 43
beyond stage eight 245
bible quotes xxv, 3, 8, 102, 184, 202
blame 225, 230
bottom line manifestation 232
business 70

C

calling 228
caregiving 206
causality 229
causative emotions 232
cause and effect xxiv, 138, 229
Celtic 61
certification 159
challenges 217
channel love to others 245
chaos 144, 159, 160
chaotic 159
characterizing 200
character weakness 155
Cherokee Medicine Woman 6, 77
children 206
clarity 133
cleanse 32, 62
cleansing 11, 22, 84, 124, 127, 190, 218, 222, 238, 241
co-creative directive 156
co-creative partnership
  begins 52
  fosters spiritual development 186
  frustrated 111
  like a marriage xxv–xxvi

co-creative potential 19, 205
Co-creative thoughts xxvii
  Alchemical Transformations
    Compassion 200–203
    Egoless 208–210
    Forgiveness 211–215
    Honoring 203–206
    Learning to attract, Opening to receive 185–186
    Multidimensional Perception 193–195
    No-Self 218–219
    Receive More than Your Fair Share 187–188
    Self-sufficiency Moving to Wholeness 192–193
    Silence and Reflection 189–191
    Trust and Faith 215–217
  Old thoughts
    Disabling Need or Dependency 192–193
    Distrust 215–217
    Ego Armada 208–210
    Even Steven Reward System 187–188
    Guilt 211–215
    Judgment 200–203
    Mental Constructs 197–198
    Open Minded 197–198
    Possessiveness and Control 203–206
    Reality Deception 193–195
    Self 218–219
    The Do-It-Yourself Fantasy 185–186
    The Mental Ghetto 189–191
codependent 205, 230
cohesive whole 232
coincidental xxiv, 138
collective unconscious 154
commitment 206
Communication guidelines
Communication Guidelines 91–96
  daily 94
  feedback 94
  instantaneous coincidence 74
  milestones 94, 95
  rule of three 92, 93, 94
  specific symbol 91-92
Communications with God
  distinguishing characteristics 82–90
Communications with God are not
  controlling 83
  critical 83
  no fear-based messages 84
  not about others 83
  not about your ego 83
  rarely predictive 84
  subtle 94
  won't condone anger 85
Divine Communications are like 86
  challenging 86
  encouraging 87
  individualistic 86
  insight 88
  insightful 87
  loving 86
  protective 88, 89
  supportive 87
  uplifting 86
  wisdom 88
  wise 87
Communicating with God
  ability to listen 69
  coincidence 74
  communication 68–81
  daily basis 70
  difficulty versus ease 74–76
  distinguishing characteristics 69
    ease 74–76
    establish guidelines 69
    God whisper 75-76
    listening 69–70
    lucid dreaming 76-77
    meaningful language 69
    questions 70
    sightings of animals 73
    signs 73–74
    spiritual insight 69
    subtle 69
    symbols 71–72
    talk to God 70
    visions 77
    wisdom 69
compassion 11, 42, 189, 201, 204, 208, 214, 218, 219, 222, 224, 225, 230
compensation 212
competition 5
complementary companion 192
complexity 161
complex visions 161
complications 145

compliments 32
compression of creative energy 194
condensation 194
conditional hate 205
conditional love 203, 205
conductivity xxx, 235
conflict, internal or external 102
confused 21, 243
confusion 128, 133
consciousness 138–139
  midpoint 250
  rise in consciousness 249
consensus 235
consistency 114, 123, 135, 165
consolidation 40
contemplation 218
contract
  addendum 121
  adjustments 54
  amendable 91
  amend your contract 134
  business 46, 51
  complex 29, 47
  concrete 36, 37, 39
  contract format 44–45
  contract media 44
  creating your contract 44–59
  empowering your contract 58-59
  group contract 46
  healers 46
  health contract 46–47
  individual contract 45–46
  multifaceted requests 48–52
  one-word contract 29
  organize 48
  overly complex 122–123
  professional 46
  relationship 46
  reminder 135–136
  rewrite 121
  simple 29–31, 47-48
  specific 37–38
  start over 121
  surrender contracts 41
  technical writing tips 52–56
  themes 48
  too specific 38
  types of contracts 45–47
  verbal 45

control 42, 125, 126, 137, 204, 205, 206, 208, 209, 210, 216, 225, 226
control and love, mutually exclusive 209
controlled 205
controlling 83, 207
controlling emotions 230
controlling others 203
corporal mortification 4
corrective action 142
correct timing 27
counterproductive behavior 213
counterproductive character traits 155
credentials trap 159
creed 131
crisis management 119, 135, 144, 159
critical mass 154
criticism 83, 189
crystals 15

D

deadline 155, 160
death 169, 176–180, 207
death coaches 177
debt 166
decision 201
decision-making process 228
defense mechanisms 208
defensive response 209
defensive tactics 210
defensive techniques 209
deficiencies 113
delay 146-148, 173
delicate art of skillful navigation 110, 167-168, 187, 236
delusions 193
dementia 206
dependency on others 192
depression 214, 215
desire xxx, 12, 40, 41, 104, 247
  active 99
  as fuel 99
  attached 40
  balanced by surrender xxvii
  balance of desire and surrender 98
  balance with surrender 129
  competing desires 102
  confused 21
  confusion 20
  descends from spirit 236

desire as fuel 17
desire balanced by surrender 20
desire to surrender 21
evaluate 47
fluctuations 129
fuels attraction 100
fosters attraction 186
God's desire 21
heart's desire 17–25
instability 124
mutually exclusive 39
negative desire 53–54
passion 40
passion as a twin sister 23
passive 99
prioritize 47
superseded by surrender 240
stable 39
strong 47
surrender 40
tempered by surrender 99-101, 237
translation 36–37
uncertainty 20, 21
unstable 39
versus desireless 247–248
devotion to God 11, 127
difficulty 103, 130, 133, 140, 248
dilemma 201
discomfort 177
discouraging guidance 95
discriminate 131
disease
  emotional contribution 171-172
  physical contributions 170–171
dis-empowered 205
disorganization 159
dispersion of attention 144
disrespectful 189
disruption 160
dissipation of energy 144
dissociation from emotions 222-223
distractions 135, 146, 159
distrust 216
Divine
  abundance 188
  assistance 140–141
  feedback 68
  grace 237
  inheritance 205
  input 91, 221

insight 210
mysteries 201
sparks 206
timing 111
Divine upgrades xxvii, 37, 38, 55, 126,
    130, 131, 139, 216, 240, 248
Divine Will 156, 157
Divinity xxix, xxx, 128, 219, 232
doable 35–36
dominate 203
doubt 124
drama 190, 238, 241
dreaming 139
dry spell 240, 241
duality of desire and surrender 249
dying 176–180
dysfunction 190, 205, 241
dysfunctional exchange 189

E

earning process 113
ease 26, 27, 94, 95, 103, 104, 130, 133,
    140, 141, 146, 235
ease versus difficulty 93–94, 134, 236, 241
economic depression 145
education 131
efforts 153
ego xxvii, 113, 115, 125, 126, 152, 205,
    207, 208, 209, 210
ego defense mechanisms 208
egoless 210
ego trip 241
Eight Stages of Heart Openness
  Beyond Stage Eight 245
  Acceptance and Generation 222, 235,
    244–245
  Channeling Abundance 235, 237–239
  Cognizance of Heart Closure 221, 222-224
    signs of closure 224
    reasons for heart closure 222–224
  Harmonizing Four Levels of Experience
    232–234
    Body and Physical Plane 233–234
    Emotions and Emotional Level 233
    Spiritual Input and Spiritual Level 232
    Thoughts and Mental Level 232–233
  Heart Vulnerability 224–227
  Receiving Abundance 235–237

INDEX

Spiritual Input, Thoughts, Emotions, and the Physical 227–232
  Spiritual Input, Thoughts, Emotions, and the Physical 227–229
  Body and Physical plane 231–232
  Emotions and Emotional Level 230–231
  Thoughts and Mental Level 229–230
Spiritual Stress Test and Surrender 235, 239–245
  Health issue test 243–244
  Inability to manifest 240–241
  Relationship issue 244–245
  Situational test 241–242
  Test of service to others 242
emotional debris 190, 229
emotional reaction 209, 231
emotional trauma 222
emotions 230
  mixed emotions 102
  negative emotions 123–125, 128
  positive emotion 41
  positive emotional climate 124–125
  role of emotions 40
empathy 218
empower 135, 206
energetic communication 89–90
energy follows thought 189
enlightened 18
enlightenment 234, 249
ethical integrity 167
evaluate the nature of communications 112–115
everyday miracles 16
evolution 238
Examples
  abundance through attraction 6–7
  Afternoon Delight 15, 74
  asking for information 10–11
  asking for money 9–10
  attracting and receiving 186
  ballad of Mildred 78–81
  begging for money 202
  bluebird 206–207
  car 19
  choice at the moment of death 178–179
  conscious computer 78–81
  control 206–207
  crystal mine 15
  delay, interference, and incorrect timing 148
  Divine Upgrade that is irrational 138–139
  egotistic folly 210–211
  energetic 89–90
  finding a healer 174–175
  finger pointing at the moon 198
  firewalk 217–218
  following blindly 106–107
  garden contract 58
  God whispers 75, 76
  good eye 89
  health club 162–163
  heiau 199
  hemorrhage 174–175
  herkimer diamond 195–196
  hotei 186
  hummingbird 106–107
  humorous 89
  insight and wisdom 88
  inspiration in the silence 191
  job resignation 148
  judgment 202–203
  kahuna 199
  kundalini yoga class 138–139
  lucid dreaming 77
  my father's passage 179–180
  mystical Hawaiian journey 199–200
  Native American vision quest 27–29
  one-word contract 29–30
  overcoming resistance 132
  personal symbolism 23–24
  plane ticket 103–104
  power of love in the afterlife 177–178
  preconceptions resulting in resistance 198
  protection 88–89
  quick moving flow 149
  rainbow symbolism 72–73
  receiving 239
  renegotiation 162–163
  request for assistance 132
  Sedona 103–104
  service to others 242-243
  shape-shifting 219–220
  shifting realities 195–196
  shirts 196–197
  sign 73–74
  skin cancer 171–173

snake 85
spans distance and space 196–197
standing ovation 210–211
symbolic visual contract 57
symbolism 92
tantric twin crystal 6–7
teacher or guru 75–76
the book of knowledge 139
Tibetan mandalas 89
trip to Hawaii 149
trust in God 217–218
turtle 191
uncle Frank 178
vision 78
vulnerability 226–227
written contract 56
excessive thinking 136–137
expectations 205
explanations 198
external progress 143
external synchronization 236
exude love 245

F

faith 116, 216, 217
fall from grace 241
false communications 113
false desire 18
false frame of reference 208
faultfinding 209
fear 22, 68, 84, 88, 99, 100, 101, 102, 113, 115, 123-125, 128, 149, 168, 208, 209, 216, 223, 224, 226, 227, 234, 40, 41, 43
fear of losing your mind 137
feedback 95, 133, 165
financial over-extension 240
financial security 23
flexibility 130
flow xxiv, 102–104, 130, 131
  according to ease and difficulty 103
  adjustments 141
  direction and speed 140
  Divine wind 140
  energetic flow 103
  lack of any response 142–143
  sensing the flow 104
flow and grace 237
flow of power xxv

focus 51, 96
focused 102, 131
focused and sustained potent thought 101–102, 237
  thought directs co-creative energy 101
focusing 132
forgive 215
forgiven 177, 213, 226
forgiveness 85, 211, 213, 214, 218, 225, 226, 230, 231
forgive yourself 213, 224
formation 194
free will xxvi, 85, 91, 204
frequencies 188
fulfillment 107, 205, 228, 230

G

gender 131
generate love 244
generate love in dark places 245
genetic roulette 171
God
  as Creator xxviii
  as loving 7
  as parent 7
  as vengeful 7
  fear-based image 43
  gimme God image 26–33, 152
God's blessing 97
God's concern 228
God's Desire 127–129, 247
  application of God's desire 127
God's grace 97
God's plan 164
God whispers xxvi, 199
goodness 248
gossip 136, 189, 190, 241
grace 98, 237, 238, 239
gratitude 11, 55, 108–109, 143, 149, 193, 237
gridlock 145
grief 214
guarantee xxviii, xxix, 27, 28, 85, 98, 115, 125, 126, 194, 216
guidance 154
guided meditation. 69
guilt 124, 177, 211, 213, 230

H

habitual response 231
hallucinations 137
harmonization 232
harmonizing 234
heal 220
healing 38, 169, 170, 171, 172, 173, 174, 175, 213, 215
healing powers 175
healing process 213
health 169, 174, 175
health problems 170
health warnings 173–174
heal your heart 222
heart
  atrophy 223
  closure 225
  connection 229 initiator 227
  multidimensional 227–232
  responds to stimuli 227
  limitations 86
Heart Journey group 56, 192
heart openness 5, 214
  fosters receptivity 186
  two-way street 55
heart's desire xxiv, xxv, xxvi, 16, 17-25, 40, 47
herbalist 174
holding pattern 241
honoring 205, 207, 208
hope 124
human inefficiency 145
hundredth monkey 154

I

illness 169, 170
  causality 170
illusion of separation 208, 209
impatience 111, 156, 163
impediment 126, 131, 147, 148
implementation 231, 237
inability to progress 133
inactivity 165
inattentiveness 135
inclusivity 5
inconsistency 147, 165
incorrect timing 154
indecisiveness 104

individualized program 192
inhibition 155
initiation xxvi, 6, 12, 60
injustice 209, 215
inner critic 209
inner harmony 232
inner voice 22
instant gratification
  inability to cope with delayed gratification 151
  choosing simple, effortless desires 151
  ego inflation 152
  lack of spiritual growth and maturity 152
  limited co-creative communication 151–152
intensity 168
interference 146, 147
interim success 133
internal advancement 143
internal harmony 236
interruption of the flow 155
interruptions 147
intervention 206
intolerance 223
intuition 22, 238
invisible spiritual realm 193
involution 238
irrational 216
irrational experiences 90

J

jealousy 230
jokes 190
journaling 22
joyful abundance 247
judge 200, 202
judgment 138, 189, 202, 216
  apparatus 202
  close-ended process 200
Judgment 201, 208

L

lack
  of attention 133
  of confidence 124, 159, 209
  of emotion 223
  of faith 116
  of focus 133
  of money 166–167

 of progress 111
 of specificity 133
 of trust 126, 216
layperson xxiii 12, 137
laziness 135
least common denominator love 227
life-long pursuits 161
limitations 32, 148
limit confusion 96
listen xxvi, 71, 133, 134, 136, 141, 210
listening 112, 136
logic 137
logical experiences 198
loneliness 230
long-term projects 161
loss of control 225
loss of potential 188
love xxx, 177–178, 203, 215, 218, 220, 222, 224, 230, 249–250
 allows abundance xxx
 and fear 84
 becoming love 100–101
 conditional love 125
 creates conductivity xxx
 distinguishing characteristic 69
 least common denominator 204
 love as a remedy 42
 is essential xxx
 open heart 198
 openheartedly 204
 of money 8, 9
 true love 125
 unconditionally 225, 227
 your neighbor 12

M

magnetize 99
magnify abundance 9
major setbacks 141
make amends 212, 213
mandates 41
manifestation 249
 born of desperation 160
 dry spell 243
 junkie 241
 lack of progress 111
 of abundance 4
 passive, attractive, receptive modes 186
 through attraction 100
 through receptivity 100
 timing 31
Manifestation process xxv, 6, 97–109
 four elements 108
manipulate 204, 226
manipulative 83
material abundance 247
materialistic dry spell 235
medicine wheel 77
meditate in groups 228
meditation 22, 69, 70, 80–81, 88, 104, 111, 126, 128, 132, 133, 135, 136, 190, 228, 229, 230, 232, 237, 242, 243
 guided meditation 69
 Vipassana 69
meditation teacher 84, 85
mental ability 131
mental constructs 197, 198
mental level 229
midwife 27, 167–168, 236
mind as a tool 137
miracle xxvii, 97, 98, 137, 207
miraculous 90
missed opportunities 226
mistakes 113
modifications 120
momentum 134, 135
money 8, 37, 39, 166–167
moral and ethical integrity 167
motivation 232
multitasking 135
mundane applications 228
mutually exclusive 11, 249
mystery 68, 71, 97, 98, 120, 156, 157, 198, 201, 202
mystic 14, 217
mystical
 doorways 250
 experience xxiv, 137, 208, 200
 intelligence 198, 200
 mystical journey 190, 216
 mystical path 197, 198, 200, 201, 220
 mystical relationship with God xxiv
 mystical union with God 184
mysticism xxiv, xxvii, 90, 120, 137, 184, 200, 201, 238

N

narrowness 130
Native American 73, 106, 250
Native American tradition 61
natural consequences 113
nature of abundance 245
navigational course corrections 130, 152
need for proof 137
need to know basis 115
negative emotions 113, 188, 209, 211, 230, 231
negative
  expectations 7
  feedback 165
  pattern of behavior 155
  results 18
  self-images 208
  thoughts 18
  visions 18
negativity 11, 102, 113, 124, 145, 177, 188, 189, 210, 211, 213, 214, 238, 241
negotiable 162
no feedback 142
noncompetitive paradigm 5
non-duality 249–250
non-dual pairing 249–250
nonmaterial abundance 245
nonmaterial contracts 248
no-self 10, 219
Not my will, but Thy Will xxvii, 9, 14, 26, 40, 55, 98, 100, 240, 248

O

obligations 160
offenses 208
offensive attacks on others 209
offering 55
oneness 209
one-stage requests 151
open-ended inquiry 200
open mind 198
organize 133
other realities 196
others
  emphasis on others 41, 42
  expectations of 41

out of body experience 139
overactive mind 136
overpower 206
overwhelming complications 144
ownership 203

P

pain 177
paradigm shift 87, 201
parenting 206
participation 35
partnership 30
passion 20, 23, 40, 47, 122, 159, 161, 219, 247
patience 100, 126
pattern of interaction 200
peace 111, 227, 228, 244, 248
peaceful 127
perfectionism 208, 209
perpetrator 214
personal agenda 136, 189
personal growth 205
personal power 190
personal preference 131
physical healing 171–173
physical needs 229
pilgrimage 12
Piscean Age 4
plan of action 164
politics 131
positive attraction 22
positive emotions 230
positive vision 22
possessed 205
possessiveness 203, 205, 208
poverty mentality 205
power 209
power of attraction 11, 14, 97
power of prayer 175
practical applications 228, 229, 236
prayer 8, 22, 229, 232, 242, 243
prayer vigil 175
pray the solution 124, 155
preconceived image 206
preconceived notions 200
preconceptions 198
preconditions to your contract 158–159
pre-contract considerations 34–43
prediction 84, 85, 115–117

preemptive corrections 213
prejudice 131, 189, 222, 223
prerequisites 159
prioritize 133, 161
procrastination 146, 149, 154–155
progress 114
proof 229
protection 225
psychic impressions 96
psychological complexes 218
psychological depression 145
punishment 211
purpose 248
put the fear of God in you 84

R

race 131
Rainbow Bridge 4, 62, 234
rationalism 90, 137
receiving abundance 31–32
receptive
   beauty of an open and loving heart 185
receptivity 97, 100
refinement of the translation 236
reflect 103
reflection 111, 112, 126, 128, 133, 135,
   141, 229, 230, 232
refocus 132, 133
regret 177, 211, 212, 213, 225
Reiki 70, 179, 207
reinforce 135
relationship issue 244–245
relationships as the hardest yoga 244
religion 131
remember the love 240
renegotiate 149, 151, 162, 163
reparation 212, 213
requests xxv, 3, 7, 10, 12, 14, 22
   multifaceted 48
   prioritizing 47
resistance 131, 155, 184, 225
responsibility 135, 212
restitution 212
restrictions 147
results xxviii, xxix, 97
retaliation 214
revenge 85
rigidity 130
rigid thoughts 131–132

ritual
   cleanse 62
   creating a ritual 60–64
   group ritual 62
   location 61
   timing 61
role playing 156
rule of three 94, 141

S

sabotage 160
Sacred Heart of Jesus 234
sacredness 6
sacrifice 3, 4, 219
safety 225
science 137
scientific investigation 229
scientific proof 90
self-criticism 209
self-denial 219
self-empowerment 160
self-flagellation 211
self-help manifestation 13
self-importance 208
self-interest 208
selflessness 216
self-made complications 145
self-mastery 213
self-pity 213
self-protection 208
self-protective response 209
self-sufficiency 192
self-will 74, 111, 125, 157, 205, 218
sensitization 192, 237, 238
service to others 206
sexual orientation 131
shared abundance xxix–xxx, 5, 6, 32, 125
sharing xxiv, xxix, 4, 5
shift in the flow 148
signposts 133, 134
signs of encouragement 165
silence 87, 133, 217
simplify 145
skills 153, 157–158
slights 209
solidification 194
soul 35
specific guidance 134
specificity 134

specific questions 134
spiritual
  attainment 244
  beliefs 228
  cohesiveness 229
  compass 209
  development 12, 21, 32, 127, 196, 198, 200, 206, 217, 248
  diet 34–35
  gift 204
  growth 135, 152, 211, 214, 216, 219, 220, 228, 229, 244, 247, 249
  growth spurt 244
  immaturity 243
  input 231
  insight 69
  journey 206, 210
  level of awareness 228–229
  mandate 233
  maturity 12, 128, 155, 221, 244
  practice 245
  principles 228, 232, 234, 240, 241, 243
  stress test 240
  visions 137
  warrior 219
  wind 236
  wisdom 221
spiritualization of emotions 230, 231
spiritualization of thoughts 230
spiritually adverse circumstances 188
spiritually regressing 203
stagnation 127, 148, 168
stand your spiritual ground 241
Star of David 62
strategy 212
subtle skill 98
suffering 3, 4, 9, 16
  alternative to suffering 249
supervision 206
suppression 230
surrender xxvii, xxix, xxx, 12, 13–16, 26–27, 40, 41, 47, 111, 120, 216, 235, 239, 240, 242, 247, 248
  balance of desire and surrender 98
  beauty of surrender 185
  becomes attractive 249
  control 209
  devotion to God 127
  fuels receptivity 100
  impediment 126
  inability to surrender control 125–127
  surrender balances desire 20
  surrender the results 9
  surrender to God's desire 21, 22
  troubleshooting surrender 125–129
  weak surrender to God's desire 127–129
suspend judgment 231
sustain 102
sweat lodge 15
symbolism 71–72
  bluebird 92
  deer 92
  fox 92
  owl 92
  turtle 92
symbols 52
synchronized to the flow 235

T

tantric twin 6, 7
testing tasks 240
testing the waters 134, 166
The Dark Night of the Soul 217
Thinking
  excessive 136–137
  need for logical explanations 137–138
  passive 136
  rationalism 137
  receptive role 136
Thought
  focused 37, 39, 40
  negative thought 36
  positive thought 36
  refinement 132
  refocus 133
  scattered 135
  specific 39, 41
  specificity 132
  sustained 39, 40, 41
  translation of your desire 130
  troubleshooting thought 130–139
    inability to focus 132–135
    lack of specificity 132–135
    rigid and narrow thoughts 131–132
    sustaining thought 135–136
thought patterns 11
  ingrained 136, 197, 202
  logical 197
  rational 197

thought voice 199
threat 225
tingling 177
total submission 127
transcendence of time and space 114
transform 218
transformations 184, 220
transgression 214, 215
transition 168
translate 233
translation 101, 102, 104, 115, 230
translation of spiritual beliefs 229
transmutation 231
transmutation of negative feelings 230, 233, 237
transparency 218
troubleshooting communication 110–117
  assessing the Strength 111–112
  confusion 114, 115
  consistency 114
  delayed communication 111
  evaluate communications 112–115, 113
  first step 111
  lack of guidance 111
troubleshooting desire
  clinging to expectations 119–121
  competing desires 122–123
  conflicting desires 122–123
  too strong desire 119–121
  untempered desire 120
  weak desire 121–122
troubleshooting flow
  criteria 142, 143
  delays 146–148
  incorrect timing 146–148
  interference 146–148
  limited or no input 144
  moving against the flow 141–142
  multifaceted contract 144
  overwhelming complications 144
  problems with the flow 140–149
  quick flow 148–149
  self-made complications 144
  slow moving 144–146
  stagnant flow 144–146
  unresponsive flow 142–143
troubleshooting avenue for manifestation
  problems with delayed gratification 153–168
    chaos, disorganization, and other distractions 154, 159–161
    complexity 154, 161
    counterproductive character traits and self-sabotage 154, 155–156
    impatience and overcompensation 154, 156–157
    lack of essential skills 154, 157–158
    lack of financial support 154, 166–167
    lack of moral or ethical integrity 154, 167
    lack of sincere effort 154, 156
    never getting started 154, 163–166
    preconditions 154, 158–159
    procrastination and an inability to follow through 154–155
    renegotiation 154, 161–163
  problems with instant gratification
    choosing only simple desires 151
    ego inflation 152
    inability to cope with delayed gratification 151
    lack of spiritual growth 152
    limited co-creative communication 151–152
trust xxv, 111, 127, 128, 131, 205, 216, 217, 240, 242, 245
tunnel vision 119

U

uncertainty 21, 128
unconditional love 228, 244
unconscious 116
unconscious debris 91
unconscious material 82
unknown 201
unlimited potential 85
unnecessary credentials 158
unrealistic expectations 209
untrue partnership 31

V

vacillation 149
vagueness 130
validation 165
vibration 172
vibrational continuum 193, 195
vibrational frequency 194, 203

vibrational rate 114
victim 19, 85, 172, 212, 213, 214, 215, 227
victimization 18, 19, 213, 214
visible material plane 193
vision, positive 36
visions 77–78, 217
vow 54
vulnerability 32, 124, 125, 210, 224–227, 227

W

way of the Bodhisattva 234
way of the mystic 222
weight loss 175–176
will power 176
windows in time and space 157
wisdom 69, 87, 115, 127, 207, 210, 226, 228, 229, 232
woundedness 18, 19

www.ingramcontent.com/pod-product-compliance
Lightning Source LLC
Chambersburg PA
CBHW051401070526
44584CB00023B/3245